Blue Collar, Blue Scrubs

Also by Michael J. Collins, M.D.

Hot Lights, Cold Steel

Blue Collar, Blue Scrubs

The Making of a Surgeon

Michael J. Collins, M.D.

ST. MARTIN'S PRESS ☙ NEW YORK

Chapter Twenty adapted from "A Child's Pain," originally published in *JAMA* (1997; 277[21]:1668). Copyright © 1997 American Medical Association. Used by permission.

www.stmartins.com

Library of Congress Cataloging-in-Publication Data

Collins, Michael J., M.D.
    Blue collar, blue scrubs : the making of a surgeon / Michael J. Collins, M.D.—1st ed.
        p. cm.
    ISBN-13: 978-0-312-53293-2
    ISBN-10: 0-312-53293-8
    1. Collins, Michael J., M.D. 2. Orthopedists—United States—Biography. 3. Surgeons—United States—Biography. I. Title.
    RD728.C64A3 2009
    617.092—dc22
    [B]

                                                                    2008046213

First Edition: June 2009

10 9 8 7 6 5 4 3 2 1

To Patti—then, now, and always

INTRODUCTION

Have you ever noticed that two plus two doesn't always equal four? It didn't for me, and I guess that's what this story is all about.

I'm a surgeon now. I spend my days in quiet, sterile operating rooms replacing knees and repairing rotator cuffs. A hard day in the hole would kill me. But back then I was a laborer. I spent my days breaking concrete and throwing rocks—and I liked it. The time would come when all that digging and lifting and breaking and throwing would be too much—but not then. Then it was fun. It was fun to push ourselves beyond all reasonable limits. It was fun to have some strutting, bellowing foreman threaten to fire our asses if we didn't break out some insanely long section of concrete in the next twelve hours.

We'd grumble and curse. We'd complain that this was typical Scalese slave-driving bullshit. We'd say nobody could break out that much concrete in one day. What did they think we were, a bunch of fucking mules? But somewhere, deep inside, we liked it. We liked being given unreasonable, outrageous tasks. Nothing was too much for us; and when they told us to break out three thousand feet of concrete in one day, we understood they were paying us a compliment: nobody could break out that much concrete in one day—but *we* could.

We'd kick the watercooler and we'd say Fred could kiss our asses, but all the while we'd be pulling on our gloves, rolling our shoulders, and eyeing that long stretch of concrete. *Bring it on*, we'd think. *Bring it on*.

Twelve hours later, our forearms would be scratched and bleeding from being ground all day against the broken slabs of concrete. Our T-shirts would be sopping wet and tattered. Our ears would be ringing from twelve hours stooped down next to the jackhammer. We would be stretched out in the grass, boots off, drinking beer, looking back on the seemingly endless expanse of concrete we had just broken out, and thinking we had the world by the balls.

That's what I miss about those days. It's something my friends and fellow doctors can never understand. All they see is the drudgery, the mindless slaving labor, the subjugation of the spirit. But they don't realize how liberating it can be to train your body, to make it so strong that labor enthralls it and quickens your life impulses so that all that work becomes as nothing, becomes the fuel that fires your life, that makes it worth getting up in the morning to laugh and drink and feel your muscles. Sure, somewhere inside you know it's temporary. You know you are dipping into your reservoir of youth and throwing away a little more of it each day. But that reservoir seems so vast, so inexhaustible. You know there will be a day of reckoning, but until that day comes . . .

I suppose if you had asked me what I was doing, I wouldn't have had an answer. I lacked what my college professors used to call Critical Awareness. I was about as introspective as a rebar. I worked breakout because I was good at it, because it paid well, but most important, because it told me things I wanted to hear. It told me I was young. It told me I was strong. It told me I was alive.

But toward the end it started telling me other things, too. Things I was not ready to hear. Jesse and JT and Angelo, guys who had been around for a while, they could hear it all too plainly. It fairly shouted to them. But as yet it only whispered to me. It whispered that, yes, I was young, but youth is fleeting. Yes, I was strong, but strength is illusory. Yes, I was alive, but, louder every day, it whispered that I was going to die.

And on that hot summer day when I finally heard that whisper, it hit me like a twenty-pound sledgehammer. And at that moment I knew that if I ever wanted to accomplish anything important in life, I'd better get going.

Blue Collar, Blue Scrubs

CHAPTER ONE

In the final stirrings of the night, the door opens and I'm back in the hole, throwing rocks. I've filled another truck with them. But Angelo isn't taking them to the dump. Instead, they're going somewhere else. . . .

I roll over and flail again at the alarm clock. It's 5:00 A.M. I'm late and I know it. I groan, push myself up, and run a hand across my face.

I throw off the blanket, struggle to my feet, yank on my jeans, and throw a T-shirt over my shoulder. I sleep on the floor in the attic of my parents' house, and as I pad downstairs in my bare feet, the house is quiet. My parents and seven younger brothers won't be up for another hour or two. As I pass Tim's room, I bump open the door with my hip and flip on the light. Tim is lying on his right side, sheets twisted around him. I call his name and tell him I had fun with Diane last night. Diane is Tim's girlfriend.

"I think I finally convinced her she is going out with the wrong brother," I tell him.

Tim yawns, pulls the sheets over his head, and tells me to keep dreaming. "What girl in her right mind would go out with you?" he asks.

I scratch my head, realize Tim is probably right, and turn off the light.

Down in the kitchen, Shannon is curled up in the corner. She gets slowly to her feet, stretches, and dutifully shuffles over. I bend down, scratch her behind the ears, and tell her she is beautiful. Shannon yawns and goes back to the corner.

I wolf down a couple bananas and pour a glass of orange juice. As I am drinking the juice, I grab eight slices of bread, lather four with peanut butter, four with jelly, then fold them into sandwiches and toss them in a paper bag. In the corner of the icebox I find a boiled potato, two apples, and a plastic bowl of macaroni and cheese. I throw them in the bag, too. I fill my old, quart-glass Coke bottle with water, grab my boots from the back door, and trot out to the car. I toss my boots and lunch on the seat next to my hard hat, plop down into the driver's seat, and start the ignition. Blue-gray smoke belches from the exhaust as the old Pontiac rumbles into life.

It is ten to six when I jam on the brakes outside the ten-foot-high chain-link fence that surrounds the Vittorio Scalese Construction Company. The morning sun is streaming down Grand Avenue. Bakery trucks and newspaper vans are dragging long shadows behind them as they head east into the city. I grab my hard hat and lunch bag, slam the door of the Pontiac, and sprint through the gates past the large pile of wooden stakes that dominates the center of the yard. Behind the stakes, a thirty-foot-high shed with a corrugated iron roof shelters a table saw, more stakes, and two enormous piles of black dirt.

Fred is standing at the door of his office. He looks at his watch and says, "Good afternoon, Senator. Where the hell you been? Your crew left half an hour ago."

I tell Fred I'm sorry I'm late.

"Save the bullshit," he says. "Now take The Rat and get your ass out with your crew. You're lucky I didn't send Vito in your place and let you spend a couple a days workin' here in the yard."

Working in the yard is easy, but it's punishment. The yard is for guys who are too old or too incompetent to go out on the jobs. Yardbirds, we call them. They pull nails, load trucks, and cut stakes. No one ever worked himself to death in the yard.

As I turn to leave, Fred says, "By the way, you look like shit."

So does The Rat. The Rat is Scalese's oldest piece of equipment: a battered old stake truck, its original shiny red finish bleached to a tired brown from years of baking under scorching summer suns. Its windshield is cracked and dirty. Its body is splattered with rock-hard gobs of mud and concrete. Its doors are creased and dented from collisions with backhoes, compressors, and scoops. The two white rod racks sticking up on either side of the hood list drunkenly inward. The running board on the driver's side is loose and hangs at a forty-five-degree angle.

Inside, a dirty piece of burlap and an old Chicago Yellow Pages phone book cover the worn foam rubber and springs where the driver's seat used to be. The floor is covered with cigarette butts, beer cans, hamburger wrappers, expansion joints, form tools, pick heads, oilcans, and a ragged copy of the *Sun-Times* ("33 Die in French Quarter Fire"). The dashboard is littered with nails, old lunch bags, and toll tickets. In the center of the steering wheel someone has scratched his name: Steve. Under it, someone else has written "blows."

I climb into The Rat, adjust the phone book, fire up the engine, and highball it out of the yard. From the doorway, Fred shouts at me to slow down. "What do you think this is, the Indy Five Hunnert?"

Even though it's late, I stop the truck outside Mary's Grill at Cumberland and Grand. It's not even six yet, so there aren't many cars on the road. I click on the hazard lights, leave The Rat in the right-hand lane, and jump out of the truck.

Bill is sitting on the steps outside the grill. He is bent forward, knees drawn up, hands and arms clenched in front of his chest. At least he's not passed out in the bushes again. I touch him on the shoulder.

"Hey, Bill, you okay?"

Bill lifts his head, cocks it, and looks at me out of his right eye. His left eye is swollen shut. "Hello, Tommy," he says. I've told Bill a million times my name is Mike, but he still thinks I am his nephew Tommy.

"What happened to your eye, Bill?"

Bill frowns, feels his eye for several seconds, then shakes his head. "Dunno," he says. "Dunno." He rubs his scraggly beard. "Hate to ask, Tommy, but could you—"

"Sure, Bill," I say. I reach into my pocket and hand him a five. "Now come in and get some breakfast."

"Thanks. Thanks a lot, Tommy."

Inside, four other Scalese guys are at the counter, hunched over coffee and eggs.

"The hell you lookin' at?" Vito asks as I enter. "Am I the first Italian movie star you ever seen?"

Brother-in-Law, sitting next to him, grunts. "Huh. They don't show no faces in the kind of movies you be in," he says.

I ignore them both and tell Mary she looks beautiful this morning. Mary wipes the hair back from her forehead, rolls her eyes, and says she doesn't know why in the name of God she ever went into this business.

"Sweet-talkin' bullshit," she says. "That's all I ever hear in this place. Sweet-talkin' bullshit from guys who tell me I'm beautiful and can they pay me later?" She squirts a little grease on the griddle. "You gonna order somethin' or what?"

"Bacon and egg sandwich and a carton of milk."

Vito snickers. "Put it in a bottle with a nipple on it," he tells Mary.

Mary tells him to shut up. She says if Vito drank more milk maybe he wouldn't look like such a broken-down lowlife. Three minutes later she rips off a piece of grease paper, wraps my sandwich, and slides it across to me.

"Two twenty-five," she says.

I give her three bucks and tell her to keep the change.

"Better hurry, boys," I say to the other Scalese guys as I'm leaving. "You don't want to be late. Your uncle Fred misses his little yardbirds."

Brother-in-Law pounds his fist on the counter. "Uncle Fred can kiss my black ass!" he shouts as I hustle out the door.

Outside, Bill is still slumped against the wall. I look at my watch, hesitate, then help Bill to his feet and walk him inside. He's too wobbly for a chair at the counter this morning, so I sit him in one of the booths. I take the five-dollar bill from his right hand, raise it up, and show it to Mary. "Could you bring Bill some bacon and eggs and maybe a cup of coffee?" I ask her.

Mary never says no when it comes to Bill. She waves me out the door. "Get out of here. You leave Bill to me."

I shake Bill's shoulder "Mary's gonna bring you some breakfast, Bill," I tell him.

"Thanks, Tommy," he mumbles.

I tear out the door, hop into the truck, honk the horn, slam The Rat into first, and swing her left toward the Eisenhower.

It's almost 6:30 when I pull up at the job site. We don't officially start work until 7:00, but there is a tradition at Scalese called working for the church. This means that although we don't get paid till 7:00, we start working at 6:30—or 6:00 or sometimes 5:30.

The other members of my crew are gathered around the compressor laughing and drinking coffee from white Styrofoam cups. Johnny Battaglia, our foreman, is sitting on the tailgate of his pickup reading the *Trib*. I pull up next to him. He looks up from his paper and says it's nice of me to stop by. Then he tells me to "park that piece-of-shit Rat and go help JT with the hoses."

JT is a thirty-five-year-old black man, father of six. He runs the gun on Johnny's crew. JT's forearms are each as big as a caveman's club. By the time I get over to him he already has the hoses laid out.

"Mike," he says, "the hell you been, man? Sippin' tea with the yard-birds?"

"Naw, I just slept late, that's all."

"Old Fred, he don't like that shit."

"Yeah. He let me know."

As I am pulling the gloves from my back pocket, Joe Roselli flings the dregs of his coffee onto the ground, crushes his cup, and throws it in the gutter. Then he slaps my belly with the back of his left hand. "Hey, man, I was starting to get worried," he says.

Rosie is a twenty-year-old kid who played linebacker at Eastern Illinois until he flunked out last year. He is built like a chunk of granite. Johnny Battaglia stole him from Pappy Cirrincione's crew back in April and won't give him back because he works so hard. Rosie, JT, and I have been working together on the breakout gang all year.

Scalese is in the concrete construction business. What we construct is mostly curbs and gutters. But before the new ones can be put in, the old ones have to be broken out. That's where the breakout gang comes in. First the gun runner breaks the old gutters into jagged hundred-pound hunks of concrete. Then the rock thrower bends down, his face inches from the pounding jackhammer, lifts the piece, or "rock," and throws it onto the back of a truck—rock after rock, hour after hour, day after day. Throwing rocks: the toughest job at the toughest construction company in Chicago. When people ask me what I'm doing with my Notre Dame education and I tell them I throw rocks, they say, "Your parents must be very proud."

The sun is knifing between the warehouses and factories, laying long bars of light across Western Avenue. There was rain during the night and the sidewalks are glistening and fresh. The morning wind is ruffling the burlap on the back of The Rat. Far to the north I can hear the rumble of the el. Johnny Battaglia looks at his watch. It's 6:30. He folds his paper, throws it in the cab, and slaps his hands together. "Aw right, aw right," he says. "We ain't got all day. Get that Sullair goin' and let's get to work."

JT swings the air hammer off the back of the truck and fits it with a bit. Rosie and I grab pick heads from under the seat and slide the heads down worn ash shafts. Jesse climbs onto the back of The Rat and throws off a couple shovels. Then JT fires up the compressor. He lugs his gun over to the first section, looks at me and Rosie, grins, and squeezes the trigger.

Suddenly the morning silence is shattered by the roar of the compressor, the thunder of the jackhammer, the bellowing of the foreman, and the rumble of the big trucks jockeying into position.

"Now bend down and lift those rocks," Johnny shouts. "Asses and elbows! That's all I want to see for the next twelve hours: asses and elbows."

"Asses and elbows!" JT bellows as he hammers away at the concrete, chips flying everywhere. "Asses and elbows!" Rosie roars as he lifts the first piece, walks it over, and heaves it onto the back of The Rat. "Asses and elbows!" Angelo shouts as he revs up his truck and backs it next to the compressor.

In an hour The Rat is loaded and ready for the dump. Even though I'm the one who drives The Rat every day, I'm a laborer, not a driver. Our driver is a forty-two-year-old guy named Angelo Sansonetti. We need two trucks on the job every day, so Angelo brings one truck, I bring the other. When he was young, Angelo used to throw rocks, too. "Until I finally got brains and became a driver," he says.

Ange pulls his truck up behind mine, hops into The Rat, and heads for the dump. Rosie and I then begin loading Angelo's truck.

The final member of our crew is Jesse Perkins. Jesse is a short, stocky black guy who, according to Angelo, has been with Scalese "since Jesus was a corporal."

Jesse is a little more specific. "Shee-it," he says. "I started with this company the day after old Abe Lincoln got hisself shot."

Night or day, rain or shine, Jesse wears a pair of black wraparound sunglasses and baggy blue overalls in which he keeps a half-pint of VO and three or four cans of Schlitz. He is missing three of his upper teeth and five of his lower. Jesse likes to talk and he's got a few years on him, but Rosie and I like him. We let him do the grading while we throw the rocks.

About nine o'clock, the little kids and the old men start coming out of their houses to watch us. The kids stand on the edge of the sidewalk, eyes wide, hands at their sides, afraid to get too close, but fascinated by the roar of the machines and the grunts of the laborers. The old men sit on their porches, saying nothing, watching us from under straw fedoras as we hurl rock after rock onto the bed of the truck. Sometimes we can almost see the longing in their creased faces.

An hour later, the coffee truck pulls up. JT wedges his jackhammer in a crack, and we stop for a break. As we drink our coffee, Angelo starts in again on JT.

"JT, you must really want that foreman job," he says. "Look how much you've broken out already. Fer Chrissake, you're killin' the job. We coulda stretched this section into half a day at least. Keep it up, big guy. Next thing you know they'll be giving you twenty blocks a day to break out."

Rosie is sitting on the back of The Rat, his hard hat pushed back on his head and his legs swinging free. "Hey, JT," he says, "when you make foreman, you gonna have any white guys on your crew?"

JT, whose black skin is glistening with sweat, wipes his mouth with the back of his hand and nods. "Damn right," he says. "But not just white. They all gonna be *Eye*talians. You the only ones stupid enough to work like this."

JT looks over and sees me smiling. "What you laughin' at, Shit-for-brains?" he asks. "You gonna be there, too. Mmm-hmm. That's right. Throwin' rocks is all you dumb Irish motherfucks is good for."

"And eating potatoes," Angelo says. "You ever see people who eat as many potatoes as those damn Irish? Fer Chrissake, they inhale the damn things."

Johnny Battaglia says he doesn't care who eats what as long as they work. He turns to JT. "Now get that gun running. I want the rest of this block broken out by noon." I stuff one more donut in my mouth; then Rosie and I heave ourselves to our feet and slip our gloves back on. JT starts the compressor, swings the air hammer around like a toothpick, and begins slamming away at more concrete. We spend the rest of the morning slowly moving north: JT breaking out the rocks, Rosie and I throwing them on the trucks, Jesse trailing behind us with the scoop shovel, and Angelo shuttling back and forth to the dump.

When noon comes, JT leans his air hammer against the Sullair and shuts it down. Rosie and I climb out of the hole and go back to The Rat, where we left our lunches. Jesse and Angelo grab their lunch boxes and the five of us find a spot of shade next to a fence.

Angelo picked up a couple six-packs of Old Style on his way back from the dump. We lean against the fence, legs extended, eating sandwiches and drinking beer. We are quiet until a rat sticks its nose out of the sewer. Since we spend so much time breaking out curbs and gutters we are always running across rats. Jesse throws an empty beer can at it and says he hates the fucking things.

He wipes his red bandana across his forehead and says that the rat reminds him of a young girl who used to live down the street from him. Rosie looks at me over his can of Old Style and shrugs. It looks like we're in for another one of Jesse's stories.

"She be livin' over there on Homan Avenue, up on the fourth floor," he says. "She gets her welfare check one Friday, then splits, leavin' her five-year-old to watch the baby. She come home that night and she sees that baby is awful quiet. She pulls back the covers and five rats jump out at her. Those rats had eaten that baby clean up to the chest."

I groan and look at Jesse in disbelief, but he swears it's true.

"Yeah, babe. The police took the other child away from her and hauled that woman's ass off to jail."

From rats, we start talking about other animals. JT, who was raised on a farm in Arkansas, claims there are only three animals that are untrainable: the possum, the buzzard, and the bulldog.

Jesse says he knows a whorehouse down near Forty-seventh and Calumet that has a bulldog. "Man," he says, "that place is wide open. You can get anything you want in there. Anything! A woman, a dog, a sheep, a mule, even a damn *monkey*!"

He tells us about running out of there one night during a raid with his pants around his ankles, cops chasing him, and a woman in a tiger-striped tube top screaming she hadn't been paid.

I've learned a lot of things at Scalese, things they never taught me at Notre Dame. I am twenty-four years old, five-eleven, 190 pounds. At one time I thought I was pretty hot stuff. But I didn't know what tough was until I started working here. Not one man in a hundred walking the streets of Chicago would last a day out here throwing rocks, but Scalese has a dozen of them: young, strong, intemperate, spoiling for a fight, ready to accept any challenge. There are guys here who stand five-six, weigh 140 pounds, and can outwork, outdrink, outswear, and outfight me and ten guys like me any day of the week.

But I make a good buck. I like the work. The guys are decent. All in all, I think I've got a pretty good thing going here.

CHAPTER TWO

Five thirty A.M. A dark, overcast morning. The air is damp and heavy. Low, black clouds are scudding in from the west. A soft rain is drifting across Grand Avenue, and a gentle breeze is rippling the puddles in the yard. Because of the rain, Fred has ordered all the stake trucks to be pulled under the burlap shed. He told the crews to wait for a while before they go out to their jobs.

Two dozen laborers and drivers are scattered around the furnace room praying for rain, hoping to be sent home. Rosie is stretched out on the floor, eyes closed, hands behind his head, hard hat pulled low over his eyes. Jesse and JT are sitting next to each other on a stack of bags of Portland cement. Angelo is standing at the door watching the rain. He grunts his greeting as I come in.

I grab a five-gallon bucket, turn it over, and sit down. Then I reach into my lunch bag, take out a chicken leg, and start munching.

"That all you do is eat?" JT asks. "You the eatin'est man I ever saw." He elbows Jesse. "Chicken," he says, nodding at me. "Five thirty in the morning and the boy is eating chicken."

Jesse pushes up his sunglasses and says, "We lucky he got that; otherwise he be pokin' his nose in our lunches, wantin' to know where the donuts and cookies at."

I shrug my shoulders and say nothing. We are quiet for a while when Angelo starts telling stories of an old laborer named Mario who used to live above the office. Ange swears he has seen Mario, who died five years ago, walking around the yard late at night. Angelo's not the only guy who thinks this place is haunted. Most of us laugh it off, but Jesse doesn't think it's funny.

"Don't fuck with that shit," he says. "Leave that shit alone."

We sit quietly for the next hour until it starts raining harder and a rumble of thunder rolls across the yard. We can hear the drum of rain on the corrugated iron roof above us. Jesse starts imitating the thunder, making a low, growling noise deep in his throat until JT tells him to shut the fuck up. Finally, at 7:15, Fred comes down and sends us home.

Most of the guys are happy to have the day off, but I'm not. I need the money, and these rainy days are killing me. That's why I started driving a cab. If we get rained out of construction, I've got another job to turn to. Driving a cab doesn't pay as well as throwing rocks, but the money isn't bad—especially when it's raining.

I drive over to the Blue Cab garage on South Boulevard and check in with Bernie. He gives me Blue 34 and I wheel out of the garage, splashing through the rain toward the cabstand on Harlem Avenue.

I pick up the mike and let the dispatcher know I'm in service. "Blue Thirty-four, ten-eight," I say.

"Ten-four, Thirty-four," the dispatcher replies.

Since it's raining, business is good. I take a couple old ladies to the el, bring some businessman with a big yellow bow tie out to O'Hare, and do a few local trips. Around noon I remember the lunch run with Mr. Beatty.

"Blue Thirty-four," I say into the mike. "You got anyone for Mr. Beatty today?"

"Ten-five, Thirty-four," the dispatcher says. "You want him?"

"Sure. I'll do it."

Mr. Beatty is an eighty-year-old guy who used to own some big manufacturing company. He retired a few years ago and now has nothing to do but sit around his apartment all day shuffling hundred-dollar bills and playing tiddledywinks with Krugerrands. He has a standing order with the Blue Cab Company for a driver to take him to lunch every Wednesday. This is a guy who could probably buy both the restaurant and the cab company and not miss a beat, and yet he has to pay cabdrivers to go to lunch with him. Bernie says he has a family, but I guess they're too busy spending the old man's money to hang around with him.

A lot of the other drivers don't like Mr. Beatty. The guy has more money than God, but he doesn't tip very well. ("What the hell's he gonna do with all that dough, line his coffin with it?" one of the other drivers asked me.) I feel sorry for the old guy. Yeah, he's loaded, but so what? There are bums living in alleys off Madison Street who have more fun than he does.

I park the cab in front of his apartment building and ring the bell. Sophia, his caretaker, always answers right away. She has Mr. Beatty in a chair by the door with his jacket already on. As usual, she glares at me. Sophia is about as friendly as a hungover repo man.

"Now, sir," she says to Mr. Beatty, "here's your driver. It's time for your lunch." She motions for me to help him up and take his arm.

"Otto's Restaurant," Sophia says to me, like I haven't done this half a dozen times before. "They will have a table waiting for you," she tells me.

She marches us over the threshold and quickly closes the door.

Mr. Beatty holds tightly to my left arm as we shuffle toward the cab. "Good afternoon, Mr. Collins," he says. Sophia probably has a net worth of six bucks. She has met me ten times and has no idea what my name is. Mr. Beatty has a net worth of two gajillion dollars and he not only remembers my name but is polite and formal, always calling me Mr. Collins instead of knucklehead or numb nuts.

I help Mr. Beatty into the cab and we splash down Randolph to Otto's Restaurant. The headwaiter says good afternoon to Mr. Beatty. He ignores me. He ushers us to our usual table in the corner of the big, open room.

"There you are, sir," he says, fluffing Mr. Beatty's napkin and placing it on his lap. "Enjoy your meal."

Just to aggravate the waiter, I push back in my chair, glance at my napkin, and wait for him to do the same for me. Instead he brushes by me, giving me a look people usually reserve for articles stuck to the undersides of chairs at White Sox games.

Mr. Beatty smiles as he watches me pick up my napkin and put it on my lap. Not much gets by the old guy. "I'm afraid Arthur must be preoccupied this afternoon," he says.

"Yes, sir," I say.

We pick up our menus, huge things that look like cuneiform tablets containing the Code of Hammurabi. I don't know why Mr. Beatty bothers with the menu. He always orders the same thing: a glass of sherry, a bowl of chicken broth, and some kind of salad that has tomatoes and cold meat on it.

Although I'm starving, I'm always afraid to order too much. I don't want Mr. Beatty complaining to the cab company that I'm running up his bill, so I order only two cheeseburgers, a plate of mashed potatoes, and a glass of milk.

I ask Mr. Beatty how his foot is doing. He was recovering from some kind of toe surgery when I took him to lunch a couple weeks ago.

He waves the question away with a flick of his wrist. "Fine, fine," he says. Sometimes Mr. Beatty doesn't like to be asked questions. I guess this is one of those times.

We lapse into silence. That's okay with me. I'm just the mope whose job is to talk when he wants to talk and shut up when he wants to shut up. But I would rather talk. I find Mr. Beatty a terribly interesting, if pathetic, man. To have all that money and live such a crummy life, cooped up in that apartment with the Bride of Frankenstein as a caretaker, no one ever visiting him, having to pay strangers to go out to lunch with him. I would love to ask him what he thinks of his life. Is he bitter? Does he have regrets? Would he have done things differently?

I am staring at the tablecloth, arranging and rearranging my silverware, when Mr. Beatty asks, "How goes the construction industry, Mr. Collins?"

He always frames his questions as though he is talking to some Wall Street analyst or financial guru. It's hard to tell if he is trying to be humorous, ironic, or serious.

"Well, sir, I can't tell you much about the industry in general, but we've been pretty busy at Scalese."

Mr. Beatty nods. "And that's good enough for you," he says.

I don't know if I've just been asked a question or accused of indolence. I am about to reply when he raises his finger and shakes his head. "No need to answer," he says. "I am certain this is a matter to which you have given much thought."

This is a matter to which I have given *no* thought, and I think Mr. Beatty knows this. The man does have a way of making me think about things.

When the meal is over, Mr. Beatty asks me if I'm going to have dessert today. I take this as his approval to do so, and I tell Arthur I'll have the apple pie à la mode and another glass of milk. Arthur, whose back is to Mr. Beatty, rolls his eyes and walks away.

While we are waiting for dessert, Mr. Beatty asks, "And how long do you anticipate your venture into the construction industry might last?"

"I'm, uh, not really sure."

"Surely you don't intend it to be your lifelong vocation?"

"Well . . . no."

Mr. Beatty rubs his chin and asks, "Have you considered what your next step to fame and fortune might be?"

"Oh, there are a number of things I've been considering," I say offhandedly, as though I am having a hard time deciding between Chairman of the Board of AT&T and President of the World Bank.

"How fortunate for you," he says.

That's not a question, so at least this time I don't have to answer. Mr. Beatty looks intently at me for several seconds, then asks Arthur for the check.

I am just putting the last bite of apple pie into my mouth when Mr. Beatty stands up and says it's time to leave. I gulp down the last of my milk, then help Mr. Beatty out to the cab. When we get back to his apartment, Sophia, as usual, takes forever to answer the bell. When she finally opens the door, the look on her face, although outwardly obsequious, evinces neither warmth nor welcome. She takes Mr. Beatty's arm from me and almost jerks him into the apartment. I feel bad leaving Mr. Beatty with that coldhearted old bitch. It's obvious that although he is the employer, she is the boss.

Mr. Beatty turns and nods his thanks to me. He is about to say something when Sophia pushes me into the hallway and slams the door.

"Love you, too, Sophia," I shout to her through the closed door. "Be sure to say hi to the rest of your family back in Transylvania."

The next morning I get to the yard at 5:20. Trucks are being started, their deep-throated roar echoing off the walls of the clothing factory next door. Men are scattered throughout the yard loading stakes, clamps, irons, and burlap. Everyone is working for the church.

Our crew is sent back to the West Side, moving from patch to patch, breaking out sections of curb and gutter. It is another hot day. Around ten I go for a cup of water from the cooler on the back of Johnny's truck. I ask Jesse if he wants one.

Jesse straightens up and blows a long stream of air through his puffed-up cheeks and says, "No thanks, babe. I don't want to dilute myself." With that he digs out the half-pint of VO from his overalls and takes a healthy slug from it. "No sense building a fire if you just gonna pour water on it."

Marty, one of the drivers from Material Service, is always messing with Jesse. He sees Jesse's bottle and says he wants a drink, too.

"Then get your own damn bottle."

"You old drunk," Marty says. "I think I'm gonna whup yo' ass. Yeah, I'm gonna whup it good. People be sayin', 'Look at that young man whup-pin' that old man's ass. What's this generation comin' to?'"

"Shee-it," Jesse retorts. "How you gonna whup my ass when you got yourself full of bullet holes? 'Cause that's what you gonna have in you, bullet holes."

"Keep talkin', old man," Marty says. "Keep talkin' and you gonna be the first man ever died of two foots up his ass. And I'll do it! I'll do it!"

"You ain't gonna do shit, because you gonna be lyin' in a box in the church with all kind of flowers round you."

"Hey, old man. I'm gonna make like an eagle and fly up yo' ass. And if I like it I'll build a nest up there. How you like that?"

"Shee-it," Jesse says. "I am one bad motherfucker, and no matter what happens to me I don't care, 'cause if it's bad, I know I already done it to someone else before."

Around five o'clock we have finished breaking out and are wrapping things up. We can't keep our eyes off a beautiful girl with a red halter top who is waiting for the bus. Johnny Battaglia doesn't like it. "I'll watch the broads," he yells. "You guys get this shit loaded up."

Rosie and I go back to loading The Rat. Johnny is sitting on a barricade watching us work. He starts telling another of his stories about how hard he used to work when *he* was on the breakout gang. "At sunup I'd get in that hole, put my head down, and throw rocks until sundown without lookin' up once. All you could see of me was my ass. Shit, no one saw my face for three years. They all forgot what I looked like."

Jesse is next to the compressor sweeping up. He gazes at the girl in the halter top one more time. Johnny asks him who he's kidding. "You're too old to be looking at girls."

Jesse nods and wipes his forehead. "That's the sad, gospel truth," he says. He looks at me and says, "Mike, when you gets to be my age, there is only one kind of fuckin' that you do, and that's *up*. You fuck up."

"Well," Johnny says, heaving himself off the barricade, "you're getting pretty good at that part."

The next day, Jesse and I are sent to Taylor and Ogden near the Audy Home to remove broken concrete from some defective squares that Scalese poured last year. There are just the two of us, no foreman. Around ten Jesse goes across the street and buys us a couple cupcakes. I eat mine and half of his. The whole time we are working, Jesse is eyeing the girls. He has something to say to every one of them: "Mmm-mmm! You sure are pretty. You shoulda been a princess," or, "Goddamn! You must be a angel. Where yo' wings at, baby?" Finally he tells me, in a voice loud enough for a passing woman to hear, "I can't work no more with all these pretty ladies about. They spoilin' my whole day. I can't work and watch them at the same time."

When a fine-looking but underage girl goes by, he rolls his eyes and says, "My, my, my. I sure could go for some of that." He slowly shakes his head back and forth. "Mike," he says, never taking his eyes off the girl, "there is only one problem with her. She's too young, and if you mess with her you gonna get yo'self the three Ps."

I tell Jesse I've never heard of the three Ps.

"Pussy, police—and penitentiary."

He goes on to give me some advice about women based on his years of empirical research. His surefire method of capturing the heart of any woman consists of sweet talk and persistence. He even quotes from the book of Proverbs, something about "sweet talk is like a honeycomb: sweet to the mind and sweet to the bone."

Jesse goes to a tavern over on Roosevelt Road for lunch. I lean back against a barricade with my hard hat between my knees, eating my sandwiches. I watch the secretaries laughing and grabbing each other's forearms as they stroll down Ogden Avenue.

Jesse is back at 12:40. I pick up a sledge, Jesse picks up a shovel, and we go back to work. As the afternoon rolls past, Jesse continues with the stories. Since I never once tell him he is full of shit, this encourages him. He lifts up his shirt and shows me a long, zippered scar, at least a foot long, running across his abdomen. He says he got it in a knife fight with four guys he beat in a crap game.

Then he tells me he did six years in a federal pen for kidnapping five cops.

I ask him if that was before or after he infiltrated the Ku Klux Klan.

Jesse tells me I am a smart-ass white boy and I don't have to believe him, but every word he tells me is true.

·   ·   ·

Johnny Battaglia wasn't supposed to say anything, but he let it slip to Rosie that in order to keep their contracts with the City of Chicago, Scalese was "encouraged" to hire a couple guys from the Projects. The next day, a tall, skinny guy everyone calls Bean Pole, and his partner Bake, were hired.

Whatever beat Bean Pole and Bake march to, it isn't Italian. They are always coming late to work, getting drunk or high on the job, and loafing every chance they get. Apparently no matter what they do, they can't be fired. They are a source of great amusement to the laborers and great consternation to the foremen.

Bean Pole tells me he is a "come freak."

"That's right. Uh-huh. I fuck anything with a hole in it," he says. "Shee-it. I'm so horny I could fuck the crack of dawn."

When we got paid last week, Bean Pole asked me, "Mike, what you goan do with yo' paycheck: get drunk or get yo' flagpole polished?"

I guess I hadn't realized those were my only two options. When I explained to Bean Pole that I was trying to save some money, he told me I was "twenty kinds of fool." He said I ought to go out with him and Bake some night and they'd show me a good time. "When we done with you, you be walkin' bowlegged for a month," he said.

He and Bake are always chopping and kicking at the air, jabbering about what badass kung fu fighters they are and how last weekend they beat the shit out of fifteen cops in the Seventh District.

This afternoon the two of them slip into the Taquería María for an hour. They only come out when some guy, whose driveway we just broke out, brings us a case of Stroh's. Bean Pole and Bake each grab an armful before Johnny Battaglia yells at them to leave the beer alone.

"Where the hell you guys been?" Johnny asks.

"We been wit m'man here all day," Bean Pole says, gesturing at me.

Johnny tells him he is a lying sack of shit. "I ought to fire both your asses right now," Johnny says.

Bean Pole just smiles.

.   .   .

The next morning Johnny sends me to break out sidewalks with a sledge-hammer. Bean Pole and Bake are supposed to help me, but mostly they just sit under a tree and talk about women and drugs. When Johnny comes back an hour later he tells them to get their asses to work. As soon as Johnny leaves, they throw down their shovels.

Bean Pole says, "I ain't gonna slave-drive myself for no *Eye*talian fore-man." He and Bake keep talking about 5:30 when work will be over and they'll have a few drinks and a couple joints. "Then we be smilin'," Bake says.

After lunch, Bean Pole and Bake hop in The Rat with me. We drive over to Forty-fourth and King Drive, where we join the rest of the crew who are breaking out. By five o'clock the work is done, but we have to stay till five thirty just for propriety's sake. The guys from the other crews—the carpenters, finishers, drivers, and laborers—all come over and we sit on the backs of trucks or lean against the compressor, drinking beer and laughing. Jesse tells us how he stole a cop car one time, drove it to Calumet City, and left it on the front lawn of a whorehouse. JT says it's a wonder there is any shit left in the world since Jesse is so full of it.

Rosie is sitting on the back of The Rat with a can of Stroh's between his knees. He stares at Bean Pole and Bake and says it's been a long day and the two of them must be exhausted.

Those two know better than to mess with Rosie, so they say nothing.

"You think we work hard now?" Jesse asks. "Shee-it. This ain't nothin' like it used to be. Nothin'!"

He goes on to tell us how laborers used to work for a dollar an hour and how they really got slave-drived, as Bean Pole calls it. When he tells us about sixteen-hour days and how there were no scoops and everything was done with sledgehammers, shovels, and wheelbarrows, all we can do is let out a long, slow breath and shake our heads.

When Jesse finishes his story, Bean Pole says, "You always talkin' about the old days and all these tough men. Where they at now, these tough old men? I want to see them."

Jesse straightens up, leans on his shovel, and thinks for a moment. "They all dead," he says finally.

The rest of us burst out laughing, but Bean Pole stamps his foot on the ground and says, "You damn right they all dead. They worked their motherfuckin' selves to death."

Jesse looks at him and then spits on the ground. "That ain't something you ever gonna have to worry about," he says.

The next day we are sent to Park Ridge. Rosie and I both get there at six. Rosie brings the *Sun-Times*, and we go through the racing section, picking today's horses at Arlington. We've been booking each other's bets all summer. So far, Rosie is up a whopping seventeen bucks. JT says it's a good thing neither of us has to make a living picking horses.

We spend the morning breaking out a long section on Merrill Avenue. As JT is hammering at the concrete, a chunk flies off and tears a gash in Roselli's arm. It looks pretty deep to me, but Rosie just pours some water on it, says, "Ah, screw it," and keeps working.

We have lunch under a shade tree in front of Lutheran General Hospital: five dirty, sweaty guys stretched out in the grass, a twelve-pack in the middle of us, lunch bags resting in our hard hats at our sides. I found some ham in the icebox this morning and made five ham and cheese sandwiches. They have been sitting in the sun on the front seat of The Rat all morning. The cheese has melted, and the warm sandwiches and cold beer taste so good that I close my eyes, lean my head back, and let out a sigh.

Jesse hears me and says to JT, "What is this, the Last Supper? I ain't never seen nobody eat like this boy eats. Look at that pile of food in front of him." He jabs me on the shoulder. "What the hell you got there, boy, half a buffalo or what?"

JT tells Jesse to leave me alone while I am eating, then he says to me, "Man, I wish to hell I was single like you, with no one to spend my money on but myself. Shee-it, now I take my check home and have to split it eight ways. If I was single I'd be drivin' a big old Cadillac and livin' like a damn king."

"Like Shorty," Jesse says.

"Fuck Shorty," JT says. "That dumb son of a bitch."

Shorty, one of the laborers on Pappy's crew, inherited six thousand dollars a couple months ago when his daughter and son-in-law died of carbon monoxide poisoning. Exactly one week after he got the money, Shorty came up to JT and asked if he could borrow two bucks.

"I told him to go fuck his self. Goddamn fool goes to spending six thousand dollars in one week! What the fuck. All he goan get from me is a foot up his ass."

To make it worse, when the money was gone Shorty's wife left him and took everything but the bed and the TV. Then she showed up at the yard at 5:00 A.M. last payday and, in front of a yard full of hooting, catcalling laborers, took Shorty's paycheck from him and sashayed out of the yard, turning the hoots to cheers and whistles.

We finish breaking out the last patch around two thirty. Johnny is checking on his other crew, so we go across the street to the liquor store and get a couple more six-packs. As always, as soon as there is beer around Bean Pole and Bake show up. They each grab a beer. Then Bean Pole starts talking about the clap. He and Bake have each had had it several times.

"Man," Bean Pole says, "that last time, I had to hold on to the wall every time I took a leak. It hurt so bad I like to died. That's when I knew it was time to get my funky ass to the doctor."

Jesse says maybe he ought to keep it in his pants once in a while; maybe he's had enough.

"Only one way I goan know I had enough," Bean Pole says, "and that's when I go to take a leak and my dick falls into the toilet. That's when I'll stop, brother."

Johnny comes back twenty minutes later. He says we should all go back to the yard and finish the day there, since we are done here.

"What about our break, Johnny?" Bean Pole asks innocently. "Don't we get ten minutes for our break?"

"Ten minutes? I know goddamn well you guys been sittin' on your asses here for the last half hour. What the hell do you call that?"

"That weren't no break," he says. "That was time we done *stole* from you. Now we want our break!"

On the way back to the yard we stop at Mazullo's on Irving Park Road. We pull the trucks around back where no one can see them. Then we go inside, shoot a few games of eight ball, and have a few more beers. We leave the tavern at 4:30 ("Before some foreman finds us here and fires our asses," Jesse says) and get back to the yard at 5:10. Fred has us load stakes till 5:30.

There is no clock in the yard. The yardbirds know it is quitting time when the church bells over on Fullerton Avenue begin to chime. As we file out of the yard, Fred tells us that listening for the church bells at quitting time is the only time any of us pays attention to religion all week.

The next day we are breaking out on King Drive when Bean Pole and Bake show up—an hour late again. Bean Pole isn't working for more than two minutes when he hits himself in the ankle with a pick and begins shivering and shaking all over. A nice old black lady with a chest as big as Wisconsin comes out of her house and gives Bean Pole some ice wrapped in a towel. Bean Pole is howling like a werewolf in heat. Bake and I help him into The Rat. Then Johnny tells me to drive "that dumb son of a bitch" back to the yard. When I get to the yard, Fred tells me to drive "that dumb son of a bitch" to Gottlieb Hospital.

When we get to the hospital, Bean Pole really puts on a show: moaning and groaning and rolling on the ground, flinging his arms around like an octopus putting up a lawn chair. He makes me get him a wheelchair, and as soon as we are in the ER he demands a shot of morphine or heroin for the pain.

I leave him in the ER and go back to King Drive to rejoin my crew. Jesse, who's had to throw rocks while I was gone, is really glad to see me.

"Babe, I thought you was *never* comin' back," he says.

Jesse digs into the folds of his overalls and pulls out a can of Schlitz. He drinks it down in long, slow pulls. When he finishes the Schlitz he takes a couple slugs from his bottle of VO. Finally, he pulls out a blue medicine bottle full of pasty white fluid. He grimaces and swallows a mouthful of that, too.

"I'm a damn fool," he says to me as he screws the lid back on the medicine. "I drink the VO, knowin' that it's hurtin' me, and then I take the medicine right behind it and it don't work for shit." He holds up the medicine, gazes at it, and puts it back in his pocket with a quiet laugh. "I'm a damn fool," he says again.

Behind us stretches a long, jagged section of broken concrete. Ahead of us, Johnny's other crew is breaking out the next section. The roar of engines, the thunder of jackhammers, and the shouts of foremen fill the air.

"This ain't no construction company," Jesse says as he picks up his shovel. "No, sir. No damn way. This ain't the Scalese *Con*struction Company. This is the Scalese *De*struction Company. We come out with our picks and sledges and jackhammers and we destroy things. We hook up those hoses and fire up those compressors and then all hell breaks loose. We make so damn much noise, ain't nobody can hear nothin' but the destroyin'. We destroy the curbs and the gutters. We destroy the jackhammers and the hoses. We destroy the shovels and the picks—and we for damn sure destroy ourselves. For *damn* sure."

He pauses and wipes his forehead with the red bandana from his pocket. "But oh, that destruction!" He rolls his eyes and smiles. "We goin' down, motherfucker. We goin' *down*! But we goin' down in a blaze of glory, a white-hot blaze of glory!"

Bean Pole and Bake don't show up for work the next day. Our crew finishes breaking out the section on King Drive around three. Then Johnny has us go back and strip the sections that were poured yesterday. After breaking out all day, stripping is a cakewalk. We hop down behind the curbs with our picks and walk down the line, swigging beer and swinging picks, knocking the stakes and frames loose. After we heave all the stakes and lumber out of the hole, we load the lumber; then Johnny tells me to climb up on the back of The Rat and catch stakes.

Angelo hops in the cab and keeps the truck moving at a crawl while JT, Rosie, and Jesse pick up armfuls of stakes and throw them up to me. I catch the stakes and then stack them on top of the lumber.

The stakes have nails sticking out of them, so JT, Rosie, and Jesse have to be careful how they throw them. Johnny never bitches at us for being careful. Some of the other foremen don't care about their laborers. Pappy sometimes drives his men so hard that the arms of the guy catching stakes are dripping blood by the end of the day.

I have a vague feeling that I won't do construction work forever, but I don't know what else I might do. It would be easy to settle into this life, working hard, drinking beer, playing a little softball and hockey, only to wake up someday and find I'm forty-five years old and still on the break-out gang. I'm not sure what God has in mind for me, but I'm pretty sure it isn't throwing rocks for the rest of my life.

But as quickly as these nagging thoughts of the future come into my mind, they leave. How like a little boy I am. How little I care for intro-spection. I do what I have to do—work—but like a little boy I want to spend the rest of my time playing. In the summer this means softball; in the winter, hockey. But always, summer *and* winter, it means the bars.

CHAPTER THREE

When I'm not driving the cab at night (and sometimes even when I am) I spend my time with the guys I grew up with, drinking beer and shooting pool in one of the many Irish bars scattered around the West Side: Sullivan's, Naughton's, Durty Dick's, Guilfoyle's, Callahan's, and O'Neill's. But the place that has come to be my home away from home is O'Dea's.

The Notre Dame Inn, it's called, a little hole in the wall on West Division Street owned by a bandy-legged old Irish football player from Clare named PJ O'Dea. The name Notre Dame Inn is PJ's effort to capitalize on the cachet of an established American institution while still respecting the ethnicity of his clientele. But no one ever calls it anything but O'Dea's.

It is a one-story brick building built back in the twenties. PJ says it was a funeral parlor years ago, but he insists there are more stiffs in the place now than there were when he bought it.

There is a Harp sign in the window and something PJ claims is an air conditioner perched precariously over the front door. No one has ever seen it work. Inside, a long wooden bar with a mirror behind it stretches halfway down the length of the pub. The floor is warped and slightly off-keel, making everything conveniently run downhill toward the bar. A quarter-a-game pool table, its rails pocked with cigarette burns, lurks within stumbling distance of the bar. A dusty upright piano, its keys cracked and yellow, decomposes in a corner.

PJ has three machines in his pub: a cigarette machine that won't work without being kicked, cursed, or beaten, a pinball-bowling machine that stopped working the day JFK got shot, and a jukebox, well-stocked with Clancy Brothers, Dubliners, Big Tom, the Kilfenora Céili Band, and an assortment of jigs and reels. Late at night you might even hear a little Bing Crosby or Carmel Quinn. If you play C7, "McAlpine's Fusilliers," you get three extra plays for your quarter.

There were glasses flyin' and biddies cryin'.
The Paddies were going to town.

O'Dea's is a workingman's bar. It is not a place to bring a woman unless she is extremely thick-skinned or extremely available. It helps to be both. I first started hanging around here five years ago, back in the days of the Vietnam War when eighteen-year-old kids were being plucked from West Side neighborhoods and shipped off to jungles on the other side of the world. At that time, neither publicans nor policemen paid much attention to laws prohibiting eighteen-year-old guys from drinking, accepting the maxim that if you're old enough to fight, you're old enough to drink.

I was nineteen but looked sixteen the first time I stepped up to the bar, took a deep breath, looked PJ in the eye, and asked if I might have a beer. Please. Sir.

From the end of the bar, an old guy with a tweed cap pulled low on his head snickered and mumbled that choir practice at St. Kate's must have let out late today.

"Shut yer durty mouth," the man next to him said. "Can't you see the lad's a fine oul toper? G'wan, PJ, I'm gettin' the next round. Give the lad a schooner. On me." He nudged the pile of bills on the bar in front of him.

PJ frowned and cocked his head. "How old might you be?" he asked me.

"Never mind how old he is," the man said. "Give yer man a drink before he collapses from the thirst."

PJ sighed, filled a glass, and slid it across to me.

"By God, the nuns at St. Kate's will have your ass for this, PJ," the first man muttered.

I lifted the glass and raised it to the man who bought it. "Sláinte," I said, "agus bas in Eirinn."

The head of every man at the bar snapped up. "Bejasus, we've a lad from the Gaeltacht! What county are you from, boy?"

"County Cook," I said with a laugh. "I was born right down the street at St. Anne's."

The guy who bought me the beer got up and shook my hand. "I'm suffocated with pleasure to have the opportunity to meet a man of your qualifications," he said.

I bought the next round. Jimmy Moylan, the man who said I was from St. Kate's, bought the next. John MacDonald, a carpenter from Westmeath, got the next, and we were off. By the end of the night, PJ, Ambrose O'Brien (who bought the first round), and I were locked arm-in-arm, mangling the words to "The Men Behind the Wire" and "The Fields of Athenry."

Finally, an hour after closing, when the only light in the place was the pale glow from the glass-fronted fridge behind the bar, PJ opened the back door and let me into the alley. "Get ye home, lad," he told me, "and if a copper smells your breath, forget you were here. Tell him you were served in one of the Polack bars up on Milwaukee Avenue."

That night was my introduction to a remarkable world—not just of alcohol, but of the companionship of workingmen. At O'Dea's there are alcoholics who come for the booze, and teetotalers who come for the camaraderie. There are single men on the prowl, and old bachelors who stammer and blush on the rare occasion when a woman comes in. There are carpenters who can recite great swaths of Shakespeare, and ironworkers who think Chekhov is something you do in the bathroom late at night when no one is around.

I have grown up in a family not of wealth but of stability, where everyone loves everyone else. Right and wrong are laid out in front of us. We are told what to choose and how to choose it. It can be a little smothering at times, but overall it is immensely comforting and reassuring. *Adultery, theft, sloth*, and *greed* are only words. I have never seen them.

At O'Dea's I see a lot of things I've never seen at home.

Although he might get the odd Puerto Rican bus driver or Polish mechanic, 90 percent of PJ's customers are Irish immigrants. From them I learn about the land of my ancestors. Ambrose O'Brien leans his elbows back on the bar and tells me what a "crazy, priest-ridden, superstitious, downtrodden, oppressed, hopeless" sort of a country it is and thank God he got the hell out. Five minutes later he tells me it is the most beautiful place God ever put on earth.

Our crew is still working breakout on the West Side. We get two hours of overtime today, so I don't get home until eight o'clock. My mom tried to save dinner for me, but my brothers have picked at it until nothing's left but a couple shriveled pieces of cauliflower and half a baked potato. I finish those while I'm frying myself a couple hamburgers. I turn the fire down low, then sprint upstairs, take a quick shower, and change into my softball uniform. I fly back downstairs just in time to find my brother Pete scooping up one of my burgers with a fork.

I elbow him aside. "Don't even think about it," I tell him.

I shovel down the burgers and head to our softball game. It's the middle of the fourth when I get there. We're playing a team from Avenue State Bank and beat them easily. The game is over at 9:30 and we head for O'Dea's.

I'm the first one to arrive. The place is empty except for PJ and old Mick Brennan down at the end of the bar, nursing a schooner and a shot of Bushmills. Mick is a janitor at St. Anne's Hospital. He always comes in here when he gets off work. Since his shift rotates, he sometimes comes in at noon, sometimes at 5:00 P.M., and sometimes at midnight. Today he has been here since noon. I say hello to him.

He turns his head and looks at me. It takes his eyes a few seconds to focus. "Hello, Michael," he says.

I swing a leg over a stool and order a schooner of Old Style. "Let me get one for you and Mick, too," I tell PJ.

PJ nods his thanks. "How'd the lads do tonight?" he asks as he fills our glasses.

"Okay. We played a bunch of bankers and beat 'em 11–2. They weren't very good."

Last spring my friends and I talked PJ into sponsoring our softball team. In return for his sponsorship we promised to patronize his establishment after each game. The deal was: he'd give us two hundred dollars now if we'd give him five thousand dollars over the course of the summer. We congratulated ourselves on the shrewd bargain we had driven.

The team drifts in, dirty and dusty, with sweat-streaked faces and damp, tousled hair hanging carelessly on their foreheads. There is a fight on TV, so we all throw in a couple bucks and draw rounds out of a baseball cap. The fight is stopped in the eighth. Chet Ryan, who is sitting in a chair along the wall, feet up on the table, spikes glinting in the light from the pool table, tells PJ to put his winnings on the bar. The rest of us drink for free for half an hour.

It is a hot night and PJ has the front and back doors propped open with slivers of wood. Pat Murtaugh is standing in the door, trying to catch a breeze, his right hand gripping a bottle of beer, his left hand tucked in the side of his grass-stained sweatpants. Pat likes it here. In fact, Pat likes just about any place that has four walls and a roof. He got kicked out of his parents' house last month and has been living in the bushes at the House of Studies ever since. He has now perfected the art of taking showers in the sink of the men's room in every bar on the West Side.

At 2:00 A.M., PJ eases the last of us out the back door. We walk around to the front of the building. Division Street is quiet at this hour, and we stand there, holding our beer bottles by the necks, taking an occasional swig, and talking about the Sox.

Two of our cars are parked right in front of the bar. The others are scattered in a half-block radius. Several of the players are leaning against the wall of the tavern. Dick Murphy and Tom Burns are leaning against the grille of Murph's car. Murph has his arms folded across his chest, his beer bottle cradled under his armpit.

It is a clear, moonless night. Across the street, the lights in Salerno's Pizza are out. A couple hours ago, we all kicked in fifty cents or a buck. Murph walked over to Salerno's, got an extra-large cheese and sausage, brought it back, and laid it on the bar. It lasted three minutes.

The conversation slowly peters out until at length we are quiet, listening to the occasional sound of a car passing down Austin Boulevard. It doesn't seem that big a deal to me that I have to get up for work in another two and a half hours, but I mention that I probably ought to get going.

Murph pushes himself up from the grille of his car, balances his empty bottle on top of the fire hydrant, and says, "Yeah. Me, too."

When I get home, my brother Tim is in the kitchen. He has just shoved something under his chair. When he sees it is only me, he reaches down and puts his can of beer back on the table.

I haven't seen much of Tim recently. He just got back from Colorado. He was there for an hour and fifteen minutes.

Tim and his friends are obsessed with Coors beer. They think it has mystical powers. I guess when you're a senior in high school, if you drink enough of any kind of beer you will think it has mystical powers.

Coors is sold only in Colorado. A week ago Tim decided that if he had a trailer full of Coors he could make a fortune selling it to his friends. Of course, since Tim and his friends are only eighteen, if he had a trailer full of Buckhorn he could make a fortune selling it to his friends.

Tim rented a U-Haul, drove all day and all night to the first town inside the Colorado line. He bought every case of Coors they had, filled the trailer top to bottom, then turned around and drove home.

Word has now spread throughout the juvenile delinquent community that some kid from Fenwick High School is selling a trailerful of Coors. He has kids from Austin, Cicero, Melrose Park, La Grange, Berwyn, and

Western Springs beating a path to our door. I bought a couple cases my-self. I might be Tim's only customer who is actually twenty-one.

My mom can't understand why Tim is getting so many phone calls. He tells her he is selling scapulars for the Altar and Rosary Society.

I grab a chair and have a can of Coors with Tim. After a couple minutes I ask him, "How's business?"

He says business is great. He's made a bundle. He has only twelve cases left. It seems funny seeing my little brother drinking a beer. He still seems like such a kid to me. Now that he has sold a trailer of beer he thinks he is on the road to a career as some sort of bootleg beer distributor, a modern-day teenaged Al Capone. Tim says he is thinking about going up to Canada to get a trailer full of Molson's or maybe heading down to Mexico to load up on some Corona.

Tim might be serious, he might be kidding, but he is for sure gassed. I tell him it is 2:30 A.M. and he'd better get to bed before Mom or Dad hears him. Tim grunts his agreement. We finish our beers, turn off the lights, and stumble up the stairs in the dark, each of us whispering to the other to shut up and stop making so much noise.

CHAPTER FOUR

The early-morning sun is streaming through the trees as I rumble past the eastern edge of Oak Park Country Club. The thick, green bushes bordering the course are bent low with dew, and mist clings to the low spots along the creek. Inside the fence the fairway is still deep in shadow, but in the distance a red flag rises out of the mist, and the rolling hills glow a luminescent green in the slanting rays of the sun.

On the crest of a hill, three greenskeepers are moving toward me, pushing their mowers ahead of them, dragging their hoses behind them. I used to caddy at this course years ago, and I wonder if any of the guys I know still work here. One of the greenskeepers shoves the other playfully and I can almost hear him say, *"Pinche pendejo."*

It is 5:45 A.M. when I pull up to the job. Already the temperature is seventy-eight degrees. Jesse is sitting on the tongue of the Sullair eating an oatmeal cookie. As much as the man drinks, he is always the first one on the job in the morning.

As I hop out of The Rat, Jesse says, "Hey, babe," and hands me one of his cookies. He slides over and I sit next to him, gobbling the cookie and waiting to see if he'll offer me another.

I notice that Johnny's other crew is here, too. I point at them. "What're they doing here?"

"I don't know," Jesse says, "and long as they don't get in our way, I don't care, neither."

Ten minutes later, Johnny waves a hand at our crew. "Get your asses over here," he says.

The five of us walk over to Johnny's truck. He points at a driveway and a long section of curb stretching away toward Central Avenue. "I want this whole thing broken out by noon," he says.

Jesse shakes his head. "Shee-it," he says. "We'd need a ton of dynamite to break out all that shit by noon."

The guys on Johnny's other crew snicker at us behind Johnny's back. Rosie gives them the finger and tells them all to get bent. Johnny tells us to quit bitching and do what we get paid to do. Then he takes the second crew off to another spot.

We don't even wait till 6:30. At 6:15 we begin working for the church. By 7:15 Angelo's truck is loaded. He swings himself up into the cab and heads to the dump. Rosie, JT, and I each give him a couple bucks to get some beer. Jesse always has plenty of his own.

When Ange is gone, I pull up The Rat and the four of us—JT, Rosie, Jesse, and I—go back to work. It is only 7:30, but already my T-shirt is sopping wet. Rosie is sweating so profusely that even his jeans are soaked. With no foreman around, Jesse won't push himself, but we don't mind. We let him take the shovel and follow behind us, cleaning up the smaller pieces.

Angelo returns in half an hour with two six-packs of Old Style. Since Ange is off the sauce, that leaves four beers apiece for the rest of us. We take a short break and guzzle down two beers each. Jesse has a Schlitz and a couple swigs of his VO.

We finish our beers, throw the cans in the back of The Rat, and get back in the hole. The beers kick in, and JT, Rosie, and I start hauling ass. Sweat flies off our faces and arms. JT runs the gun nonstop, breaking loose piece after piece of concrete, never taking his hand off the trigger. Rosie and I have to run just to keep up.

No one is forcing us to work this hard. It is something we want to do. The three of us don't just *do* the work; we *attack* it. We want to work harder and harder, faster and faster. We want to grunt and sweat and holler and roar. Rosie and I run from the driveway to the truck with our chunks of concrete, hurl them over the edge, and tear back for the next one.

Our ears are battered by the thunder of the jackhammer. Our noses, thick with filtered grime, can still smell the sweet exhaust from the compressor running wide open next to us. Our throats and tongues are dry and raspy from inhaling the desiccating clouds of limestone. Little pieces of grit coat our skin. We can feel them in our hair, under our shirts, down our pants, in our boots. They flow in rivulets of sweat that drop from our chins and wrists.

As I heave another piece of concrete onto the truck, I glance back to the spot where, twenty feet away, Rosie is bent over to pick up the next rock. The sun is behind him, and as the sunlight filters through the soot and dust, it catches a drop of sweat poised on the tip of his chin. Time stops for a moment as the drop glistens in the thick, dusty air. The glimmering bead of sweat looks so startlingly fresh and pure as it hovers, swells, and then drops to the ground.

Rosie and I leave our cans of beer on the side of the truck. We grab a mouthful when we can. But even twenty feet away, pieces of grit and bits of concrete find their way into our beer. I can taste the grittiness as I swig down another mouthful. Then it's back to stoop, lift, run, throw. When we finally finish the first section, Rosie and I are gasping for breath. We lean against the compressor, panting, and pound down the last of the beer.

Jesse says we are two dumb-ass white boys for working so hard. But he doesn't mean it. Jesse knows. He was young once, too.

Angelo comes back from the dump. He sees us leaning against the compressor. He hops out of his truck and grins. "Well, boys," he says. "Congratulations. You've broken out a driveway, knocked off a coupla hundred feet of curb, loaded three trucks, and got yourselves drunk—and it's only nine o'clock in the morning!"

We still have several hundred feet of concrete to break out. We continue to attack our work, but not as furiously as we did with the first section. Whatever effect the beer had is gone in an hour, but we continue pushing. We want to finish this section by noon.

We toss the last rock on The Rat at 12:10, just as Johnny pulls up.

"You guys done? Good. Come on over to Thirty-first Street. I got a couple sections there for you."

"What about lunch?" Rosie asks.

"Lunch? You guys ain't had lunch yet? The hell you been doin', jaggin' off?"

"No, asshole, we've been workin' our balls off. You think Jurgis and Stew and those guys on your other crew could have broken out this whole section in one morning? Hell no! We just busted our nuts for you, and now you don't want to give us lunch?"

Johnny backs off. He knows damn well we are his best crew. "All right, all right. Have your lunch and then get your asses over to Thirty-first Street."

When Johnny leaves, Rosie turns to me, Jesse, and JT. "What the hell's with you guys? You lose your voices or something? How come I'm the only one stands up to Johnny?"

"Johnny's not going to listen to us," I say. "You're a *paisano*, a goombah. Johnny listens to you. We no speaka the language, *capeesh*?"

Rosie says we're full of shit and let's eat. We find a nice shade tree and stretch out on the grass, our lunch bags beside us. Angelo pulls up in his truck and saunters over to eat with us. Rosie takes off his T-shirt and hangs it on a parking sign to dry. There is a faint breeze and it is so deliciously cool in the shade that it feels like heaven.

My mom made chicken for dinner last night. When I finished raiding the icebox this morning I left no survivors. I have two breasts and four legs—plus three peanut butter and jelly sandwiches, two oranges, a can of peaches, and a sleeve of fig bars.

I spread my lunch out in the grass in front of me. Rosie looks at it, shakes his head, and says, "What's the matter, you losing your appetite?"

Rosie should talk. He's got four sandwiches himself. JT, on the other hand, spends the whole half hour working on a battered peach and a brown hunk of meat loaf wrapped in aluminum foil. Jesse is happy with a couple cans of Schlitz and more oatmeal cookies.

When I finish my lunch Jesse sees me eyeing his cookies. He grabs them, clutches them to his chest, and says, "Ain't gonna happen, babe. Ain't gonna happen."

Two minutes later, lunch is over. As we grunt and struggle to our feet, Jesse hands me his last cookie. I smile and say thanks. Jesse pushes up his sunglasses and says, "Fuck you."

When the day ends, both crews come together. Jurgis is the gun runner on Johnny's other crew. He is a huge, lumbering tree trunk of a guy from some Eastern European country that no one ever heard of. Johnny called him a Polack one day and Jurgis reared up. "*Not* Polack!" he shouted. He told Johnny he was from Lutherania or Lithovackia or somewhere. Johnny says what the hell difference does it make? He can never remember the name of the country anyway, so he calls it Lesbomania.

Jurgis always works with a rock thrower named Stewart. Stew is a white guy. No one knows his last name. We figure it's gotta be Italian. What we do know is that Stew is not a rocket scientist. He's not a rocket janitor, either. Johnny was pissed at him one day and said he was dumber than a vegetable, so now everyone calls him Vegetable Stew. Stew doesn't care. He works like a mule.

The other rock thrower who works with Jurgis is a skinny little black guy named Lester who was the laziest guy in the company until they hired Bean Pole and Bake. Lester always works with Vegetable Stew, who does the work of two men, which is good, because Lester does the work of half a man.

I casually mention this fact to Lester, who immediately tells me to "shut the fuck up. You and that muscle-bound dago Roselli is only two men. Me workin' with m'man Stew here is like havin' two *and a half* men. Ain't that right, Stew?"

Stew just smiles. He never says much.

Sometimes I envy Stew. Not that I would want to trade places with him, but Stew has no concerns about anything. He is perfectly content to throw rocks for the rest of his life. My problem is that recently I find my- self *not* content.

Being from a family like mine makes things difficult. I am surrounded by such good people—so good that it is intimidating. Everywhere I look there is some larger-than-life, legendary character: my father's father, the alcoholic, who beat the booze; my mother's father, who left the family farm at age thirteen to seek his fortune in British Columbia; my uncle, a tail gunner on a B-17 who got killed in the war; another uncle who carried a machine gun in Patton's Third Army—typical West Side guys whose toughness in fights, whose exploits on the gridiron, whose valor in the war, whose devotion to their families have set the bar so high that I wonder if I will ever measure up.

But I don't really allow myself to think much about it. It's easier to throw rocks and drink beer. The problem is that I've been throwing rocks and drinking beer for too long. More and more I find myself longing to in- volve myself in something bigger, something more meaningful.

I just don't know what that would be.

CHAPTER FIVE

They drive us. All day long they drive us. They drive us until the heat sears our lungs and each breath rasps the back of our throats. They drive us until we pant like dogs and our tongues hang from our mouths like hams on a curing hook. They drive us until our sweat dries up and black blood congeals between the cracked calluses on our hands. They drive us until we cramp up so bad we can't stand up straight and we stagger back and forth like a crew of hunchbacks working the mines of hell.

It is the hottest day I have ever seen. It is the hottest day any of us have ever seen. But the foremen say they don't give a shit how hot it is. They tell us we are behind schedule and we gotta finish this section—today.

The thermometer at the Pure Oil station reads 104 degrees, but it must be 140 on the highway. The concrete reflects the heat of the sun back at us, and the air is so hot we can breathe only in shallow gulps. The pavement burns our hands if we touch it. It disintegrates the adhesive that holds our boots together, and we trudge across the highway with the soles of our boots flapping. Pavement buckles, and black tar oozes up from the expansion joints.

The cooler on the back of Johnny's truck is empty by 10:00 A.M. and we have nothing else to drink for the rest of the day. There is not the least breath of wind, not the least hint of shade. There are no breaks, no lunch. We gotta finish this section today.

The heat sucks the strength from us, but we force ourselves to go on. No one wants to be the first to give in. JT has been running the gun without stop since 6:30 this morning. He has been breaking the rocks into smaller and smaller pieces, but as the day goes on, they seem heavier and heavier to us. Rosie and I have filled ten trucks today, but we still have several hundred feet to go.

Up and down the line, foremen are screaming and waving their arms. The shimmering waves of heat rising off the highway warp my vision, making the scene even more nightmarish. Trucks are scurrying back and forth, compressors are dangerously overheating, and above it all the roar of the machines obliterates all other sound.

I have a little warm water left in my Coke bottle. I take a mouthful and give the rest to Jesse. He has his red bandana hanging from the back of his hard hat, Foreign Legion style, but he can barely lift his shovel. I'm worried he's not going to make it.

We finally finish breaking out the last section around three. For the first time in nine hours, JT shuts down the compressor. I heave the last rock onto the back of The Rat. JT, Rosie, and I stand next to one another, bent over, heads down, hands on our thighs, panting slowly. We are looking for a place to sit down when Johnny pulls up in his truck. He tells us to start lining up the lumber and stakes.

"The carpenters'll be here any minute," he says, "and they gotta get this thing framed up."

We can't believe it. The only thing that has kept us going this last hour was watching as the end of the line approached, thinking that we were almost done, that in a short while we could finally rest.

Now Johnny wants us to start lining?

Rosie straightens up, balls his fists, and glares at Johnny. "You gotta be shittin' me," he says.

Johnny lifts his hands. "Look, kid. This ain't my idea. Fred says this job's gotta be wrapped up today. I know you guys been bustin' your ass, and I'll make it up to you, but this lumber's gotta get lined up—now!"

Rosie doesn't move. He continues to glare at Johnny. I am afraid Rosie is going to take a swing at him. Finally, JT turns, grabs a sixteen-inch board, and drags it into position. I grab the next one and line it up next to JT's.

Rosie won't let us work alone. He clenches his teeth and growls out a long stream of profanity directed at the Scalese family lineage, with particular emphasis on the unorthodox and incestuous methods by which they were all begotten. Then he turns and drags the next board into position.

JT, Rosie, and I, who thought we could handle anything from anyone, are hardly able to stay upright. But we keep working.

The carpenters arrive ten minutes later and are right on our asses. Usually they bitch about having too much or too little lumber, too few or too many stakes. Today they don't say anything. They grab the boards and start framing. They don't look much better than we do.

Everything is almost framed up at four o'clock when the Material Service trucks arrive. The foremen are worried that it is so hot that the concrete will harden before the finishers can get to it. The foremen scream and swear and throw clipboards, but the laborers and finishers are too beaten, too worn, to do more than plod on. Finally, around six, when the last of the concrete is poured, we stumble into the shade and drop to the ground.

Jesse is sitting on the ground, slumped against the side of a stake truck. He looks up and sees me slinging angle irons onto the back of The Rat. "Boy," he calls in a soft, raspy voice, "you tryin' to kill your damn self? Sit your white ass down here."

I can hardly lift my feet. I trudge over to Jesse and drop down next to him. I think how good it would feel to lie down. I lay back and stretch out, but immediately cramps tear through my stomach, back, and shoulders. I sit back up and hook my arms around my drawn-up legs and lay my head on my forearms.

A few minutes later, I struggle to my feet, stumble over to The Rat, pull out a warm can of Old Style, and ease back down next to Jesse. I point the can away from us and pop the top. A shower of white foam shoots into the air and drips down my hand. I shake the foam from my hand and offer the can to Jesse.

"No thanks, son," he says, shaking his head. "Save it for my damn funeral."

I take a long pull of the Old Style and close my eyes. I don't care that the beer is warm. All that matters is that it is wet.

Jesse is in awful shape. He takes off his hard hat and gets some kids to fill it with water. Then he slowly pours the water over his head, turning his gray Afro into a soggy batch of seaweed. He lets his head hang down, swinging it slowly back and forth as the water streams from his forehead and lips.

"This is the worst day I seen in thirty years," he says. "You gonna tell your grandchildren about this day." He is panting as he speaks, and his words are torn from him like rusted barbed wire ripped from a weathered fence post.

"Look around you, boy," he says.

I nod. "Yeah," I murmur without looking up.

"No, goddamn it. I said *look around*!"

I lift my head and look at the men around me, suddenly realizing how much everyone else is suffering. Men are slumped against trucks and leaning on trees. Three of the older guys are lying against the shady side of a compressor, boots off, eyes bulging, mouths open, panting miserably. Lester is in the bushes, bent over with the dry heaves.

"You're young," Jesse says, "and it ain't too late. Look around and remember what you see. And then you get the hell out of here or you'll wind up like me: an old sack of shit lyin' in the dirt."

"Jesse, you're not—"

"Don't you fuck with me, boy," he says. "Don't you fuck with this old man."

He raises his bloodshot eyes and fixes them on me. "I'm tellin' you God's own truth. You don't wanna listen, that's your business, but don't you fuck with me. I'm too old to be fucked with. And pretty soon you be old, too. And there ain't nothin' you can do about it. But you *can* do somethin' about this." He gestures around us. "You can spend your life on the breakout gang throwin' rocks like the rest of us no-account fools, sweatin' our lives away, waitin' to be throwed on the junk pile—or you can get out before it's too late."

Before it's too late. Sometimes I think it already is.

For the next few days I can't get Jesse's words out of my mind. It's not that I suddenly don't like being a rock thrower. I do—and that's the problem. It's not exactly prestigious, but that's not what's bothering me. Anyone who wants to look down on me because I work with my hands can go take a flying leap for himself. But I'm beginning to feel that something is missing. I'm heading nowhere. All I do is throw rocks, shoot pool, and drink beer. My life isn't evil or slothful; it just lacks direction.

Sometimes I think it would be easier if I had one of those miserable Irish Catholic childhoods people talk about. It would be easier to want things to change, to dream of something better. But to me a miserable Irish Catholic childhood is an oxymoron. For twenty-four years I've had a pretty nice life—and it's hard to admit that it's coming to an end. But I'm starting to realize that I can't be a child forever, that I don't *want* to be a child forever. I've had my turn, and now it's time to grow up. It's time to start asking myself the question my friends must have asked themselves years ago: "What do I want to be when I grow up?"

My friends are now in law school, working for accounting firms, or getting started in the Secret Service and the FBI. I'm throwing rocks on a breakout gang for the Vittorio Scalese Construction Company, and as Jesse says, I'm goin' down.

So what, then? I want to do more than just make money, more than just live for myself. It sounds corny, but I want to do something important, something noble. I want to make a mark on the world.

I don't know where I get the idea of being a doctor. No one in my family has ever been a doctor. But the more I think about it, the more I like it. No other profession offers such opportunity for altruism and compassion. If I truly want to help other people, I may have found what I'm looking for.

But *me*? A doctor? Give me a break.

.   .   .

I make the mistake of mentioning to my brothers that I'm thinking about becoming a doctor. Denny says that's interesting because he's thinking about becoming Pope. Tim says he's thinking about becoming a boxer and kicking Muhammad Ali's ass. Rog says he didn't know they let guys with half a brain into medical school.

Jack tells me to ignore those other guys. He says if being a doctor means I will be able to help him get some fake IDs then he's all for it.

Bill is only seven years old. "What's a doctor?" he asks. Pete tells him doctors are guys who stick needles in your arm and fingers up your butt.

Bill looks at me funny and says he will sit on the other side of the dinner table tonight.

I make tentative inquiries at several Chicago-area medical schools. I learn that all applicants have to take a test called the MedCAT, the Medical College Admissions Test. It's supposed to be very difficult.

What is worse, all applicants must have taken a minimum number of science courses in college. The only science course I had in college was a geology course everyone called Rocks for Jocks. It turned out to be harder than we thought. I also tried to get into a physics course known as Quarks for Dorks. It, too, was supposed to be an easy A. Unfortunately, too many other students applied before me and I couldn't get in.

"No chemistry? No physics? No biology?" The schools I talk to are astounded that someone lacking these most basic of requirements would have the temerity to consider medical school.

"But I've read Yeats and Shakespeare and Wordsworth and Woolf."

No one's impressed. "Come back when you've read Watson and Crick and Mendel and Einstein."

"But I want to be a doctor, not a scientist."

What I want does not matter here. They will send me a list of their requirements. "Come back when you've met them; then we'll talk."

.   .   .

I imagine myself being called into the office of the dean of admissions at Northwestern med school. The dean is a tall, thin gentleman with well-coiffed silver hair and immaculate nails. He has a long, hyphenated last name like Haversham-Blitsington. The last time someone with a name like his sat across the table from someone with a name like mine, it probably involved salmon poaching or gunrunning. Fortunately for me, this modern-day Haversham-Blitsington no longer has the power to sleep with my wife on our wedding night or have me transported to Van Diemen's Land if the potato crop goes bad and I can't pay my rent.

I introduce myself to His Lordship, I mean His Deanship, and immediately try to hide my hands behind my back. My nails are broken; my hands are calloused and dirty. I scrubbed them for half an hour this morning but just couldn't get all the dirt out. It must be tattooed into my skin.

I sit quietly as he leafs through my file, frowning and muttering things like, "Good heavens," and, "By Jove."

Finally he looks up at me. "Now let me see, Mr. Corchoran," he says with his very proper English accent. "It appears that you spent the last several years working for"—he glances back at the file—"the Scalese Construction Company? Hmmm. Most interesting. Were you by chance in their medical department?"

"Their *medical* department?" I clear my throat. "Well, no. Actually I was in their, uh . . . *propulsion* department."

"Their propulsion department?"

"Yes. I threw rocks."

"You . . . threw . . . rocks." The dean pronounces each word with the type of distaste usually voiced after observing lewd behavior by caged monkeys. He sighs and then begins polishing his glasses on the end of his white lab coat. "I am afraid, Mr. Costello, that your transcript does not mention your grades in chemistry or physics or biology."

"I didn't take those courses in college."

He shakes his head. "Unfortunate. Most unfortunate indeed."

He clears his throat, closes the folder, and snaps open the lid of his gold pocket watch. Where *has* the time gone? It must be time to wax the old yacht. The dean rises to his feet and extends his hand. "It certainly has been nice to meet you, Mr. Connolly."

"Collins."

"I beg your pardon?" He glances back at the file. "Oh, yes, of course. Collins. Well, thank you, Mr. Collins, and we'll be getting back to you soon."

I wonder when the next ship leaves for Van Diemen's Land.

Okay. So I have to go back and take some pre-med courses. That's doable.

But then I think, *What am I, nuts?* Taking all those pre-med courses is not something I can knock off in a few weeks. I'd have to go back to school for *two years*! All that work, all that tuition, all that time—on the outside chance that some medical school *might* let me in?

It's too bad I didn't take those science courses in college. It's too bad I didn't major in pre-med. It's too bad I didn't do a lot of things—*but I didn't*, and that's that. Get over it. It's time to accept the fact that this door is closed. It's time to move on.

But I can't move on. I try, but I can't, and now I'm stuck with this stupid, hopeless dream of becoming a doctor. I'm about to throw away two years of my life chasing a dream that has very little chance of coming true.

Well, no one's holding a gun to my head. No one is saying I have to do this.

But a line from Tennyson keeps running through my head. " 'Tis not too late to seek a newer world," the aging Ulysses tells his men.

Maybe, just maybe, it's not too late for me, either.

CHAPTER SIX

Perhaps because I'm thinking about leaving this life, I suddenly start seeing and feeling things that weren't there before. At the end of the day, when JT levers the last rock free, lays the jackhammer on the pavement, and shuts down the compressor, I notice, for the first time, how the silence becomes not just the absence of something but a living, tangible thing that flows up from the ground and wraps itself around us: silence we not only hear but feel, silence that flows over the tired men and the trucks and the broken piles of concrete, caressing our foreheads and soothing the back of our sunburned necks.

For the first time, I notice when I'm on the back of The Rat catching stakes how Rosie throws them to me so perfectly that when his stack of stakes reaches the top of its parabolic arc, it is neither rising nor falling but is suspended there, and I can reach out and grab it as if it had been floating motionless all the time.

And the mornings, especially the mornings: the rainy mornings when I see the gray light of day rise warily over Lake Michigan and seep into the sodden city over the roofs of muffler shops and all-night diners, or the sunny mornings when I lean back in the cab of The Rat, my feet up on the dashboard, drinking coffee and watching the sun slip through the gaps between the warehouses and the factories and throw refulgent bars of light over sheets of soggy newspaper clinging to the broken pavement.

I'm asking a lot of questions but finding no answers, and it's beginning to take a toll on me. One minute, I'm yelling at Jesse for not keeping up with us. The next, I'm grabbing a shovel, giving him a hand, and telling him I'm a jerk and he should pay no attention to me.

"What the hell's with you, man?" Rosie asks.

I don't know what the hell's with me. This whole decision about going to medical school is harder than I thought—and I haven't even done anything yet. I'm not sure I even have the tools to make the decision. What do I know about medicine? What do I know about anything? I'm in uncharted territory. I'm the octopus who wants to fly—it's not like he has a lot of other flying octopuses he can go to for advice. I can't just walk into some office somewhere and exchange my pick and shovel for a stethoscope and a reflex hammer.

Today at lunch I see a dragonfly, a big, old, hoary prehistoric-looking thing that has no business living in the twentieth century. It looks like some fossil you would see etched in sedimentary rock on the banks of the Tigris or Euphrates. Its body is so bulky, so ungainly, so primitive, that even when I see it in the air, I can't believe it can fly. I watch it for a while as it hovers, then darts around the edge of the canal, unconcerned that it is ugly, unconcerned that it shouldn't be able to fly, and unconcerned that, by rights, it should have been extinct centuries ago.

For the last four days we've been working on the Southwest Side. Today we are at Thirty-first and Sacramento along a slip of the Sanitary Canal. Around us, grimy brick smokestacks belch white smoke. Above us, sagging strands of high-tension wires, strung between giant pylons, stretch east toward California Avenue. Next to us, a long, gray barge is moored on the far side of the canal cowering under two black winches. Great mounds of earth and coal are piled next to a squat, brick warehouse lined with small paneled windows, most of which are broken. Two men are propped in chairs, leaning against the loading dock, reading the *Racing Form*.

Our crew is gathered around the back of The Rat, drinking coffee. Even at 6:00 A.M. we have to shout to be heard above the grating of gears, the roar of diesels, the blast of air brakes, and the crash of shocks from the truck traffic along Thirty-first Street. As I lean forward to grab another donut, Rosie pulls the paperback book from my back pocket.

"*The Making of a Surgeon*," he says. "What's this shit?"

I grab the book back from him. "It's a good book," I tell him. "You ought to read it sometime."

"I'm done with books," he says. "Books suck. Books are what got me kicked out of college."

I tell Rosie he has an interesting way of looking at things.

It is quarter after six. I glance to the east where, behind the Sanitary Canal, the sky is glowing orange and red. "Ah, rosy-fingered dawn," I say.

"I don't care *what* he did to her," Johnny Battaglia says. "We got a shit-load of work to do today." He hooks both thumbs in his belt and leans back. "You guys get a good night's sleep?" He doesn't wait for an answer. "I hope so, because you're gonna earn those paychecks today."

Jesse spits on the ground. "What we gotta do, break out the whole damn Dan Ryan Expressway? Why don't you just say you're gonna fuck us over?"

Johnny tells him to quit bitching. "This ain't no country club we're running out here," he says. "The carpenters are gonna be here at eight and they gotta have everything framed so Normie's crew can pour it this afternoon. So quit your bellyachin'. Get that compressor running and get the last of this shit broken out. Then we're moving over to California Avenue."

JT hops off the back of The Rat, clasps his hands behind his head, and tilts right, then left. He stares off to the east. "Red sky at morning . . . ," he says.

We finish breaking out the last of the curb on Thirty-first Street at seven o'clock. Then we shift over to California Avenue, just south of the Stevenson. By nine o'clock we have a nice rhythm going. We are loading a truck an hour and moving steadily south. Over the roar of the jackhammer we can hear Jesse talking to himself as he shovels. "Country club, my ass," he says as he flings a shovelful of stones and rocks at The Rat. About half of it makes it onto the bed; the rest clatters against the side and falls onto the road. "Goddamn bullshit, that's what it is. Goddamn Scalese bullshit."

Around ten the sky darkens, the tops of the trees stir, and a light rain begins to patter against our hard hats. We don't even slow down. It's a warm rain, so Rosie and I strip off our T-shirts and toss them in the front seat of The Rat.

The rain picks up, and by eleven the hole we're working in has an inch of water. Rosie and I slop around in the muddy water bending and lifting the endless string of rocks JT is breaking out. Soon our boots and our pants are soaked. Water streams off our bare backs and forearms, but there is no thought of stopping. Fred and the guys in the office may cancel work if it is raining, but once the foremen have us out on the job they aren't going to send us home for anything less than a Category 5 hurricane.

Johnny drives by in his pickup twenty minutes later to be sure we are still working. Jesse shakes his shovel at him. "That's right. That's right," he shouts at Johnny. "You just sit there in your truck, while we out here workin' in the rain like a bunch of goddamn fools."

For lunch, we pull our shirts back on and troop into the Czech bar across the street from the Campbell's Soup plant. We get there just before noon. Within five minutes, the workers from the plant start streaming in. They aren't pleased to find a bunch of muddy construction workers sitting in their booths and playing on their pool table. But they aren't fools, either. They take one look at us and keep their mouths shut.

The owner's wife serves up a hot lunch. I finish my four sandwiches then borrow three bucks from Angelo for a plate of bratwurst and potatoes. I tell Angelo it's really good and he ought to try some.

"That ain't bratwurst, you dumb Mick," Ange says. "It's Polish sausage. Fer Chrissake, don't you even know what you're eating?"

"What's the difference?" Rosie asks. "They're both made outta leftover shit like hog livers and rat noses that blind old Polack grandmothers grind up in their basements on the north side and serve to suckers like you two."

When Johnny Battaglia scratches on the eight ball he slams his cue stick on the table and throws a buck to JT. "Aw right, that's it," he says. "Party time's over. We got work to do."

I shovel down the last forkful of potatoes and follow the rest of the guys out the door. We slog down Thirty-fifth Street in the rain to the job site. JT pulls the jackhammer out of the crack where he wedged it and starts slamming away at the concrete. He at least gets to stand on the curb. Rosie and I have to get down in the hole, where there are now three inches of muddy water.

My back has stiffened up during lunch. I have to bend my knees when I lift the first few rocks. Rosie sees this and says, "You gettin' old or what?"

I say nothing but elbow him aside and grab the next rock, which should have been his.

The rain finally stops around three, but that makes things worse. Rosie and I are still slogging around in a mud pit, still getting splattered by slop from the jackhammer, still lifting dirty, jagged pieces of concrete—but now there is no rain to rinse us off. By the time I throw the last rock on the back of The Rat at 5:45, we are so black you can't even tell we aren't wearing shirts.

Rosie and I straighten up and wipe our foreheads. All this does is smear dirt across our faces. We are standing there catching our breath when some asshole in a Cadillac drives by and yells out his window, "Typical City loafers."

Jesse's eyes bulge and he tries to say fifteen swearwords in three seconds. The only one I recognize is "cocksucker." Rosie points at the guy and says, "Come here, chickenshit."

The guy gives Rosie the finger and speeds away. Rosie starts chasing him down the street, but Johnny hops out of his truck and grabs him. "Let it go," Johnny says. "I can't afford to have you in jail for ripping the head off some Gold Coast dickhead."

He walks Rosie over to the back of his pickup where there is a twelve-pack of Schlitz. JT finds a few pieces of burlap in the front of The Rat. We try to dry off but end up smearing mud all over ourselves. We give up and sit on the back of The Rat, drinking beer and looking like a bunch of cam-ouflaged Navy SEALs waiting for the next chopper to Da Nang.

At 5:30 the next morning I'm sitting at the counter in Mary's Grill having a bacon and egg sandwich. There are only four other guys in the place. One of them is old Bill, who is in the corner booth, sleeping. The sun still hasn't risen, and the sky is a weary gray. I watch the rain gusting against the window. It's been raining all night and I expect Fred is going to send us all home today.

Mary is running a spatula back and forth across the grill. "You're quiet this morning," she says.

At first I don't realize she is talking to me. Finally I look up at her and smile. "Sorry. I was thinking."

"Then you're the first guy in this place who ever did."

I sit with the rest of my crew in the furnace room until 7:30 that morn-ing, when Fred sends us home. I pick up my cab in time to catch the tail end of the morning rush hour. I take a guy with a huge briefcase to the el, a housewife to Marshall Field's, and an old lady to the doctor's of-fice next to West Suburban Hospital. Around eleven I take an old couple out to O'Hare and hustle back in time to do the lunch run with Mr. Beatty.

With the rain, I keep busy all day. For dinner, I grab a quick burger and a beer at Goldie's, and am back in the cab in fifteen minutes. When things finally slow down around ten, I bring the cab back to the garage, gas it up, and check out with Burt, the night manager. It's been a good day. With tips, I clear a hundred bucks for fourteen hours.

Ten minutes later I'm sitting at the bar in O'Dea's with a schooner of Old Style and six bags of pretzels in front of me. PJ pulls up a stool and sits down next to me. He rests his elbow on the bar, puts his chin in his hand, and tells me Clare got robbed in the Munster finals last weekend.

" 'Twas a travesty," PJ says. "The game was stolen from us."

Jimmy Moylan wipes the foam from his upper lip and winks at Ambrose. "They say Cork were the better team," he says innocently.

PJ explodes. "Cork were bullshit! That little whoor O'Sullivan is a piece of shite. He couldn't even make the Clare *junior* team."

The bar erupts in laughter and PJ realizes his chain is being yanked. "Ye can go to hell, the lot of ye," he mutters.

Ambrose asks me if I want to shoot some eight ball. He puts up a quarter, and the two of us play the winners. At 1:00 A.M. we still have the table. Ambrose has just run the table for the third time. We've been playing for a buck a game, and even with all the rounds I've bought and the beers I've had, I'm still up five or ten bucks.

PJ closes the front door and says, "Time, gents. Time now."

No one pays any attention to him. Mick Brennan says to me, "Michael, would you give us 'The Banks of the Roses'?"

I oblige him, and then we're off. For the next twenty minutes the whole place is roaring with foot stompers and rebel songs. Finally PJ says again that it's time we all got the bloody hell out of here.

Jimmy Moylan orders another glass of Schlitz. PJ calmly pours it for him. Five minutes later PJ slaps his towel on the bar and shouts, "It's half-one. For the love of God, have yez no homes to go to?"

Ambrose tells him to shut up or he'll have the cops on him for being open after hours.

Finally, at two o'clock, PJ turns off the lights. This ends the pool game, but it is another half hour before he ushers the last of us out the back door.

When I get home, the rain has finally stopped. I park the car and walk toward the back door of our house. Brilliant white clouds are drifting across the face of the full moon, and the sky is a dark steel blue. It's too nice to go inside just yet, so I sit on the steps, watch the clouds, and think about my dad. I asked him recently how he got started as a salesman.

He shrugged and said when the war ended and all the guys came home there were so many guys and so few jobs that you were glad to take any job you could get. Then he met Mom, they got married, started having kids, "and there you are."

He makes it all sound so natural, so easy. But he's not telling me what I want to know. He's telling me facts, but facts can lie. My dad didn't just come home when the war ended and pick right up where he left off. The home he left in 1942 wasn't there anymore. His younger brother had been killed in Holland. His best friend had been killed in the South Pacific. There were things he had to overcome, things he had to get past. How did he do it? What got him through it?

When I try to get him to talk about that stuff, he just smiles and says I am making too much of nothing. "We did what we had to do," he says. "Same as you will."

I tell my dad that's not much of an answer.

My dad shrugs and says he thinks it's a pretty damn good answer.

Good or not, my dad's answer is not helping me figure out what to do. I've discovered that saying you want to be a doctor is like a fat guy farting in an elevator: things are going to get a whole lot worse before they get better.

I make a few calls. I write a few letters. I talk to a few people. Everyone agrees that if I go back and take all the required pre-med courses there is a *chance* some medical school will accept me—but no one's going to bet the ranch on it.

And how would I live if I went back to school? I could drive the cab at night, but I wouldn't be able to work construction. I've got a couple thousand dollars saved, enough to cover one semester's tuition, but not much else. I suppose my parents would continue to feed me and let me live up in the attic, but I'd hate to do that to them. The whole thing is a tremendous gamble, and I'm not sure I want to take it.

So, in the meantime, I keep throwing rocks.

When I get home from work the next day, I drop my hard hat and boots at the back door. Shannon shuffles over to lick my hand, but she doesn't have much time. The mailman should be here soon. Shannon has two overriding passions in her life: her love of my mother and her hatred of the mailman. Shannon has seen too many movies. She thinks she is John Wayne defending her family against marauding outlaws and ax-murdering mailmen.

Shannon is not what you would call a thoroughbred. In fact, Shannon is what you would call a flea bag. My brother Jack found her in an alley ten years ago. My mom said we could keep her for a week. It's hard to tell what her parentage might have been. When people ask, we tell them Shannon's mother was a Great Dane and her father was a Chihuahua—a very lonely Chihuahua.

Every afternoon Shannon plants herself at the front window watching the mailman on his appointed rounds, growling deep in her throat as he finishes the other side of the street and then crosses to ours. She stays in the front window until the mailman starts walking up our sidewalk. Then she tears over to the mail slot in our front door, crouching like a panther, teeth bared, eyes narrowed, growling low. The instant the mailman sticks the mail in the slot, Shannon lets out a roar, leaps at the door, and tears the mail to shreds. After she has sufficiently destroyed everything the mailman has just delivered, she relaxes. Mission accomplished. Another family saved. We are the only family on the West Side that thinks it's normal to open letters full of teeth marks and dog saliva.

While I am listening for Shannon's daily assault on the mail, I grab an orange from the counter. My mom is at the sink peeling potatoes. She takes one look at my filthy T-shirt and blue jeans and refuses to allow me to sit on one of her kitchen chairs, so I sit on the floor next to her, peeling my orange while she peels her potatoes.

Mom tells me there are problems on the home front. My brother Jack is in trouble again. He's flunking religion. When my dad gets home that night he is furious.

"Religion!" he says. "How can you flunk religion?" He threatens to ground Jack until the next ice age. Then he calls Fenwick and reams out the teacher. He says he understands how someone could flunk math or English. "But how does a kid flunk religion?" he asks. "What'd he do, rape a nun?"

Father Fogarty patiently explains that Jack did not rape a nun, but he has been inattentive and disrespectful. Last week, Father asked the class if anyone could tell him the greatest miracle in the Bible. Jack raised his hand and said it was in the book of Exodus, where it says after riding all day in the desert Moses tied his ass to a tree and walked five miles.

My dad is sputtering with rage. He tells Jack if he ever wises off to a priest again he will break his neck. Jack gets off with a few whacks from the old man's belt and a month's grounding. Tim says it's a good thing Dad didn't find the *Playboy*s under Jack's mattress. A chastened Jack replies meekly, "Let he who is without sin cast the first stone."

We stay pretty busy right into early October, but by the end of the month they are starting to lay guys off. One of the first to go is Jesse, but they don't just lay him off; they fire him. Years of hard work and hard living have caught up with Jesse. He has been with Scalese for thirty or forty years, but the foremen have been complaining that he can't cut it anymore. Nobody wants him on their crew.

On Monday morning while we are waiting in the furnace room, Fred calls Jesse into the office and tells him he is being let go. We all knew it was coming. When Jesse comes out of Fred's office we try to avoid his eyes. He walks over to the far corner of the furnace room and stares out the window, saying nothing to anyone. He is still standing there when it is time for us to go to the job site.

I tuck my hard hat under my arm and walk over to him. "Hey, Jess," I say. "I'm really sorry."

Jesse says nothing. He doesn't turn around. He just slowly nods his head and continues to stare out the window. I stand behind him, trying to find something else to say. I'm afraid to even pat him on the shoulder. After a couple minutes I turn and walk out to my truck.

.   .   .

"It's a damn shame," JT tells me at lunch. "That man works for this company for forty years, bustin' his ass. Then he gets old and can't work no more, so they fire his ass."

JT doesn't have to say any more. We all feel bad about it.

Jesse sits on the steps outside Fred's office all day. He has no car and has to wait for JT to get off work at six to give him a ride home. He is back at the yard on Wednesday morning to collect his check. He comes with his work clothes on, hoping he will be offered his old job back. Fred hands him his check, tells him good luck, and walks him out the gate.

Our crew isn't the same without Jesse. JT sees him now and again and tells us he is drinking too much and fighting with his wife.

Rosie, JT, Angelo, and I are no longer doing just breakout. This late in the year we do a little bit of everything. Some days we break out; other days we strip or line or backfill. We aren't getting as much overtime, but we are still giving to the church every morning.

October has been mild, but on Halloween the weather changes, and for the next two weeks we are pelted by a stream of cold, sleety days. There are jobs that the state or the city wants finished by winter, so we keep breaking out, keep framing, keep pouring, keep stripping. It is impossible to stay dry. Our hands are red and raw from the rain, cracked and dry from the concrete, splintered and gouged from the lumber.

Thank God The Rat has a heater. It grinds and it wheezes, but it throws off plenty of heat. At lunch, Rosie and I sit in the cab. We drape our sopping wet jackets and gloves in front of the vent, hoping to dry them before we start back to work again.

I stand on the bed of The Rat in the declining light of a November day. My raincoat is open and flapping in the wind. Rain is streaming off the brim of my hard hat as I catch stakes and pile them against the back of the cab. I drive back to the yard with the wipers smearing the glaring light of traffic across the streaked and broken windshield.

.   .   .

It gets dark early in December. I pull The Rat into the yard and switch off the ignition. I am the last one in. All the other crews finished before me and the yard is quiet as I step out of the truck. The wind is whipping under the eaves at the north end of the shed, and a bare bulb swings back and forth, throwing shadows across the dusty stacks of burlap. As I gas up the Rat I see dust devils tearing across the empty yard.

This is my last day. I'm not being laid off; I'm quitting. But I'm going to miss this life. I love working hard and being outside. I love the growl of the backhoe and the roar of the compressor. I love throwing rocks and stripping forms. I love sweating and grunting.

But the time has come for a change, and I'm going to go back to school. It's foolish, I suppose, a construction worker wanting to be a doctor, but there it is. There's my dream.

I have checked it out. I have done my research. I will have to take four science courses. I have enrolled at a local college and will take physics and inorganic chemistry in the winter and summer sessions. Then I'll take organic chemistry and biology next fall. If all goes well, I'll finish the following spring. That means it will be almost two years from now before I can even *start* medical school. Then four years of medical school. Then five years of residency. Hell, I'll be toothless, bald, and incontinent by the time I finish all that.

When I finish gassing up, I park The Rat in the back of the yard, grab my hammer and hard hat off the seat, and go into the office. Fred is hunched over papers at his desk. He glances at the clock on the wall when I come in.

"Where the hell you been, jaggin' off?"

"Come on, Fred," I say. "I stripped that whole job by myself in four hours."

"Hunhh."

That's as close as Fred ever gets to complimenting anyone.

"So, this your last day?" he asks.

"Yup. I'm going back to school."

"School. Hunhh. You learn more out here in a week than you learn in school in a year."

"I'd like to come back and work once in a while—you know, on vacations and stuff," I say. "I'm going to need the money."

"You'll probably be too soft by then."

When he sees the look on my face, he says, "All right, give us a call. We'll see if we can use you."

Fred and I shake hands and I walk out of the office. I stand at the door of the furnace room looking out on the dark and silent yard. The stake trucks are lined up in front of the burlap shed. The streetlight out on Grand Avenue shines on the stake pile, throwing a long shadow that stretches back to the stacks of lumber and angle irons piled against the chain-link fence by the railroad track. I stand there, waiting for something, looking for something. Finally, I take off my hard hat and walk out the gate.

I have a long road ahead of me, going back to college for two more years. It seems like an eternity. I have to take four tough science courses, and I have no background in science. It all seems so improbable, so incredibly risky. What if I go through all that and still don't get into medical school? After all, who's going to want some Joe Schmoe construction worker in their medical program? Just because the octopus takes flying lessons doesn't mean anyone's going to give him a pilot's license.

But it's a challenge, just like breaking out three thousand feet of concrete in one day. I have to forget the distractions, forget the pain, forget the logic. I have to put my head down and work.

Asses and elbows, I think. *Asses and elbows.*

CHAPTER SEVEN

Back in school again. Joe College. I'm taking only two classes—inorganic chemistry and physics—but they're both killers. And I'm not sure how ready I am to return to school. Although I have always been an avid reader, I'm certain my study skills have eroded. These two courses are going to be difficult for me not only because I have taken no previous science courses but also because I am not particularly drawn to science.

I'm taking inorganic chem and physics not because I *want* to but because I *have* to. Not every doctor wants to be a scientist. Some of us just want to take care of sick people. I can't help thinking that medicine is more closely aligned to the humanities than to the sciences. I can't help thinking I could learn more about being a good doctor from William Shakespeare than I could from Isaac Newton. After all, isn't understanding *people* at least as important as understanding *pathology*? Well, no one is asking my opinion. If I want to get into medical school I have to take chemistry, physics, and biology. Period. "Ain't goan *be* no Shakespeare."

I don't know who I'm trying to impress, but for my first day of class I actually shower, shave, and put on a collared shirt. When I get to school, it takes me a while to find the right classroom. Since it is January, most of the students already know one another. They stand together in groups talking and laughing. When I walk into class with my calloused hands and weathered face, everyone looks at me, wondering why the maintenance man is here—and why he has a textbook under his arm. I find a seat at the back of the classroom and start leafing through my chemistry book, opening it to the fascinating chapter on polydentate ligands.

After a couple minutes, I sneak a look at my fellow students. Most of them look like freshmen or sophomores, which means they are five or six years younger than I am. This makes me feel even older and more out of place.

My first day back in school is like a trip to another planet. I am learning not just a new subject but a new language—and none of it seems to have anything to do with medicine. Our first class is on something called the Electron Configuration of Neutral Atoms in the Ground State. I can hardly write fast enough. What did she say: "The Electric Conflagration of Neutered Adams in Ground Steak"? This is not exactly something I have been thirsting all my life to learn.

I picture myself standing in an Emergency Room someday, stethoscope around my neck, one of those reflector things on my forehead. There's been a car crash and I'm about to take out somebody's liver or maybe put her spleen back in—something important anyway. My patient is a beautiful twenty-year-old supermodel in a crocheted bikini. Her eyes flicker open. She doesn't know me from Adam, so she needs a little reassurance. She clutches my sleeve and whispers faintly, "You do know the Electron Configuration of Neutral Atoms in the Ground State, don't you, Doctor?"

I smile at her, pat her on the shoulder, and tell her she has some of the most nicely configured electrons I have ever seen and I will be sure they stay that way.

I'm still reeling from the electron thing when our teacher tells us to memorize the permittivity of vacuum, the Newtonian constant of gravitation,

Avogadro's number, the Rydberg constant, and the proton-electron mass ratio. By Monday.

Already I feel like I am drowning. Electrons? Ratios? Constants? How can anyone memorize all that esoteric nonsense? But then it occurs to me that I can immediately rattle off Gail Hopkins' batting average, Bobby Douglass' completion percentage, and Tony Esposito's save percentage. There must be some chemistry nerd sitting in a laboratory somewhere wondering, *How can anyone memorize all that esoteric nonsense?*

I give myself a pep talk. *Get with it, boy. What did you expect—Big Bird lecturing on tricycle safety? This is college. This is pre-med. This is the wheat being separated from the chaff.*

The problem is that I am now starting to realize how the chaff must feel.

Although a few of the students in my class seem eager—probably pre-meds anxious to get started on their pathway—most seem to be here against their will, as if this class were a punishment. To me it's not a punishment; it's an obstacle. It's what stands between me and my dream. Inorganic chemistry isn't a subject that needs to be mastered. It is a dragon that needs to be slain. If I don't succeed brilliantly in this and every one of my pre-med classes, I can kiss med school good-bye. I *have* to succeed. I *have* to get good grades. Anything less than an A is unthinkable. Getting a B is as bad as getting an F.

To my classmates, this may be just another course, but to me, this is war. This is an all-out, full-scale, no-holds-barred battle for survival, and I'm going at it full bore. *You want me to memorize the Faraday constant? Bohr radius? Thomson cross section? Fine. Bring it on. Give me your best shot.*

I start out methodically. The important thing is not to fall behind. I have to master each day's assignment. When our first class is over I head for the library and start to memorize. One part of me realizes how absurd this is: I am memorizing Avogadro's number, which is the number of molecules in a mole—but I have no idea what a mole is (I'm pretty sure it's not that blind little furry creature with the mustache who likes to dig holes on golf courses) and only a vague notion of what a molecule is. Nevertheless, like a little parrot I am now able to recite that Avogadro's number is $6.02214179 \times 10^{23}$.

As weeks go by, I become less analytical and more pragmatic. I don't care *why* I must do these things; it is enough to know that I must. I become proficient at intellectual regurgitation. I can barf up numbers and constants and ratios with the best of them. I am the parrot in the cage who has been taught to say, "Four score and seven years ago." Like the parrot, I have no idea what any of it means. But also like the parrot, I know that if I say the right thing, someone will give me a cracker.

I now live for crackers.

It takes me a while to get back into the routine of school. I'm used to being on my feet all day, sweating and lifting. It's hard sitting in one place hour after hour. I fidget and squirm, tapping my pencil on the book and bouncing my right leg up and down. I have to keep motivating myself because now there are no foremen to do it for me. No one is screaming at me to get my ass in gear. If my ass is to be in gear, I'm going to have to get it there myself.

There are too many distractions at home, so I go to the library—the last carrel of the far corner of the top floor. I refuse to let myself go home until I have mastered whatever has been assigned that day.

On the first physics test I get a hundred. I'm on top of the world. On the first chemistry test I get a 90. I'm ready to slit my throat. The only thing a 90 is going to get me is a seat on the next bus to Nowheresville. So I work even harder. I practically live in my chemistry book. I breathe electrons and pee neutrons. On the next chem test I get a 94; on the next, a 96.

In Chicago, winter doesn't "give way" to spring. Winter is hauled away kicking and screaming by dirty salt trucks and battered snowplows driven by bleary-eyed Sanitation workers with cups of coffee in one hand and cigarettes in the other. By the time March staggers into April, I am three months into my pre-med career and wondering if I am in over my head.

I knew this stuff would be hard—but not *this* hard. I am becoming almost paranoid about studying, deathly afraid that I must master every nuance of every footnote of every subtext in every book. But time is a limited resource and I have to be better about rationing mine. I spend four days studying my brains out for a ten-point quiz only to realize that I have a two-hundred-point test coming up two days later.

It's one thing to tell yourself that you have to memorize everything on this page. You can do that. But try to tell yourself that you have to memorize everything on these *forty* pages. You threaten yourself. You flog yourself. You tell yourself you are a gutless wimp if you don't master these pages. You know there is a limit to what you can demand of yourself, but lowering your standards is not going to get you into medical school.

Nothing matters, nothing. Not your friends, not common sense, not exhaustion, not the verbalized concern of your parents, nor the concern-masked-as-ridicule of your brothers. *They don't get it*, you tell yourself. They don't realize that if you don't master this stuff you are screwed. If you don't get a 96 or more on this test then you won't get an A for this quarter, which means you won't get an A for the semester, which means you won't get into medical school, which means you have failed. And you have invested so much time and energy into this quest that to fail means everything. Fail, and you might as well jump off a bridge.

I close the library, not just most nights, but *every* night. I walk home through silent streets, wondering where all the snow went, wondering when the trees started to bud. Over the past three months there have been blizzards and tornados and eclipses. Water mains have burst in my own neighborhood. Wars have been fought in Asia and Northern Ireland. Planes have crashed in Europe. Revolutions have occurred in South America. And I know nothing of any of it. Nothing matters to me anymore except beating the shit out of chemistry and physics. That's what it has become for me. Those courses aren't stepping-stones or pathways; they are mortal enemies.

I hate them. I want to destroy them. I will fight them with every bit of strength and courage I have, for if I don't, if I let them win, I am done. My dream is over.

One o'clock on a Saturday morning. A cold April rain is whipping against my windshield. Usually rainy nights are busy, but tonight things have been slow. I'm sitting on the cabstand in front of Laurie's Bakery on Madison Street, dying for a bismarck, but Laurie closed the place hours ago. As the minutes tick by, I curse myself for not bringing my chemistry book. I could at least be doing a little studying.

Not many guys sit on this cabstand late at night. It's too close to Austin. There is a lot of crime in Austin, and most of the drivers refuse to go there. They think every time they cross Austin Boulevard they are going to get shot or robbed. In a way I don't blame them. They don't care if a neighborhood is Irish or WASP or Abyssinian; if there is a chance they will get shot or robbed, they don't want to go there.

But I was born in Austin. I was baptized at St. Thomas Aquinas on Washington Boulevard. I know there are some punks with guns in Austin, but there are also a lot of good people, too, people who don't have guns and just need a ride to work. I'm always a little more careful when I go there, but I'm not about to refuse the call. I've already picked up a couple fares in Austin tonight: a nurse working the night shift at West Suburban Hospital and an operator at the Illinois Bell office on Lake Street. Neither was a crook. They were just people who needed to get to work.

Since it's getting near closing time, I decide to head west for the long row of bars on Madison Street in Forest Park. I have just splashed across Harlem Avenue when a guy coming out of Doc Ryan's hails me. He looks like he's had a snootful. He keeps tilting to the left as he staggers toward me. He plows into the back door of the cab, straightens himself up, yanks open the door, and pours himself into the backseat. He is half-sitting, half-lying there. I can't even see him in the rearview mirror, so I turn around, lean over, and ask, "Where to?"

The guy's eyes are a blind date gone bad. One eye is looking at me; the other keeps drifting off to left field. I get dizzy watching his eyes, so I watch his lips instead. He says he wants to go to the all-night bowling alley on Roosevelt Road.

I should have seen this coming. That's what all the boozehounds do. The all-night bowling alley has an all-night liquor license. Guys who can't guzzle down enough beer and schnapps by 2:00 A.M. always want to go to the bowling alley—just in case there is one part of their liver that isn't already totally fried.

The guy doesn't say much, and we splash through the silent streets till we get to Roosevelt Road. When I pull up to the bowling alley, the meter reads $3.20. The guy throws open the back door of the cab, steps out, trips on the curb, and falls flat on his face. He picks himself up, turns around, and leans in the window on the passenger side. "Ya know whass the biggest problem in America?" he asks me.

The biggest problem in America. Where did *that* come from? Well, let me see: Poverty? Racism? Bad schools? Leisure suits? The guy has both hands on the door but is swaying all over the place. Finally realizing that his question is rhetorical, I say, "No, I don't know the biggest problem in America."

The guy wags his finger at me. "It's these fuckin' high curbs, that's what."

Before I can reply, he throws me a ten, tells me to keep the change, and stumbles into the bowling alley. With that stroke of good fortune, and having now learned my country's most pressing problem, I decide it's time to go home.

My brothers think something is wrong with me. As spring rolls around, I don't watch the final round of the Masters. I don't go to O'Neill's to watch the Stanley Cup play-offs. I don't go to the Sox opener. All I do is study. They offer to chip in and buy me some Coke-bottle glasses, a pocket liner, and a bow tie so I won't just *act* like a nerd, I'll *look* like one, too.

My brother Timmy isn't as hard on me as the others. That's because I recently gave him an Irish work permit that I got from one of the guys at

O'Dea's. The permit says his name is Liam Dougherty from County Kerry, Ireland, and he is twenty-one years old. Tim is nineteen but looks fourteen. Even with this fake Irish ID there is only one bar, Wrobel's over on Sixteenth Street, that will serve him. And when he goes there he has to remember to speak with an Irish accent.

"Ah, well, sure Jaysus," he says by way of introduction when I go into Wrobel's with him one night, "I'd like yez all t'meet me own cousin, Michael, born right here in Americay."

I whisper to him that isn't he laying on the brogue a bit thick? He tells me to shut up. He'll handle this.

I am only twenty-four years old, but no one asks me for my ID. I guess when you are drinking with a guy who looks fourteen they cut you a little slack.

Tim (I have to remember to call him Liam in the bar) orders us two beers and begins talking about the "low, durty English blackguards" who are oppressing his native land.

"Blackguards?" I whisper to him. "*Blackguards?* How did you come up with *that* one?"

Tim elbows me in the gut and tries to ignore me.

A couple of Latvians down at the end of the bar sympathize with Tim. They tell us that their native land is also being oppressed—by low, dirty *Russian* blackguards. They tell Tim (I mean Liam) that he is a fine boy and they buy a round for us. When we finally leave the bar three hours later, Tim and the Latvians have concocted a foolproof plan to free their native lands. Unfortunately, none of them can remember it the next morning.

"We thought you'd joined the IRA or somethin', Michael. Where in the name o' God have you been?"

The guys at O'Dea's can't get over the change in me. I come in only once every week or two and stay for just a couple beers.

"Before we know it, you'll be takin' the Pledge," Ambrose O'Brien says. "You'll be one of Father Matthew's boys."

I sit down at the bar and tell them once again that I am back in school and have to study every night. They shake their heads in pity. "It's your funeral," PJ says as he pours me a schooner.

The neighborhood around O'Dea's is changing, getting a little rougher all the time. Jimmy Moylan says there are now rats in the place as big as dogs. "Sure, you'd need a whip to keep 'em away," he says. Jimmy is in a bad mood. He had the Daily Double at Maywood tonight and it paid only $23.60. "What kind of bullshit is that?" he asks.

Fights are more common in the bar now. Guys are shooting craps in the women's bathroom. Kids are throwing beer bottles at buses and selling dope outside the door. It has gotten so bad that PJ has actually started carding kids once in a while. A lot of the Irish guys are leaving and moving farther north.

I mention to Ambrose that I don't see a lot of the old guys around anymore.

"The place has gone down all right," Ambrose says. "It's rejuiced," he says. "Rejuiced entirely."

From the end of the bar Mick Brennan lifts his head from the glass of Bushmills in front of him. "The corse o' God is on this place," he mumbles.

I say hi to Mick and ask if I can buy him a drink.

He nods his approval. "No bird ever flew on one wing," he says.

When Ambrose mutters that no bird ever flew on twenty, either, Mick tells him he can shut his durty mouth.

But the guys are right. The bar is going down. The floor hasn't been swept in a week. The bathroom door is hanging from one hinge. The pool table has a rip in the felt that has been glued back down. A couple of the light fixtures no longer work.

PJ is hanging on, but I wonder for how much longer.

As May rolls around, finals are coming up. In spite of my almost fanatical single-mindedness, things aren't going well. This stuff is hard. The fact that I don't like it makes it even worse. I would much rather be reading Yeats or Goethe or Hemingway. Heck, even John Bunyan is starting to look good at this point.

I continue to do well in physics. Physics is practical and sensible. It is like a giant puzzle. They give you facts; they give you laws; then they ask you questions. The answer can always be found—you just have to work hard enough to find it. The laws are immutable, the conclusions irrefutable. It is always logical. It is never arbitrary. I have a solid A there.

But inorganic chem is another story. Most of it is confusing and irrelevant: "A solid will sublime at any temperature below the triple point when the pressure above it is reduced below the equilibrium vapor pressure."

Huh?

My average in inorganic chem is hovering between an A and a B. If I get a B, this whole med school thing is over. I'll be back on the breakout gang—for life. In desperation I go over the material time after time, night after night. I check and recheck every homework assignment, every lab assignment. I go over and over everything that might be asked on the final exam. In the days before the test I'm a mess. I don't sleep. I don't eat. (Well, I don't eat that much. . . . Okay, fine, I eat—but that doesn't mean I'm not really stressed.) I go over notes and study guides and texts. I think of every possible question our teacher might ask.

I try to ignore the possibility that all of this might be in vain. I try to ignore the possibility that even if I get As in all these pre-med courses no med school will want me anyway. I can't let myself think that way. I need to stay focused, stay positive. I have to keep slugging away.

But my desire to succeed is not meant to be at the expense of my fellow students. They are nice kids, and I want them to do well, too. Over the course of this semester we have studied together and shared notes. We have pulled for one another and tutored the stragglers, but there is no question that my fellow students are a little in awe of me. I'm not your typical college kid. I'm not interested in parties or drinking or girls—or anything. I am a pre-med machine. I never miss a class. I never miss an assignment. I never come unprepared. I never let anything get in the way of studying.

But I'm starting to worry that my best might not be good enough. Going into the chem final I have a 94 average—an A, but just barely. If I mess up on the final, I'm toast. In physics I have a 98. It would take a major screwup to blow that A, but I still have to be careful that in my desire to do well in chem I don't entirely neglect physics.

Our chem final is on a Tuesday. When we finish our last class the Friday before, I get out my books and spend virtually the next ninety-six hours studying. I nod off for an hour or two every now and then. A couple times I go outside for five minutes just to breathe in the cool night air, but otherwise I study with an intensity that borders on desperation, realizing that how I do on this stupid exam will have an extraordinary impact on the rest of my life. It seems so ridiculous. You mean to tell me that just because someone hasn't mastered the Fourier Expansions for Basic Periodic Functions he won't make a good doctor? I think a good argument could be made that anyone who *has* mastered the Fourier Expansions for Basic Periodic Functions won't make a good doctor.

But what I think, what I want, what I believe doesn't matter. What matters is the answers I put on that piece of paper next Tuesday morning. Medical schools want regurgitators, not philosophers. It's time I accepted that.

Fine. You want regurgitation? I'll give you regurgitation. I'll cram and stuff and jam so many facts and figures inside me that I'll be like Vesuvius getting ready to erupt. Come Tuesday morning it'll be zero hour. Then back up, baby, because Mount Collins is gonna blow.

CHAPTER EIGHT

I get a 97 on my chem final and a 99 on my physics final. I finish the semester with an A in both classes. When the finals are over, I go to bed at 7:00 P.M. and sleep till three the next day. My mom is sure I'm having a nervous breakdown, but my brothers tell her not to worry. They say I am no more screwed up than usual. Mom isn't convinced, so she decides to have an intervention—a culinary intervention. She makes my favorite dinner: pot roast and noodles. At dinner that night, Jack says he can't believe this crap. "Just because Mike acts like an idiot, you make him his favorite dinner?" Jack wants to know if Mom will make him *his* favorite dinner, corned beef and cabbage, if *he* starts acting like an idiot.

Timmy tells him it hasn't worked so far.

Pete says he will hang from the chandelier and scratch his armpit like a monkey if Mom will cook him a chicken.

I have dinner, drink a few beers, watch *Starsky & Hutch* with my brothers, and go back to bed until nine the next morning. When I wake up, Denny is downstairs telling Mom he has been having visions of bald-headed nuns beating him with rosaries, so could she please make him some French toast.

.   .   .

I will be taking second-semester chemistry and physics in summer school, which begins Monday. I spend the next few days sleeping, going for runs, and reading—real reading, things like Steinbeck and Woolf and Dosto-yevsky. I decide it would be good to read something that is both literary *and* medical, so I check out some of William Carlos Williams' stuff, and I like it. I find myself enjoying A. J. Cronin and Somerset Maugham. When my brothers see that I am reading stuff that is neither a textbook nor a glossy magazine with a centerfold, they decide maybe Mom is right after all and I *have* lost my marbles.

School begins again the following week. The college I am attending is several miles away, and I can't always use my parents' car. Four of my younger brothers are old enough to drive, and they, too, are clamoring for the car. I am saving up to buy a car of my own, but all I have so far is seventy-five dollars. I have been checking the car ads in the *Tribune* and figure I could get something decent for a couple hundred dollars. In the meantime, if I can't use my parents' car or if I can't get one of my brothers to drive me, I hitchhike. Sometimes it takes fifteen minutes, sometimes an hour. The fact that I am a clean-shaven guy carrying a physics book under my arm helps. It would be a lot more difficult if I were a bearded guy with an ax, although in Chicago even *he* could probably get a ride—unless he was wearing a Green Bay Packers jersey.

Even though I won't be able to make every game, I tell my friends I will play on the softball team again this summer. It's one of the few ways I have to keep my sanity. We are sitting in O'Dea's after a game one night when I mention how hard it is for me to get a ride to school.

PJ has never been in favor of this med school thing from the start. He tells me this is just one more sign from God that I am wasting my time: "When the good Lord wanted the Israelites to get across the Red Sea, did He make them wait to see if one of their brothers would give them a ride?

Not at all. He parted the waters for them." PJ fills my glass and says as far as he can see, the only thing God has parted for me is my brain.

Our shortstop, Tom Burns, is a little more sympathetic. One of his younger sisters is taking an anatomy class this summer at the same college I am. She drives to school every day. He tells me she can give me a ride.

I vaguely remember Burny's sister. As I recall, she is a nice girl, but frankly, I don't care if she is a four-hundred-pound bucktoothed flatulence champion; I am delighted to have a reliable means of transportation.

My physics class runs from six to nine four nights a week. At 5:30 the next afternoon, a white Oldsmobile Vista Cruiser station wagon pulls up in front of our house. I hop in the front seat. Sitting next to me is a pretty twenty-year-old girl with a freckled Irish face and beautiful blue eyes. *This* is Burny's little sister? When did this happen? The last I can remember of her she was a flat-chested, giggly high school kid who looked like Laura on *Little House on the Prairie.*

Her name is Patti. She is a nursing student at the College of Saint Teresa in Minnesota. She tells me that in the fall she will be moving to Rochester, where the nursing students spend their junior and senior years working at the Mayo Clinic.

I am impressed. To someone like me, stuck in undergraduate chemistry and still dreaming of the real world of medicine, it sounds like a dream come true.

"I heard you are a medical student," Patti says.

"Well, I'm *trying* to be a medical student. First I have to finish my pre-med courses."

"Where do you want to go to med school?"

"Oh, Harvard, the Mayo Clinic, Oxford, Juilliard, the Sorbonne, the Lyceum, Frank's Barber College—depends who makes me the best offer."

Patti looks at me out of the corner of her eye. "Tommy *said* you were nuts—just like the rest of your brothers."

"My brothers? Oh, they're way worse than I am."

We separate in the parking lot, Patti promising to meet me back at the car when our classes end.

When I get back to her car at 9:00 P.M. it is locked. I stand there until 9:15, when Patti arrives, breathless, apologizing for being late. "We had a test and it took me forever to finish it."

Fifteen minutes later we pull up in front of my house. "It was really nice of you to give me a ride," I tell Patti.

"Tommy told me I had to."

"Oh." So much for my having swept the girl off her feet.

"But I'm really glad I did," she says.

I close the door and lean back in through the window. "Me, too," I say.

After Patti has driven me to school three or four times, I ask her if she would like to stop for a beer on the way home.

"It's the least I could do to repay you for driving me every night," I say.

Patti agrees, and every night for the rest of the summer we stop at Durty Dick's or Callahan's, maybe venture out to the Come Back Inn or down to O'Rourke's, where they draw the best pint of Guinness in the city. We also spend a lot of time at Sportsman's on Roosevelt Road. The waitress there, Dani, has been serving and mothering me and my friends for years. The fact that Patti is only twenty doesn't matter. I had been a regular there for almost three years when they threw a twenty-first-birthday celebration for me.

Patti has a beautiful smile, and I love talking to her. We talk a lot about our families and our dreams: hers of becoming a nurse, mine of becoming a doctor. But I quickly learn that Patti is different from my brothers. When I played high school and college hockey, we didn't have to wear face masks. Consequently I have had my front teeth knocked out, my nose broken, and a face full of stitches. I keep sitting by the phone waiting for *GQ* to call about the cover shoot, but they must have lost my number.

Anyway, my brothers and the guys I played hockey with always thought it was hilarious when we would go out for a few beers and I would crack my nose or take out my teeth and lay them on the bar. I assume Patti will get a kick out of this, too, but the first time I do it for her, she looks at me like I am some kind of a bug. She doesn't think it is funny—at all. In fact, she says it is vulgar. I thought only moms used the word "vulgar." Now that I think of it, my mom used the word "vulgar" a lot.

Patti asks if I have any other anatomic abnormalities she should know about. I tell her no and promise not to be vulgar anymore.

Even though Patti and I are going out three or four nights a week, I never take her to O'Dea's. It is a little too rough in there, and besides, I don't want everyone on the team to know I am going out with Burny's little sister. Patti, however, begins taking a much greater interest in her brother's athletic pursuits. Before long she is coming to all our softball games.

Our center fielder, Dick Murphy, is one of my best friends. I stood up in his wedding the year before when he married Mary Ann, his high school sweetheart. Over the years, Murph and Mary Ann have fixed me up with several of Mary Ann's friends, but I never really hit it off with any of them.

We are sitting in O'Dea's after a game when I see Murph rubbing his chin and eyeing me.

"Hey, Burny," he says to Patti's brother, "wasn't that your sister at our game tonight?"

"Yup."

"She still going out with that mob enforcer from Melrose Park?"

"That *what*?" Then he notices Murph tilting his head in my direction.

"Oh!" Burny says. "You mean Big Mario. Yeah. He's been a lot meaner since he got out of prison this last time."

"Yeah, yeah, I know," I tell them, "and he swore if anyone touched his *bresaola* he'd slice 'em up like a beef sangwidge."

Even though my relationship with Patti hasn't progressed much beyond talking, I find myself thinking of her during the day. We have been going out for beers after class several nights a week, but I have never asked her out on a formal date. On the way home one night, I ask Patti if she would like to go out Saturday night. She agrees, and when she drops me off that night, for the first time I lean over and give her a little peck on the cheek.

Our first date is to Ravinia, a large park up on the North Shore where all the rich people live. Ravinia hosts a series of outdoor concerts every summer. I get a bag of charcoal, a small grill, a couple steaks, and a twelve-pack of Old Style. I pick Patti up at 5:00 P.M. It feels strange having *me* drive *her* for a change. We find a spot on the park grounds where we spread our blanket, grill our steaks, and have a nice picnic before the concert begins.

When it's time for dessert, Patti looks in the picnic basket and asks what's the point of bringing a whole bag of cookies for dessert. "Who's going to eat them all?" she asks.

When I finish the last Oreo, she looks at me funny and asks if I have a metabolic disorder. I tell her that life has not been easy for me. I explain that I am actually the illegitimate son of Queen Elizabeth. I was abandoned at birth and raised by seals in the Aran Islands. I am getting to the part about crossing the Atlantic in a dinghy when Patti says she has to go to the bathroom. When she comes back she says she is my date, not my therapist, and wouldn't we rather just listen to the music?

I agree. I stretch out on the blanket next to Patti, but after about ten minutes we aren't listening to the music as closely as we should. When the concert ends an hour and a half later, we hardly notice. We are finally shooed away at midnight by the groundskeepers who want to clean up the place. Ours is the only car in the parking lot when we get there.

It's been wonderful going out with Patti, but that doesn't change the fact that, as my brother Rog said the other day, "Your life really sucks." Squeezing a semester of physics and a semester of chemistry into a summer means I am in class from eight to twelve five mornings a week and six to nine four nights a week. I study every afternoon, most nights, and all weekend. I have a solid A in both classes but live in constant paranoia. What if I forget to study something? What if I turn in the wrong homework assignment? What if I blow this next test? I have no leeway. All it takes is one screwup and I'm finished.

When finals roll around in mid-August, I burrow into the library and scarcely come out for a week. We get our grades a few days later. I get an A in both chemistry and physics, but I'm almost too worn-out to care. I have now completed half of my pre-med courses. I'm on course. I've aced my first two courses, but the thought of another year of this stuff is crushing me.

Patti and I have two weeks before she goes back to Minnesota and I resume classes here in Chicago. Patti spends those last two weeks working, as she has all summer, as a nurse's aide at Oak Park Hospital. I go back to throwing rocks at Scalese.

"Where the hell you been, man?" JT says to me on my first day back. "We heard you was back in school studying how to be a millionaire."

Johnny Battaglia looks at my soft hands and says, "Aw, Christ." He points his finger at me. "You ain't in school now, pal. And we ain't carryin' nobody's ass. When you get down in that hole, I better see you throwin' rocks like a fuckin' steam shovel or you're outta here."

I take a step closer and get right in Johnny's face. I tell him it's almost six thirty and what are we waiting for?

Johnny stares hard at me for a few seconds, then laughs and slaps me on the shoulder. "Fuckin' Irishman," he says. He turns to the rest of the crew. "Aw right, you heard the man," he says. "This ain't no fuckin' country club. It's time to start givin' to the church. Now get that Sullair fired up and get your asses to work."

I picked a hell of a day to come back. We are breaking out both sides of Blue Island Avenue down near Nineteenth Street. I am on one side of the street with JT. Rosie is on the other side with Jurgis. Today Rosie and I won't have to carry our rocks to a truck and throw them on; we'll just throw them into the street. Then Hiram, in the Michigan, will scoop them up and drop them in the back of a big dump truck. Since there is only one rock thrower in each hole, Rosie and I will have to throw twice as many rocks as usual. And to make it worse, the two crews can't help trying to compete with each other. JT is a better gun runner than Jurgis, but Rosie is hardened from a summer of throwing rocks and clearly has the advantage over me.

Because JT is so good, the two crews stay even until midafternoon, when my lack of fitness starts catching up with me. By five thirty the other crew is a good five minutes ahead of us. As we are loading up, Rosie sees me leaning against the side of the stake truck wiping my forehead. Just to rub it in, he asks if I want to go to the Y with him to do a little lifting. I tell him no but say I will gladly join him for a few twelve-ounce curls.

For the last two weeks of summer, I am up every morning at four thirty, throwing rocks all day, playing softball or going out with Patti every night, and rolling into bed at one or two.

The night before Patti goes back to school we have a long, bittersweet night listening to Irish music down at the Emerald Isle. We close the place, and as I am kissing Patti good night at her door I ask if she would like me to visit her in Minnesota sometime.

She returns my kiss and says quietly, "I'd like that."

The next morning, Patti heads back to Rochester. A day after that, I put my hard hat and hammer in the basement and begin my second year of pre-med with organic chemistry and biology. More big books, more big words, more big headaches.

Within a week I'm having trouble concentrating. I don't seem to have the focus I had last semester. It doesn't take me long to figure out why: I need to go to Minnesota.

The problem is I have no way to get to Minnesota. Although my parents let me use their car once in a while, there is no chance they'll let me take it to Minnesota for a whole weekend. I'm going to have to buy a car. A week after Patti leaves, I go to see my cousin Mike, who sells used cars at Ed Fanning Chevrolet.

"I need a car," I tell him. "A used car. Something that's cheap but runs well and is dependable."

My cousin claps his hands to his cheeks. "Something very cheap but very dependable. Gee, I never heard *that* before!"

He shows me a few old clunkers before finally remembering one that just came in today.

"I think you're gonna like this one," he says, leading me to the back corner of the lot.

"Let me guess," I say. "It was owned by a little old schoolteacher who only drove it to church on Sundays."

"Hey, Mr. Rockefeller, you want a car or not?"

He shows me a ten-year-old white Chevy Impala. The engine thunders into life when I turn the key. There is no muffler.

"Whadda ya want a muffler for?" my cousin shouts over the rumble of the engine. "It's just one more thing that could go wrong."

He tells me he can let me have it for two hundred dollars. I tell him I don't have two hundred dollars.

"You come here to buy a car and you don't even have two hundred dollars. What do you think this is, Catholic Charities?"

I tell him I have $150. Mike rolls his eyes and says okay, "but this doing business with my relatives is killing me."

There is no spare tire, so as a gesture of goodwill Mike hunts through the trunks of several other old clunkers until he finds one that has a spare tire. He throws it into the trunk of the Impala. I don't want to insult him by pointing out that it is bald.

When I get home, Shannon sees my new car. Her eyes narrow and the fur on her neck rises. She begins circling the car, growling deep in her throat. My brother Jack asks, "Where'd ya get that thing? At the Salvation Army?"

He calls my other brothers. "Hey, you guys, come and look at the beater Dr. Einstein just bought."

My brothers tumble out the back door. They see the car and begin laughing. "Hey," Rog says, "Fred Flintstone has a car just like that."

Denny asks if you need a crank to start it. Pete says the people at the Museum of Natural History are going to be pissed when they find out I have stolen part of their exhibit from the Middle Ages.

They start calling my car Dr. Einstein's Beater.

.   .   .

The following weekend I pile my books in the backseat, fire up the Beater, and point her north toward Rochester. It is a beautiful fall day. The trees on either side of I-94 are sparkling in red, orange, and yellow. I've got the Notre Dame game on the radio. The Beater seems to be running great, but I'm a little concerned when I get off the interstate just north of Madison to get gas. As I come up the exit ramp, the oil light flickers on. I made sure the oil was full before I left, so I'm not sure what's going on. I pull into the Standard station and check the oil. It doesn't even register on the dipstick. I put in two quarts and it just barely registers. I put in two more and get it up in the normal range. When I cross the Mississippi at La Crosse I have to put in two more quarts. By the time I exit I-90 at Rochester I have burned seven quarts of oil.

Patti is waiting for me when I pull up in front of her apartment. It is a two-bedroom place that she shares with three other nursing students. There is no room for me there, so Patti has gotten me a room at Mrs. Prust's Boarding House down the street. Five bucks a night for a room just barely bigger than the bed, bathroom down the hall. It's perfect.

Patti seems glad to see me until I show her my car. I guess I misled her on the phone when I told her I bought a new car. She thought "new" meant "off the showroom floor." When she sees the rusted wreck in front of her apartment, she gasps.

"What is it?" she asks.

"What do you mean, 'What is it?' It's my new car. Isn't it great?"

Patti looks at it like it is something out of a Hitchcock movie. "You drove all the way up here . . . in *that*?"

"Yeah. And look, it even has a radio."

"Does it have a respirator?" she asks when I start it.

Against her better judgment, she gets in and we drive around Rochester. She shows me the Mayo Clinic, the Plummer House, the Zumbro River. We even drive out to Mayowood, the beautiful country estate of one of the old Mayo brothers. Patti makes me park the car in the far corner of the lot, next to the port-a-potty.

We take a tour of the home and talk about how neat it would be to live in a place like this and how much fun it would be for kids. When the tour is over we stroll around the grounds, her hand in mine.

Patti works part-time as a nurse's aide at St. Mary's Hospital in Rochester. She has to work that night, so I study until ten, when she gets off work. Then we head to the Depot House, Rochester's one and only singles bar. We have a few beers and attempt to talk above the blare of the band. About midnight Patti gives up waiting for me to ask her to dance. She asks me.

I tell her I don't dance.

"Oh, you do, too," she says, grabbing my hand. "Come on." She tries to pull me onto the dance floor where other young couples are writhing and shaking.

"I can't," I tell her. "You see, well, it's on account of . . . uh, my grandfather. Yeah, that's it, my grandfather. He died of . . . of creeping jungle fever. Or was it galloping? You never know with jungle fever. Sometimes it creeps; other times it gallops. Anyway, old Gramps had jungle fever . . . of the brain. Stage Four. On his deathbed he made me promise never to dance again until the Sox win the pennant."

"You're bizarre."

"It's a family thing. My brothers are the same way. We all got dropped on our heads when we were kids."

"I think you got dropped the hardest."

It's been a great weekend, but on the drive back to Chicago I start thinking about the MedCAT, the Medical College Admissions Test. I will be finished with pre-med next June. If I want to apply for admission to next year's freshman medical school class, I will have to take the MedCAT this fall.

There is a science section on the test with special emphasis on organic chemistry and biology. But I just started organic chemistry and biology last week. That means if I take the test this fall I will be tested on two courses I just barely started. Talk about a recipe for disaster!

But what choice do I have? If I don't take the MedCAT this fall, I will have to wait an extra year before I start med school. But if I *do* take it, I am almost certain to do poorly on it—which means I might *never* get into med school.

John Devlahan and I went to high school together. He is now a med student at Creighton. I wonder if he might be able to give me some advice, so I give him a call.

Dev listens quietly while I explain my dilemma. "So what do you think?" I ask him.

"Basically," he says, "I think you're screwed."

I decide to take my chances. I sign up for the MedCAT this fall. On a Saturday in October I sit in an auditorium with a couple hundred other hyper pre-meds answering questions about proton shifts, alkene resonance, covalent bonds, and parallel plate capacitors. Every now and then, as a concession to English majors, they ask what an ellipsis is or why Hamlet had Rosencrantz and Guildenstern bumped off.

It is the hardest test I have ever taken. There is so much stuff that I've never heard of, so much stuff I've never studied, so much stuff I don't understand, that I might just as well have taken a test in Swahili.

I get the results six weeks later. I do very well on the verbal, quantitative, and general information parts of the test. I don't do nearly as well on the science part. It isn't quite as bad as I feared: 515. That's still better than half the people who took the test—not bad considering I hadn't taken two of the courses I was tested on. But who am I kidding? Medical schools aren't interested in guys who score in the fiftieth percentile.

For the next few weeks I find it hard to study, hard to stay focused. I call Patti in Rochester almost every night. She tells me not to worry. She says I'm going to get into lots of medical schools. Her confidence is sweet and I'm grateful for it, but there is no getting around the fact that my chances of getting into med school just got a lot longer.

CHAPTER NINE

Now that I've taken the MedCAT, it's time to start applying to medical school. I send away for something called the *AMCAS Instruction Booklet,* containing the standardized application form used by all medical schools. I fill out the forms, arrange for transcripts to be sent and letters of recommendation to be written. But when I look over the completed application I have to admit that I'm not very impressed. My grades in college were pretty good but not exceptional.

So I write an essay explaining why my grades weren't better and why med schools should accept me anyway. I talk about the demands of playing major college hockey. I talk about not having any money and having to take an accelerated course load so I could graduate in three and a half years. I talk about shoveling furnaces at South Bend Foundry to help pay tuition.

But while everything I say is true, I feel hypocritical. I know damn well why my college grades weren't better: I didn't work hard enough. Don't give me this "college hockey was a burden" stuff. It was fun. Don't give me this "don't you feel sorry for poor old me working in an iron foundry" stuff. It wasn't that big a deal.

But it occurs to me that maybe I am selling myself short. Maybe there is something to be said for the lessons learned when the puck is dropped and two teams want the same thing, but only one is going to get it. And maybe there is something to be said for waking up in the early morning and trudging across a silent campus, past the mist-covered lake to Highway 31 to hitchhike to the foundry. And the amazement you feel at the end of the day when every inch of your body is filthy black from dirt and soot and you never have trouble getting a ride home. Never. Guys in pickups, guys in old beaters, guys in fancy Cadillacs—it doesn't matter. They all stop to give you a ride. And after a while, you wonder why that is.

So I bundle all these forms and letters and transcripts and essays together and send them off to eight different medical schools. They all want twenty or twenty-five bucks, and it takes five or six nights of driving the cab to pay for that. Within two weeks I receive a letter from each of them thanking me for applying and saying that no decision will be made for several more months.

As my second year of pre-med drags on, I continue to hack away at organic chemistry and biology. Organic chemistry is one more slug in the gut, one more kick in the groin—but that's fine. I'm now wired for slugs in the gut and kicks in the groin. I'll take whatever is dished out and I'll come back for more.

Biology, on the other hand, is a godsend. It isn't exactly med school, but it's a chance to finally study real, living things. As opposed to the tedium and trivia of chemistry, it's fun to learn about circulation and respiration and reproduction—stuff that will be useful if I ever get into med school.

I'm still living at home. Although I am paying my own tuition, I feel the shame of being twenty-five years old and still living off my parents, who have seven younger boys to feed and educate. My parents, for their part, are very supportive of my efforts to get into med school, but I'm embarrassed to be sponging off them. To make it up to my parents, I do my best to be a good influence on my younger brothers. I tell Jack that vomiting out the car window the whole way home from Cicero is really not that cool. I tell Tim that lighting garages on fire is irresponsible and dangerous. But I guess I am not that good a role model. When I find out that Rog blew up a toilet in the Lake Theater with an M-80, I laugh my head off—and then quickly tell him it's not funny and he should be ashamed of himself.

I'm getting an A in both biology and organic chem, but it isn't easy. Except for visiting Patti, I do nothing but study, drive the cab, and work the odd day of construction.

Patti is home for a few days over Thanksgiving. We have Thanksgiving dinner at my house. My brothers think it's funny to tell Patti about various venereal diseases they suspect me of having, about other girls I used to go out with until they learned of my prison record, and about my hockey equipment that they say is so toxic that it is registered with the Environmental Protection Agency. My mom tells my brothers to "shut your traps and leave that poor girl alone or no one's getting any dinner."

Patti tries to pet Shannon, but Shannon doesn't have time for petting. She is a dog on a mission, and she is focused on the mailman. Shannon is a very smart dog, but the concept of holidays has thus far eluded her. The entire time we are eating Thanksgiving dinner Shannon is at the window looking for her archenemy. She is convinced he is trying to trick her. As the minutes tick by she becomes more frantic. He should have been here by now. Her eyes bulge and saliva drools from the corner of her mouth. Occasionally she slinks like a jaguar over to the mail slot, where she crouches and growls. Patti slides a little closer to me and says in a low voice, "That thing has had all its shots, hasn't it?"

Patti goes back to school on Sunday afternoon. Before she leaves I tell her I'm sorry, but I have to study and I won't be able to come to Minnesota for at least two more months.

After I finish my last class the next Friday, I stay in the library until eleven, studying for our next quiz. When the library closes, I shut my book and trudge out to the dark, empty parking lot. A little dusting of snow covers the Beater. I bend over and brush off my half of the windshield with my hand, then drop down into the front seat. I put the key in the ignition but don't start the engine. I feel like just sitting there for a while. I lean forward and rest my head on the steering wheel. I'm tired, but it's not the physical aspect of all this that's getting me down.

Ten minutes later I can't stand it anymore. I don't care that it's 11:15. I don't care that I'm tired. I don't care that I have no money. I'm going to Rochester. I stop at home, throw a change of clothes, four apples, and a box of Salerno butter cookies in a bag, and head for Minnesota. There aren't many cars on I-90 at this hour. I cruise north with the semis and hog trailers. It's 5:30 when I ring the bell at Patti's apartment. Her roommate answers the door after the fourth ring.

"Sorry, Sue," I tell her. "Is Patti here?"

Sue restrains the impulse to split my skull with a tire iron. She lets me in and wakes up Patti.

Patti comes out of her bedroom, pulling a bathrobe around her, eyes squinting, wrinkles from her pillow creasing her cheek. We look at each other, smiling for different reasons.

She shuffles over and gives me a hug. I love the warmth coming off her. "I knew you would come," she says. "But I didn't think it would be at five o'clock in the morning."

"Me, neither."

A week later, Patti is home for Christmas. We have two weeks together, but I spend most of it with my nose in a book because finals are coming up. Our dates consist of me taking her to the library to study. If she's lucky we stop for a couple beers on the way home. When Patti goes back to school again after the first of the year, I spend two furious weeks preparing for finals. I do fine. I regurgitate with the best of them. I get two more As, but all this is starting to wear on me.

As winter deepens, I feel as if something in me is dying. I am beginning my final semester of pre-med. For the past year I have devoted myself so completely to getting into medical school, have so assiduously excluded anything that isn't related to studying, that I am starting to feel over-whelmed. All I do is study and work.

To make it worse, O'Dea's has closed its doors forever. I stopped there a couple nights ago and found a notice slapped on the door:

THE LICENSE AT THIS PREMISE HAS BEEN SUSPENDED
By order of the City of Chicago
Richard J. Daley, Mayor

There were too many fights, too many drunken disorderlies, too many ar-rests for underage drinking. I drive by the place sometimes in the cab. The same old air conditioner is dangling over the door, but the lights are out, the door is padlocked, and the place is gone forever. "The kegs have all run dry," as Ambrose used to say at closing time. I have a beer in Sullivan's or Durty Dick's or O'Neill's once in a while and occasionally I run into Ambrose O'Brien or Jimmy Moylan, but those other pubs just aren't the same as PJ's place.

I still haven't heard anything from the eight med schools to which I ap-plied. My lousy score on the science part of the MedCAT haunts me. I keep asking myself, *What good are As when I did so poorly on the one test all med schools pay attention to?*

I quit playing hockey, quit playing softball, quit shooting pool. I rarely see Murph and the rest of my friends. I never read anything that isn't as-signed in class. I look sometimes at the collection of books I have amassed over the years, running my hands over their spines: Dostoyevsky and Tol-stoy, Yeats and Synge, Farrell and James. I think of the joy they have given me, the perspectives they have opened for me. I haven't read anything worthwhile in a year. I haven't *done* anything worthwhile in a year. I haven't fished or climbed or gone backpacking. I haven't run or worked out. I am a single-minded, one-dimensional fanatic who has cast all his eggs in this one medical basket.

"Too long a sacrifice / Can make a stone of the heart." I think about Yeats' line a lot. I feel the ossification of my own heart has already begun. But what can I do? I knew this was going to be hard. I went into it with my eyes open. Whining isn't going to help. I just have to keep working, keep pushing, keep attacking. It's only five more months. Hell, I can take anything for five months.

I sit down, ponder my situation, and resolve to do three things: First, I will read. Whatever it takes, I will read: between classes, in bed at night, eating lunch. Whenever I get the chance I will read. I will start bringing Tennyson or Rilke with me to work. When I am parked at cabstands or when I have to wait while some Romeo walks his date to the door, I will pull out my book and read.

Second, I resolve to stop neglecting my friends. All the unreturned phone calls, all the begging off about meeting for a couple beers, all the turned-down invitations to Hawks games and barbecues and parties—from now on I will do everything I can to spend at least a few hours a week with the guys I grew up with. I don't know if I'll ever make it into medical school, but whatever path my life eventually takes, I want those guys to be there with me. I want to be a part of their lives and I want them to be a part of mine.

And, finally, I resolve to do one more thing: something so bizarre, so foreign, so out of character that I can hardly believe I thought of it.

I'm going to take piano lessons.

My parents have a piano in the living room. I bang on it once in a while, thundering out the bass notes of "In-A-Gadda-Da-Vida," or pounding out snatches of various Irish rebel songs, but no one in their right mind would ever call what I do playing the piano.

The world's greatest symphony orchestra is in Chicago. They have delighted audiences all over the world. I have never heard them play. I have never heard *any* orchestra play. Occasionally when I come home at night, my parents will be sitting in the living room with the record player on, listening to Renata Tebaldi singing Puccini, or Sir Thomas Beecham conducting Grieg, or Jascha Heifetz playing Tchaikovsky. I find myself moved by what I hear. I marvel at the power of the music. But it is all foreign to me. It is a world of which I know nothing—but I'd like to learn.

So, when I fill out my course selection for the spring semester, I spend an extra forty bucks to take Piano I with "Miss Wilson."

It is my understanding that in order to fully qualify as a piano teacher, one must be at least seventy years old, single, thin as a rail, and own no fewer than three cats. Being homely is desirable but not mandatory. I assume there is a Piano Teachers Union where fuzzy-haired, cackling old crones with cups of herbal tea in hand hunch over applications looking for just the right mixture of decrepitude and irascibility before deciding to admit each applicant. I am shocked, therefore, when I show up for my first class. Miss Wilson is just old enough (thirty) to seem out of reach, but she is vivacious and attractive.

Piano I is not really a class, it is a lesson, and I am the only student. Miss Wilson seems as intrigued by me as I am by her. *Why*, I wonder, *is this pretty woman teaching piano to dumb college kids? Why*, she wonders, *is this clumsy construction worker taking piano?*

Miss Wilson doesn't waste any time. "Michael," she says (I like it that she doesn't resort to the proper, but farcical, "Mr. Collins"), "why are you taking this course?"

I think the answer I give her is the one she is hoping for: "I've never had much exposure to music," I tell her. "I want to learn what music is all about, and I want to be able to play it."

But before we go any further I have to lay some groundwork. I explain that I am not a music major and that my main priority is getting into medical school. But I tell her that I'm beginning to understand that there is more to life than studying the periodic table and throwing rocks.

"Throwing rocks?"

"Never mind," I say. "It's just a way of saying that I sense my life is incomplete."

"And what would you like to learn to play?" she asks.

"Beethoven," I say immediately. I don't know why I pick Beethoven except that from what little I know of music he seems to be the most revered, the most powerful.

She nods. "All right. Beethoven it is."

It turns out that I am not one of those prodigies who can play the

Polonaise in A-flat on his first day. Miss Wilson begins by teaching me how to read music. Then she has me work on scales until I can play them all. Finally she considers me ready for the set piece of all little kids' piano lessons: "Für Elise."

But I'm not insulted; I'm thrilled. I've never heard "Für Elise" before, so I go to the college library and take out a recording of it. I like it immediately. It isn't all that difficult, and within a week I am hacking away at it. Within two I have mastered it.

Over the next few months my repertoire grows. Sometimes Miss Wilson lets me pick what to play; sometimes she picks it for me. Rather than my grades suffering because of playing the piano, the opposite seems to be true. Once, sometimes twice, each day I stop my studying for fifteen or thirty minutes to practice the piano. Then I go back to studying, refreshed and better able to concentrate.

Miss Wilson is a wonderful teacher. I think she has as much fun teaching as I do learning. Every now and then I talk her into playing for me. I scoot over on the piano bench. She comes over, sits next to me, smoothes her skirt, and plays one of Scriabin's sonatas or something from Liszt or Schumann. I love to watch her play. It isn't just the listening but the actual watching that I like: the way her fingers move over the keys, the gentle sway of her body as she plays, her facial expressions as they change with the change in the music.

Miss Wilson won't play for me very often. There is something too personal, too intimate, about being alone in that room together while she plays for me. I can never quite divorce the beauty of the music from the beauty of the musician. They come together so wonderfully every time she plays. I think Miss Wilson is aware of this, too, because she is always a bit flushed and tends to avoid my eyes whenever she finishes playing. The last note hangs in the air and the silence grows uncomfortable. When she plays for me she is sharing a part of herself, and neither of us is prepared to let our relationship go beyond the formal, professional level.

Since musical notation is still somewhat of a mystery to me, each new piece is a struggle, but once I play it a few times I can memorize it. There is a rhythm or logic that helps me sense what comes next. I never get very good at playing the piano, but good enough to take real pleasure in it. I love to sit at my parents' piano before dinner and pound out "In the Hall of the Mountain King," or come home late at night, with the house dark, and work slowly and quietly into the *Moonlight* Sonata.

I never neglect my studies. As I told Miss Wilson, pre-med is my priority, but somehow music makes the rest of my studying easier, makes life seem less like drudgery.

I shouldn't be surprised, but Piano I, like all classes, has a final exam. For my final, I have to pick two pieces and play them for a panel of professors in the music department.

I choose a couple Beethoven pieces and play them flawlessly—that is, I hit the right notes at the right time, but my playing obviously lacks the sophistication and subtlety of a more experienced pianist. I get an A in the class, but the panel gives me several backhanded compliments along the lines of "Don't quit your day job."

When my little recital is over I shake hands with Miss Wilson. She wishes me good luck getting into medical school and encourages me to keep playing. I thank her and walk out the door. I never see her again. It is years before I realize what a wonderful gift she has given me.

CHAPTER TEN

A sleety March rain is splashing against the windshield as I turn right off First Avenue and swing the cab into the parking lot. I slide the cigar box full of singles and fives under the seat.

"Blue Twenty," I say into the microphone. "I'll be ten-seven for an hour or so."

"Ten-four, Twenty," the dispatcher replies. "Let me know when you're back."

I hang the microphone on the dashboard, grab my sport coat from the seat next to me, and make a run for it. I splash through the puddles and sprint up the steps to the front door of the Loyola University Stritch School of Medicine. My appointment with Dr. Rich, the head of the admissions committee, is at 4:15.

My friend Burke Gawne is a third-year medical student at Loyola. He interviewed with Dr. Rich three years ago. "Rich is a psychiatrist," Burke tells me. "He is going to be analyzing you the whole time, so try to be relaxed and natural."

Oh, sure. This man has the power to make my dream come true or to squash me like a bug. My entire life depends on what he decides. And I'm supposed to be relaxed? I feel like one of the early Christians being led in chains into the Colosseum where the lions are waiting. "Don't worry," the centurion says. "Just try to be relaxed and natural."

I try to imagine what Dr. Rich will be like. I picture Prof. Henry Higgins in *My Fair Lady* standing in his library scrutinizing me as I stand before him like a frightened and begrimed Eliza Doolittle.

"I say, Pickering," Professor Higgins says, "what have we here?"

Colonel Pickering adjusts his monocle, walks slowly around me, studying me up and down. "Extraordinary," he says at length. "It appears to be some sort of primitive man. A rock thrower, I believe."

"Good heavens, Pickering! You can't be serious. That species died out centuries ago."

The professor walks up to me and pokes me in the belly with his umbrella. "I say, can you speak?" he asks.

"Yes, sir."

Professor Higgins slaps his knee. "It speaks! Pickering, the thing speaks! How delightful. How absolutely delightful!"

I have deliberately waited to interview at Loyola last. I wanted the experience of interviewing at other places before I interviewed here. This is the school I really want to attend. Almost every Irish and Italian doctor on the West Side of Chicago went to med school here.

This will be my eighth med school interview, and every interview has been the same. Dr. So-and-so from the admissions committee glances at my file, sees where I am vulnerable, and goes for the jugular: I didn't do well on the science section of the MedCAT. I didn't major in pre-med.

I try to get the interviewer to look at how well I did on the rest of the MedCAT, or how good my pre-med science grades are, or how badly I want to be a doctor, but by then he has stopped listening. If he happens to notice my work history, that seals it for him. But what did I think was going to happen? Who wants some stupid construction worker in his medical school?

.   .   .

I sit on the edge of my chair in Dr. Rich's waiting room. I can feel my heart pounding. Dr. Rich is late. But that's okay; the interviewers are always late. I look at my watch every thirty seconds. Four fifteen. Four twenty. Four twenty-five. Finally at four thirty-five an immaculately dressed, preppy-looking character comes out of Dr. Rich's office. He is laughing.

"Thank you so much, Doctor," he says to the man inside. "I'll be sure to tell Mother and Father hello for you."

He closes the door. As he passes by, he looks down his nose at me, dissecting me with a glance that higher life-forms often cast on their evolutionary inferiors.

"Be sure to tell Mother and Father hello for me, too," I tell him.

He seems startled that I possess the capacity to speak. He curls his lip and walks past me. A minute later the door opens and Dr. Rich comes out.

"Mr. Collins?" he asks.

I stand up and say, "Yes, sir."

"Please come in."

We shake hands and I follow him into his office. I stand next to the chair facing his desk until he tells me to sit down.

I swallow, cough, and wish I had the sense to go to the bathroom while I was waiting. Dr. Rich says nothing. He studies the chart in front of him, frowning and occasionally glancing up at me in consternation.

"I'm a little confused," he says. "I see you graduated from Notre Dame, but you took no pre-med courses there?"

"No, sir."

"And what have you been doing since graduation?"

"I worked construction for a couple years before I finally realized I wanted to be a doctor." It sounds so lame.

"Construction." He says it like he is accusing me of something.

"Yes, but I'm taking pre-med courses now."

"Are you still working?"

"Yes, sir. I still work construction whenever I get a little time off; otherwise I drive a cab."

"You drive a cab." Another accusation.

"Yes, sir."

When he asks his other applicants what they have been doing with their free time they say things like, "I've been at Johns Hopkins doing research on a cure for bone cancer," or, "I've got a little project going at MIT designing new CAT scanners." All I've been doing is figuring out shortcuts between Riverside and Berwyn.

Dr. Rich returns his attention to my file.

"I'm afraid you didn't do very well on the MedCAT exam, Mr. Collins."

I knew he would get to that sooner or later, so I go through my standard explanation. "In order to apply for next year's freshman class I had to take the MedCAT before I had biology and organic chemistry. You'll see, though, that only my science scores were low. I did quite well on the other parts."

"Yes, but unfortunately science is what you study in medical school."

My heart is sinking. This interview is going just like all the others.

Dr. Rich folds the chart and looks at me with a weak smile. "Well, Mr. Collins, I think that's everything." He rises and extends his hand.

I start to rise, then sit back down. I'm not going to let our interview end. If I walk out that door now, it's over for me.

"There is something else, Dr. Rich."

Dr. Rich hesitates a moment, then sits back down. "Yes?"

I grip the rails of my chair and lean forward, struggling to find the right words. "I know there are lots of students who have better grades and better MedCAT scores than I do. But I want you to know that . . . well, even though I don't have the best grades and best test scores, grades and test scores aren't the only things that matter. I've been around a little. I've seen life. I've worked hard. I didn't make the decision to become a doctor lightly. I had to quit my job, change my life, and go back to school—*for two years*. I took all the required science courses, and I've aced every one of them.

"I guess what I'm asking you to do is look at more than grades and test scores. You won't find a single applicant to this medical school who wants to be a doctor more than I do, who will be more grateful to be accepted here than I will, or who will consider becoming a doctor a greater honor than I will. If you admit me, you won't regret it. I will repay your confidence."

Dr. Rich looks at me for several seconds. "Well put, Mr. Collins."

On June 6 I finish my last two pre-med courses. Just as I told Dr. Rich, I aced them all, but I am beginning to wonder if it matters. Three medical schools have already rejected me. Five have put me on a waiting list. Most medical schools start in September, but the school I really want to attend, Loyola, starts June 24—three weeks from now. Things are not looking good.

For the hundredth time I try to think of something else I can do to improve my chances of getting into med school. I took the courses. I did the interviews. I got the letters of recommendation. What I really need is to have some big shot take an interest in my situation and "arrange" for me to get in. But the biggest shot I know is Judge LeFontaine down the street. He once was Deputy Grand Knight of the Oak Park Branch of the Knights of Columbus—not exactly the most influential position of all time. And besides, ever since Timmy set the judge's garage on fire, he hasn't been very fond of the Collins boys.

I ask my mom if there is any chance I might have been switched at birth with one of Teddy Kennedy's or Nelson Rockefeller's kids. If so, would she mind getting him on the phone to see if he could lend a hand here? You know, help a brother out?

My brother Pete says that if I was switched at birth it was with one of the Three Stooges or maybe Bozo the Clown.

But at least Patti is back home. She finished her junior year at St. Teresa's and is working again at Oak Park Hospital as a nurse's aide. After driving up to Rochester every other weekend for the last nine months, I'm glad to have her so near. My only regret is that we won't be taking summer school together again.

At home, my mother has made a deal with God. I feel kind of sorry for God. My mom is always making deals with Him, and He always seems to come out on the short end of the stick. This time she's made a deal to get me into medical school. My mom is not an alcoholic, but like most Irish, she enjoys a drink now and again. If I get into medical school she has promised God she will quit drinking for one year.

My brother Tim tells her she is nuts. He says he doesn't care if I get cancer of the eyeball, he's not giving up drinking for a year.

I'm back on the breakout gang at Scalese. It's almost as if I never left. The only difference is that I'm two years older; otherwise I'm still a laborer, still throwing rocks. But Jesse is gone; Rosie is gone (JT says he got hired by the Fire Department); Bean Pole and Bake are gone (they finally got themselves fired for coming to work high and crashing a pickup into one of the compressors).

Every day is pretty much the same: up at 4:30, at the yard by 5:30, working for the church at 6:30. We are getting an hour or two overtime every day. When I get home, the first thing I do is go through what's left of the mail after Shannon has savaged it. By mid-June I still haven't been accepted anywhere, and I'm getting discouraged.

School is over. There is nothing left to study. All I can do now is wait. At night I drive the cab, play softball, or go out with Patti. If we don't go to one of the Irish bars we head up to Sportsman's on Roosevelt Road. Now that O'Dea's is closed, all the guys have made Sportsman's our new home. Patti is still a couple months short of her twenty-first birthday, but no one in the bars seems to care. She is never carded.

By now all my friends are making something of themselves. Murph is with the Secret Service and tells us he might be transferred to Washington soon. Joe Muldooney and Nick Farentino have graduated from law school. Jay Standreth is teaching at St. Rita's. Others are working for insurance companies, banks, or brokerage firms. We meet sometimes for a drink after work. Most of them are wearing suits and ties. I am in a dirty T-shirt and boots. No one looks at me funny—yet. But I wonder how much longer it will be before my friends start to wonder if Mike is ever going to grow up and get a real job.

My brothers are all over the place. Denny is in South America working for some governmental agency whose name he never reveals. Timmy is a garbageman. He, too, is looking for his place in the world. Rog is a cadet at the Air Force Academy. Jack and Pete are still in high school—a remarkable achievement for Jack, who is always on some kind of probation: academic, disciplinary, moral, legal, or gluteal (my dad says if he gets in trouble one more time, he is going to kick his ass). Joe and Bill are still in grammar school and, despite all odds, are turning out to be pretty good kids.

I am glad to see my brothers and my friends succeeding. They are great guys and I wish them the best. But their success makes me feel my own situation more keenly. I am twenty-six years old. My life is totally unsettled. My future is hanging by a slim thread. My chances of getting into medical school are fading a little more each day. And if I don't get in, then what? I suppose I would just keep working for Scalese, keep throwing rocks, at least for a while, but the fight would have gone out of me, and I don't know if I would have the heart to try something else.

And worse, what about Patti? If I don't get into medical school do I really still have the right to keep going out with her? She has shared this dream with me and I don't know if I could ever look her in the eye again. Doesn't she deserve something better than a failure?

I trudge in the back door and set my hammer and hard hat on the floor next to my boots. My cousin is getting married in two hours, but before showering and changing I have to check the mail. The University of Chicago rejected me last week. Four med schools have now rejected me. That leaves four others. I am still on their waiting lists, but time is running out.

The mail, all torn and covered with dog spit, is lying on the floor. I brush past Shannon and begin sorting through the tattered envelopes until I find the one I have been waiting for. It is from the Loyola University Stritch School of Medicine.

I have been thinking of this moment for so long. I always imagined that I would be unable to restrain myself from immediately tearing open the envelope. Instead, I hold the envelope in my hand for close to a minute, afraid to open it.

A poem has been nibbling at the back of my mind for the last few weeks. Snatches of it have come to me here and there, but I haven't been able recall the whole thing. The verse comes to me now:

> *. . . I had so long suffered in this quest,*
> *Heard failure prophesied so oft, been writ*
> *So many times among "The Band"—to wit,*
> *The knights who to the Dark Tower's search addressed*
> *Their steps—that just to fail as they, seemed best,*
> *All the doubt was now—should I be fit?*

For better or worse, what is written in this letter is going to change my life forever. So be it.

I take a deep breath and tear open the envelope.

> *Dear Mr. Collins:*
> *The admissions committee of the Loyola University Stritch School of Medicine is delighted to inform you . . .*

"Sweet Mother o' Jaysus," I shout. "I'm in!" I grab Shannon on either side of her head and shake it back and forth. "Shannon, you filthy flea bag, I'm in!"

"In what?" my brother Tim shouts from the living room where he is lying on the floor watching *Gilligan's Island.*

I wave the envelope in his face. "Med school, you idiot! I got into med school!"

"They must be pretty hard up for doctors," he says. "Now can you get out of the way? I gotta see if the Professor can get Ginger out of the quicksand."

I look at the clock on the desk. Quarter after six. I am supposed to pick up Patti at six thirty. I know I should hop in the shower, but I can't wait. I run out to my car and head east on Division. Five minutes later I screech to a halt in front of Patti's house. Her little brother Terry answers the door.

He scarcely has the door open before I push my way in and grab him by the shoulders. "Where's Pat?" I ask.

"She's—"

I see Patti, still in her nurse's aide uniform, coming down the stairs. I brush past Terry, crush Patti in my arms, and begin swinging her around, laughing. "I'm in!" I tell her. "I'm in!"

She grabs the envelope from my hand. "Loyola?" she says. "You got into Loyola? Oh, Mike!"

She gives me a big kiss that stops only when her brother says, "Hello? You guys want to get a room?"

"Shut up, you little dweeb," I tell him. "I'm a med student now and if you don't leave us alone I'll dissect your brain."

"That won't take long," Patti says, sticking out her tongue at him.

She glances at her uniform, now streaked with dirt from my embrace. "Oh, look what you did," she says, trying to act upset.

"Relax," I tell her. "It makes you look like a real nurse. All you need is a little blood on that uniform." I turn to her brother. "Come here, kid."

Terry holds up his hands and starts to back away. "Use your own blood," he says.

I give Patti one more hug, ruffle Terry's hair, and head out the door, promising to return within the hour to pick her up for the wedding.

And later that night, after the wedding, after a few more beers at Sportsman's, after Patti and I spend an hour parked in my car down the street from her house, I come home to a quiet house and, for the first time since I opened that letter, have time to think about all this.

A wonderful, incredible thing has just happened: I'm going to be a doctor. Me, a twenty-six-year-old rock thrower and cabdriver. I'm going to be a doctor. All kinds of silly, childish things keep running through my head: *"The doctor will see you now." "The doctor is* in.*" "I asked my family doctor just what I had."* It seems so outlandish, so inconceivable—even now, even while I hold the very letter in my hand and reread it for the tenth time. Me, a doctor!

Loyola took its sweet time accepting me. School starts in less than two weeks. It's time to take a deep breath. One very major hurdle has been overcome: I have been accepted at medical school. But some very real problems remain. I will be in class with all kinds of egghead pre-med majors: guys who carry slide rules and read Albert Einstein for fun, guys who have Coke-bottle glasses and were members of the computer club, guys who have forgotten more astrophysics and molecular biology than I will ever know, guys who smoke meerschaum pipes and wear blue blazers with paisley ascots, guys who can kick intellectual sand in my scrawny little face any time they feel like it, guys who spend their Friday nights designing bridges, studying pi, and setting up electromagnetic fields around their bathrooms.

I wasn't a pre-med major. I took the bare minimum of pre-med courses. I'm not good at anything that will be the least use to me in medical school. I have a very rough road ahead of me.

I don't know a lot of things, but one thing I know for sure: medical school isn't going to be a picnic.

CHAPTER ELEVEN

Medical school begins two weeks later—with a picnic.

The picnic is held in the Miller Meadow Forest Preserve across the street from the medical center. I don't know a single soul, so I slip into the throng of students, residents, and interns meandering through the long grass and the maze of worn wooden picnic tables stained with white bird droppings and carved with lovers' initials and monosyllabic profanities. The tables are stacked with quarters of watermelon, bowls of potato salad, and bags of potato chips. A savory cloud of barbecue smoke drifts slowly across the meadow onto First Avenue, where it is sucked into the vacuum of passing buses and trucks.

I have been to a lot of picnics but never one like this. There are no Frisbees, no boom boxes, no halter tops, no sixteen-inch softballs. I have been dropped, unprepared, into the schizoid world of medicine: guys leaning forward, biting into hot dogs loaded with mustard and relish, talking about drunks vomiting blood; guys with stethoscopes around their necks slurping down baked beans that they say look like fecal stew; guys in gray lab coats talking about a woman in the ER who had a sweet potato in her vagina ("I swear, she had white sprouts growing around her underpants").

They are different from me in almost every way. They dress differently. They speak differently. They carry themselves with a swagger born of experiences I long to share. They are gods, and I am desperate to be like them. I want to go to picnics in *my* gray lab coat and blithely throw off phrases like "BUN/creatinine ratio" and "aortic insufficiency." I want to stand with a cup of coffee in my hand, looking tired and haggard from being up all night doing important things like delivering quadruplets and repairing ruptured aneurysms. I want to have a beeper on my belt and an ophthalmoscope in my pocket. I want a name tag that says *Doctor.* I want to be anything but a rock thrower on Johnny Battaglia's breakout crew.

I wander around the picnic, feeling out of place, wondering where to go, what to do. I am surprised to see they have a keg of beer. I like beer, but I thought beer was somehow on medicine's blacklist. Doesn't beer cause cirrhosis and alcoholism? Taken in large quantities, doesn't it make ugly girls look like supermodels? At closing time every night doesn't it make skinny little Irish guys think they can beat up 250-pound Italian bouncers? Shouldn't doctors be telling people to stay away from stuff like that?

And besides, I'm a medical student now. Don't I owe it to my patients to swear off alcohol forever? Now that I have placed myself at the service of humanity, there are many sacrifices I will be called upon to make. I imagine myself in the coming years wading across raging streams to deliver babies at isolated farmhouses, battling howling blizzards to remove appendices under flashlights in storm-tossed Maine lighthouses, sewing legs back on after plane crashes in remote parts of Manitoba, fighting off hordes of spear-throwing savages to deliver lifesaving serum in darkest New Guinea, fighting off hordes of Guinness-waving Gaels to deliver lifesaving liver transplants in darkest Ireland.

I am about to embark upon a life of selfless humanitarianism. I worry that alcohol is the seductive temptress trying to lure me from this noble endeavor. So I stand in front of that keg and hesitate. What if one of those haggard guys in a gray coat asks me to help deliver the next baby or repair the next artery? I look around. No one seems about to ask me anything. There are no raging streams or howling blizzards in the vicinity. It is a hot day. I decide that one beer wouldn't be such a bad thing, so I fill a cup. I have a burger, too. It's nice having something to do with my hands, so I grab a hot dog. When that's gone I have another burger.

"You want me to have them back up the truck for you?" someone behind me says.

I turn to see a heavyset guy with a round face, black hair, and a mustache smiling at me. *John Brennan,* his name tag says.

"I was just, uh, having a burger," I say.

"Yeah. You from Biafra or something? Looks like you might eat the tablecloth next."

"I was kind of hungry."

"Kind of? I'd like to see what you do when you're famished." He holds out his hand. "Jack Brennan," he says.

"Mike Collins," I reply, shaking with him.

Jack steps forward and stands next to me. He says he, too, is a freshman. Together we survey the scene in front of us. It's easy to pick out the other freshmen. They are all wandering around with dazed looks on their faces. Across the way, with his yellow sweater tied around his neck, talking to two of the attending physicians, is the preppy guy I saw the day I interviewed with Dean Rich.

"You know that guy?" I ask Jack.

Jack doesn't even hesitate. "That's Farthingham J. Chestworth," he says, "heir to the Chestworth dildo fortune. He parks his yacht next to mine. Wanna meet him?"

Before I can say no, Jack is calling him. "Farty! I say, Farty, old boy!"

The preppy guy is oblivious to Jack's greeting. Jack smiles and tells me Farty is a bit busy at the moment sucking up to the deans but assures me that "the two of us go way back. We even got our silver services from the same silver mongery."

I am starting to realize that Jack is nuts. I like him.

I am not fooling myself. It's great that I have gotten into medical school, but that doesn't mean my problems are over. My classmates are all hotshot

but sneaking occasional glances at the knobby knees, the shriveled penis, the contorted face. It is at once terribly alien and disturbingly familiar.

There is a professor, Dr. Martin, who presides over the class, but we quickly learn that the real teaching is done by anatomy grad students. These guys are a couple years out of college. Most of them are trying to get into med school by first getting master's degrees in anatomy. The grad student assigned to us is a stocky guy with a drooping mustache. His name is John Fleming, but everyone calls him Dog.

Our first assignment is to make an incision down the length of the body to open the abdominal cavity. Everyone in our group just stands there, our shiny new dissecting kits in our hands, waiting for someone to do something. Finally, Brian Clark volunteers to make the incision, a job we are all glad to cede to him. We move a little closer, but as yet no one touches the table.

Dog is right behind Brian's shoulder giving him advice as he prepares to slice our cadaver open. Brian draws his scalpel down the length of the cadaver's chest and abdomen. Unfortunately, Jimmy's skin is tough as leather. Brian's initial effort does little more than scratch the skin.

"You're going to have to push a little harder with that scalpel," Dog says after Brian's third attempt. It takes Brian several more hacks to complete the incision.

I know that inside we are just a bunch of organs. I know I'm not going to learn anything earthshaking, but I still can't wait to see what it's like to "look beneath the surface" and "see what's really inside." Unfortunately, the inside of Jimmy's abdominal cavity is not all that enlightening. Loops of gray bowel float in a caustic sea of formaldehyde that stings our eyes. There's not a lot of food for thought here, and I don't feel this experience has afforded me any new insight into the human condition—unless it is to reinforce my cynicism.

Dog reaches forward with his gloved hand. He pulls a few things *this* way and shows us the liver. He pulls a few things *that* way and shows us the spleen. "Tomorrow, boys and girls," he tells us, "if you're good, I might show you a fecalith. Can you say fe-cuh-lith?" We are all excited until we go home that night and consult our medical dictionaries to find what a fecalith is.

Since Loyola med school isn't far from the West Side where I grew up, I make it my responsibility to show my fellow students where to find the best burgers, the best hot dogs, and the best beer. Before the month is out, Sportsman's has become our second home.

Dani, the waitress in Sportsman's, is shocked to see this horde of unruly medical students descend upon her establishment. She can't get over the fact that all these future doctors enjoy beer and cheeseburgers.

"Shouldn't you guys be in a lab curing cancer or something?" she asks Dog at closing time one night.

Dog wipes the foam from his mustache and says he is not a medical student like the rest of us.

"What do you do then?"

"He dissects people for a living," Brian Clark interjects.

Dani's eyes get wide and she takes a step back.

"But he's very good at it," Brian tells her.

Dog smiles modestly and says he's glad to hear Brian say that. He didn't want Dani to think he was just another pretty face.

Brian tells Dani to keep Dog in mind if she ever needs anything dissected.

Dani looks at Dog like he is something out of *The Texas Chain Saw Massacre*. She hands us our check and says her mother was right. No good can come from serving strong drinks to weird guys in dark places.

My dream of getting into medical school has come true, but that doesn't change the fact that I have no money. With the money I made at Scalese I paid off all my college loans and even saved enough to cover my first semester's tuition here at med school, but that's gone and now I'm broke. I have to figure out how I'm going to pay tuition for the next three years. I guess I could talk to my mom. She seems to have the inside track with God. Maybe if she gave up drinking for *two* years, God would give me the winning lottery numbers, or at least the Trifecta at Arlington.

"That's not how it works, sonny boy," my mom says. She suggests I focus on studying and leave the divine-intervention stuff to her.

I try to think where I could possibly get the money. My brothers would do it for me, but they have a combined net worth of fifteen bucks. Finally, in desperation, I go to see my uncle Jack.

My dad has two living brothers. Both of them fought in World War II. My dad was stationed in Alaska working in Army Intelligence. His brother Jimmy was with Patton's Third Army in Europe. Jack was in the Navy in the North Atlantic. Roger was a tail gunner in a B-17. He got killed over Holland in 1944 when he was twenty-one years old.

Uncle Jim and Uncle Jack own a small painting company in Oak Park. Uncle Jim has seven kids. I know I can't ask him for help. But Uncle Jack has only two kids, both of whom are out of college. I go to see him one night to ask if he could lend me some money. We go down to his basement, have a couple beers, and talk about the White Sox. He asks me if I think Wilbur Wood can pitch into his fifties. I tell him I thought Wilbur Wood already was in his fifties.

After a few minutes I tell Uncle Jack why I have come.

"It would be a loan," I say. "I'll pay you back as soon as I get into private practice." But I also tell him I might not be in private practice for nine years.

Uncle Jack doesn't hesitate. He reaches into his drawer, pulls out a checkbook, and asks me how much I need. He then writes out a check for my next semester's tuition. "Come back when you need more," he tells me.

Twice a year over the course of the next three years I make the trip to Uncle Jack's house to sit in the basement, have a couple beers, and talk about the White Sox. I always leave with a check for next semester's tuition. I am running a tab with him, and at each visit we total up the amount of money I promise eventually to repay. Never once does he hesitate or question me about the money. The only thing he asks is that I keep his generosity quiet. For some reason he doesn't want people to know how kind he has been to me.

Uncle Jack's generosity takes care of the tuition payments, but I still need a little money for books and gas and the odd beer. I worry about spending too much time driving the cab. Med school is hard and I don't want to shoot myself in the foot by driving the cab when I should be studying. For the time being I decide to cut down on movies and enter-tainment and live off the few bucks I make from driving the cab a couple times a week.

Patti is very understanding. Incredibly, she doesn't seem to miss going to Arnold Schwarzenegger movies and Sox games. She seems content to watch TV with me, go for walks, and have an occasional beer at Sports-man's.

We have been in school about a month. Several of us, including Jack Bren-nan, are clustered around our microscopes trying to memorize the histol-ogy of various body parts: the liver with its lacunae, the pancreas with its islets, skeletal muscle with its bundles. We have been doing this for the last six hours.

Jack is having a particularly difficult time. He keeps shaking his head and mumbling to himself. Finally he throws down his pen, pushes back from his microscope, rubs his eyes, and says, "If I never see another mam-mary gland in my life it'll be too soon."

Brian Clark gasps and tells Jack not to be ridiculous. He says he's never met a mammary gland he didn't like. He says there's no such thing as a bad mammary gland. He says he wouldn't mind seeing a mammary gland any time its owner wants to air one out. Cathy Conroy sighs loudly and says she thought boys got over this stuff when they left seventh grade. Brian hitches up his pants and starts talking like John Wayne: "Some things aren't so easy to get over, little lady."

We all look at one another. We have been cooped up in this MDL for six hours. We're all getting a little goofy. It's time for drastic measures. We shut off our microscopes. Fifteen minutes later we are in Sportsman's with a couple pitchers of beer and a bowl of popcorn in front of us, listening to Brian Clark deliver a lecture titled "Famous Mammary Glands I Have Known."

Cathy Conroy says Brian is setting the medical profession back a hundred years.

Dani, our waitress, listens for a while before she announces to everyone in the bar that if the health of America rests in the hands of these medical students, then she is moving to Uzbekistan.

CHAPTER TWELVE

First-year medical school is not what I imagined. It is not stimulating. It is not exciting. It is not glamorous. It is memorization, pure and simple. It is the scholastic equivalent of throwing rocks. It is as though our teachers dropped twenty books in our laps and said, "Memorize these." That's it. That's first-year medical school. Biochemistry and pharmacology, anatomy and histology, physiology and pathology, immunology and micro-biology. Page after page, chapter after chapter, of dry, sterile facts to be memorized.

I want more. I want erudite discussions of "man, woman, birth, death, infinity." I want grizzled old surgeons telling us about the old days when they fixed ruptured aortas with bailing wire and catgut. I want beepers, and frantic calls from ERs, and desperate mothers rushing choking babies to us. I want bloody gunshot wounds and psychos whom we talk down from ledges of tall apartment buildings. ("That's not the answer, Jimmy. Now give me your hand.") I want to be a doctor, not a student.

Well, it ain't happenin'.

I plod on, memorizing everything they throw at me, but I miss college. I miss discussions and analyses and rational discourse. I wish just one of my white-coated medical school professors would put down his lecture notes and ask how the kidney knows it's a kidney and not a liver. Or what are the epistemological implications of the pluripotential cell? Or why is the human form peculiarly suited to function as the locus of the only souled animal in creation? Medicine gives rise to so many profound questions that are so rigorously ignored. It is almost as if we are afraid to ask. Kierkegaard or Montaigne wouldn't have been afraid to ask.

My medical school professors are focused. They are pragmatic. But somehow they manage to take the wonder out of medicine. They fail to impart to us a sense of awe, a sense that somewhere, somehow, our lives transcend the chemical and biological formulae that never quite succeed in explaining us to ourselves. To me that's all that matters.

There is an entire part of my brain, the analytical part, that is going fallow this year. Never once have I been asked Why or Whether—only What. What is the degree of nuclear hyperchromasia in anaplastic astrocytomas? What is the role of immunophenotyping in hematopoietic neoplasms? What is the role of glucose 6-phosphate dehydrogenase deficiency in falciparum malaria?

Say what?

I come home at night shaking my head and wondering if this is really happening. How is any of this stuff going to help me deliver a baby, take out an appendix, or replace a knee? It's like I'm trapped in a trivia game for idiot savants—except that I'm not a savant, just an idiot. The stuff we are studying is so esoteric that it's almost comical. I suppose in a sense I am being educated, but it feels more like I am being disciplined. I'm the Spartan boy left on a mountainside to see if he is tough enough to survive the winter. I feel like I am stuck in one long rite of initiation, one long hazing ritual.

I imagine my professors sitting together at night over beers, laughing about the sadistic tricks they played on their students that day. "You're never gonna guess what I made 'em do today," Dr. Smith says as he reaches for the pretzels. "I made 'em memorize the Krebs cycle. A ha ha ha! The freaking Krebs cycle!" The professors slam their beer bottles on the table and nearly fall off their chairs laughing.

"That's nothing," Dr. Jones says. "I made my class memorize the pathway of biosynthesis for—are you ready for this?—*for type-three polysaccharides*!"

"No way!"

"Swear to God! You shoulda seen 'em. They all got green and looked like they just swallowed a bottle of ipecac!"

The professors roar with laughter and order another round.

Not all my medical school experiences have been disappointing. I have made some great friends. Cathy Conroy is temporarily living at her grandmother's house just down the street from me. She and I take turns driving each other to school every day. Brian, Jack, Dog, and I squeeze in a night up at Sportsman's every week or two.

Dog has applied to next year's freshman medical school class but says he's not sure he will be accepted. We can't believe it. I tell Dog he would be twice as good a doctor as any of the rest of us. Brian tells him if it doesn't work out, "maybe Collins could get you a job in the coal mines or wherever it is he came from."

Another thing I like about medical school is that, for a change, not all my fellow students are guys. It has been a good experience for me to go to school with women. I was raised in a family of eight boys and no girls. I went to an all-boy high school and an all-boy college. I spent two years before medical school working in all-male environments. Girls have always been exotic creatures to me. I don't understand them. But it is refreshing and healthy to work and study alongside people who don't think burping is cool, who don't care who can fart the loudest, and who don't have to have sharp objects kept away from them every time the Bears lose.

As I slowly get into the swing of things in medical school, I find myself torn between what I *have* to do, study, and what I *want* to do, spend time with Patti. Patti will start her final year of nursing school in September.

Although she is familiar with the sacrifices doctors have to make, I know she is a little hurt when she sits at home Saturday night after Saturday night while I study.

As summer draws to a close, it's time for Patti to head back to Minnesota again. She is leaving on a Sunday. I decide to splurge and take her to dinner at one of Chicago's premier restaurants, The Bakery. I have to call two months in advance to make the reservation.

Unfortunately, the night before this farewell dinner we go bowling with Dick and Mary Ann Murphy and Joe and Lucy Muldooney. We have a lot of laughs, and wind up closing the bowling alley at 2:00 A.M. Patti and I say good night to the Murphys and the Muldooneys and then spend the next hour in a secluded corner of the parking lot. It is four o'clock before I get Pat home.

She calls me the next morning to say her parents are furious. They are threatening to ground her tonight and not let her go out to dinner.

"Oh, no!" I reply. "Tell them it's The Bakery. Tell them I made reservations two months ago. Tell them we're really sorry. Tell them it was Murph's fault. Tell them I'll have you home by twelve tonight. Tell them I promise to make you stop kissing me till all hours of the night—"

"*What?*"

"Just kidding." I am quiet for a moment, then add, "But you really should learn some restraint."

Patti sputters and chokes. She threatens to wring my neck and scratch my eyes out. She says if I want restraint, she'll give me restraint.

Neither of us has ever been to a fancy downtown restaurant before. Even though The Bakery is one of the premier restaurants in the city, it does not have a liquor license. You have to bring your own wine, which the waiter will open and pour for you.

To date, my life's experience with alcohol consists of 4,867,239 beers, thirty shots of Irish whiskey, and eight sloe gin fizzes (consumed in rapid-fire fashion one night after hockey practice at the Junior Olympic training camp in Lake Placid when I was eighteen years old. Those were the last sloe gin fizzes that will ever cross my lips in this lifetime). I know nothing about wine except that everyone thinks it's okay for priests to drink it at 6:30 in the morning at Mass.

I want to impress Patti with my expertise in vinology, so I go to the local liquor store and hunt for some wine. It's in the back corner behind the cardboard figure of Bill Melton holding a Schlitz. After poking around for a few minutes, I discover there are three kinds of wine: white wine, red wine, and a pink wine called rosé that presumably is a mixture of both.

The manager, Duke, asks what I'm doing in the wine section: "You buyin' somethin' for your grandma or what?"

When I tell him I'm taking Patti out to dinner at a fancy restaurant he asks, "Since when is Old Style not good enough for her?"

I have no idea if you drink red wine or white wine with dinner, so I decide to get a bottle of each. Fifteen minutes and eleven dollars later, I leave with a bottle of Mogen David red and Julius Gallo white.

Duke says I must be in love to be spending that kind of dough on Tommy Burns' little sister. "Is she built like a brick shithouse or what?"

I tell him not to talk about Tommy's sister that way.

Duke is right about the wine, though. I've gone overboard. For eleven dollars I could have gotten two cases of Old Style and a bag of pretzel rods. But the girl I love is going away to college, so why not splurge?

I go home, find an old cooler in the basement, fill it with ice, put the two bottles in it, and put the cooler in the trunk of the Beater.

When I pick Patti up that night, her father, arms crossed, is waiting at the front door. He says he doesn't want a repetition of last night. He says keeping Patti out that late is an insult to her. He says he hasn't raised his daughter to be the kind of girl who stays out till dawn. He says he has half a mind to make her stay home tonight just to teach us a lesson. He says he is disappointed in both of us. He says in *this* family girls come home at a decent hour. Finally, he says my car is a piece of junk.

Patti kisses her dad and says, "Don't worry; we'll be home early." I shake hands with Mr. Burns and say, "Don't worry; we'll be home early." As Patti and I walk to my car, her dad calls after us, "You'd better be home early."

When we arrive at The Bakery we see a sign for a valet service, but neither of us knows exactly what a valet service is, so I drive around for twenty minutes until I find a parking place three blocks away. Then I open the trunk, take the two bottles of wine from the cooler, and bring them into the restaurant with us.

"Bonjour, monsieur et madame. Bonjour," the maître d' says, bowing slightly from the hip. "Allow me take madame's coat." He tells us our table is ready and would we like to be seated?

I think that is a good idea since I don't want to eat standing up.

When the maître d' seats us, he calls our waiter, Philippe, who also bows and then hands us our menus. Philippe takes the two bottles of wine, promising to open them and bring them back to the table.

"There are no prices on my menu," Patti whispers to me after he has gone.

"There are on mine," I say with a gulp as I peruse the pheasant under glass, pan-roasted squab, and other delicacies. I'm not sure what a squab is, but there's no way I'm going to eat one. It sounds like some kind of groin rash you get from not showering enough. I try to stop swallowing and act as though I always spend thirty or forty dollars to get my squab roasted.

Philippe is back in two minutes with our wine. The white wine he places in a large bucket of ice; the red wine he sets on the table. "Excellent choice, monsieur," he says as he wipes off the bottle of Mogen David. He pours us each a glass of wine and tells us he will give us a few minutes to make our selection. When he is gone I notice that he has forgotten to put the red wine on ice, so I squeeze it into the bucket with the white.

We clink glasses and Patti says how great it is to be at such a famous restaurant. While Patti is looking at the menu, I slip out my wallet, put it on my lap, and count my money: eighty-four dollars. Hopefully it will be enough.

Philippe returns, frowns, and takes the red wine out of the ice bucket, wipes it down, and sets it on the table. "Have you made your choices?" he asks.

Patti orders lamb chops and the *salade niçoise*—whatever *that* is. ("I like the name," she tells me later.) I do a quick calculation and figure I have enough money to get the *petit filet*.

"Would monsieur care for some soup or salad?" Philippe asks.

I have just finished my sixth roll and am wiping the crumbs from the corner of my mouth. "No, not for me, thanks," I say. "I'm on a diet."

"A diet . . . *oui,* monsieur."

When he is gone I lift the bottle of red wine and put it back in the ice bucket. "It'll never get cold if he keeps leaving it out," I say to Patti, who nods in understanding. Through the rest of the meal we alternate between red and white wine. Each time the waiter comes he takes the red wine out of the bucket, wipes it down, and sets it on the table. Each time he leaves I stick it back in the ice.

When the meal is over, Philippe comes by with the dessert menu. I do another quick calculation and figure we have enough money left for one dessert. There are flans and flambés and mousses and tartes and crème anglaise and ten other things I've never heard of. I tell Patti to order something and I'll split it with her. She tells Philippe she will have the *clafoutis aux pommes.* We never do figure out exactly what it is, but it tastes good. By then we have finished the last of the wine. I turn the bottles upside down and stick them in the ice bucket. Philippe winces slightly, turns them right side up, and then takes away the bucket. "Was the wine to your liking?" he asks us.

"It was really good!" Patti says, trying desperately to keep her eyes in focus.

Philippe then hands me the bill. I look at it and inhale sharply. Seventy-eight dollars. Something is wrong. I very carefully totaled the bill each time we ordered and was sure the bill was only going to be sixty-eight. That would leave a sixteen-dollar tip. From driving a cab I know how much guys depend on tips, and I've vowed to always leave a decent tip no matter where I go and no matter how poor I am. But if the bill is seventy-eight dollars, that means I can leave only a six-dollar tip.

I look at the bill and notice there is a ten-dollar "decantation charge." I ask Philippe what this is all about.

Philippe explains that the restaurant charges us to open the wine. "That is what we call the corkage fee."

I tell him I don't want the corks. He can keep them.

Philippe bows and says, "Monsieur is very witty."

Even though he wasn't very good at keeping our red wine cold, Philippe seems like a decent guy, and I don't want to stiff him. Embarrassed, I turn to Patti and ask if she has any money.

"All I have is ten dollars," she whispers.

"Can I have it?"

Patti smiles and passes me two fives under the table.

I count out ninety-four dollars and lay it on the table. "Mercy bo koo," I tell Philippe as he helps Patti into her coat.

"Pas de quoi, monsieur," he replies. "It has been a most . . . interesting evening." He bows once again and holds the door for us.

"What a wonderful place," Patti says as we are walking back to our car. Patti has had quite a bit of wine and at this moment everything is wonderful. She takes my arm and leans her head against my shoulder as we walk. "I just love that Philippe. He is such a gentleman."

"Yeah," I reply. "He was a good guy. Too bad he kept forgetting to put the red wine on ice. But he's young. He'll learn."

We are home by eleven o'clock. Patti's father is waiting for us.

"That wasn't so hard, was it?" he asks.

The next morning I give Patti a ride to the Woodfield shopping mall to meet her roommate Cathy, who is going to drive them back to Rochester. Patti and I stand outside Cathy's car having a long hug and kiss that ends only when Cathy begins coughing so loud that we think she must have emphysema.

"I hate to break up this little lovefest, but if we want to get to Minnesota before Tuesday we'd better get going," Cathy says.

As Pat is getting into the car, I tell her I have a big microbiology test next week and maybe I will come up the weekend after that.

"You'd better," she says, leaning out the window and giving me one more kiss.

Cathy laughs and says, "You guys need help."

CHAPTER THIRTEEN

When Patti goes back to school, I do nothing but study. I put in a lot of hours, but our courses are hard and there are lots of them. It's great having a lot of smart people in the same boat I'm in. My classmates and I share notes, study together, and prepare for tests together. In anatomy we have a special weapon: Dog. He singlehandedly is getting us through that course. To show our gratitude, we buy him a couple pitchers at Sportsman's and try to figure out ways to help him get into medical school next year.

Sometimes in the halls I see senior medical students and residents heading to or returning from the hospital. I envy them. They are practically doctors. I am just a student. But I never forget where all this is leading. In a couple years I will be the one with the gray coat. I will be the one assisting at surgery. I will be the one trying to figure out which antibiotic works best for this infection.

I am still having a hard time adjusting to the fact that I am actually going to be a doctor. In one of the halls of the medical school I run across a long row of pictures of all the previous graduating classes, going back to before I was born. They are almost all white, almost all male, but there is one other thing that strikes me about these pictures: everyone seems so much older, so much more focused, so much more intense. Even as senior medical students, these guys *look* like doctors. They *look* like someone you would want to take care of you when you are sick. How did they get that way? Presumably they were just knuckleheads like me when they started. What happened along the way that made them so different?

It's hard to believe, but our medical center has its own bar. It's down in the basement, and it's kind of hard to find. It's called The Pub and they serve pizza and beer. It isn't open to the public, just to students and employees of the medical center. Dog is the one who introduces us to The Pub. He loves the place. Jack Brennan, Brian Clark, Cathy Conroy, and I often meet him there on Friday nights when the place is packed with students, residents, and nurses.

I am having a beer in The Pub with Steve Byrne, who was a year ahead of me in high school and is now a resident in internal medicine. Steve tells me one of the patients on his service died this morning and would I like to watch the autopsy with him? I tell him I'd love to. Here is an opportunity to get away from all the books and do something a real doctor would do. Steve tells me to meet him in surgical path at ten o'clock tomorrow.

The idea of witnessing an autopsy both excites and repels me. I am not too keen on seeing someone cut up a body, but it seems like such a "doctorly" thing to do. I can almost hear the announcer in the background doing the voice-over: "Come with us now as we join the man of science dispassionately observing the dissection of a human body in his continuing struggle to understand and eventually conquer disease." The camera zooms in on me as I put my hands on my lapels and gaze off into the distance, my mind filled with Important Thoughts.

I just have to be sure it isn't one of my brothers doing the voice-over. He'd be saying something like, "Come with us now as Joe Dipshit pukes his guts out watching some stiff get carved up."

But to hell with my brothers. I'm over the squeamishness I first felt in the cadaver lab, and I'm finally comfortable, almost casual, with Jimmy Hoffa, our cadaver. But this autopsy won't be performed on some shrunken, embalmed, scarcely human cadaver; it will be performed on someone who was walking around, breathing the same air I'm breathing, just a few hours ago.

I wonder if the body will bleed when the pathologist makes the incision. I don't think it will. All the blood should be coagulated by then. But will it be stiff as a board? Will it smell? Will the experience open my eyes or reinforce my denial?

I wonder if the pathologist will want me to participate. The thought of actually cutting or assisting at the autopsy is a bit unnerving. What if he asks me to identify certain vessels and nerves? What if I don't know the answer? What if I faint or vomit? If I do, will he report me to the dean of the medical school as being unfit for a career in medicine?

I arrive at the path department the next morning at five to ten. There are three other med students there, but no Steve. The secretary tells me Steve called to say he is still on rounds and won't be able to make it. She then leads me and the other med students down the hall to a set of double doors.

"Wait here for Dr. Valinskas," she tells us.

At 10:15 a tall, thin, serious-looking man in a white lab coat comes out and says, "Good morning, Doctors. Come with me."

He leads us down the hallway and pauses outside another set of double doors. "How many of you have ever seen an autopsy?" he asks.

No one.

"How many of you have ever seen surgery?"

Again, no one.

"How many of you have ever seen *M*A*S*H*?"

We all raise our hands.

"Good. So you are all very comfortable around dead bodies, right?"

One of the other students gives a short, polite laugh. The rest of us don't know if he is kidding or not. Dr. Valinskas is starting to fit my preconceived notion of a guy who dissects bodies for a living: weird.

"I am here to perform an autopsy," he continues, "not to resuscitate medical students. If you feel faint, if you feel sick, if you feel grossed out, please leave. If you leave, I won't be mad. But if you pass out, fall down, and fracture your skull I *will* be mad, and I will drag you into a corner of the morgue and leave you there. I will withhold medical treatment and you will remain a vegetable for the rest of your life."

I look at the student next to me. *Is this guy for real?*

Dr. Valinskas tells us that once we get to the path lab we are to touch nothing. He will tell us where to stand. We are to stay there and observe. "Understood?" he asks.

We all nod, and then he leads us through the double doors into the path lab, where, in the center of the room, on a dull silver table, lies the object of our visit. It is a woman who looks to be about fifty or so, but it is hard to tell. I'm not used to guessing the age of dead people. This isn't what I expected. This person isn't anything like Jimmy Hoffa. She isn't like a cadaver at all. She is like a person.

I try to act professional, but it is hard to know what to do. I am both fascinated and repelled by what I see. I try not to stare at her breasts or the thin, dark patch of hair at her crotch. Not that there is anything in the least attractive about either. Her breasts and her genitals, while retaining their fascination, do so mockingly. This *is what you are so desperate to see? Look, then.*

"Our subject this morning," Dr. Valinskas says, pulling on a pair of thick, brown rubber gloves, "is a forty-three-year-old woman with metastatic, Stage Four carcinoma of the cervix. She was transferred to our service yesterday morning."

Transferred to our service? I've heard a lot of euphemisms for dying, but this is the strangest. Again I wonder if Valinskas is trying to be funny or if he is just plain weird.

"This patient has had X-rays, CT scans, bone scans, and countless blood tests. And yet none of these has told the whole story." He reaches over to the instrument stand and picks up a scalpel. "*This* will."

He takes the scalpel, steps up to the body, and without a moment's hesitation cuts her open from the bottom of her neck to the top of her pubis. I can't help but wince. From behind me I hear a quiet groan. The student next to me inhales sharply and looks away.

Valinskas looks up from his work, the scalpel poised in his right hand. "There is no disgrace in leaving," he says. "It's perfectly normal to feel a little squeamish. Better to leave now than to keel over and be condemned to spend the rest of your life witless, chained to a table here in the path lab."

No one moves.

"No takers? Very well then, Doctors, let us proceed."

As the autopsy progresses I find it difficult to sort through my feelings. I am fascinated one moment, disgusted the next. It doesn't take long before our "patient" ceases to look human. All that we recognize as human is on the surface, but we're not interested in the surface here. In a few short minutes Valinskas has turned the woman inside out. She is no longer someone's mother or someone's wife. She is a bag that holds organs. It is much tidier that way.

Part of me wants to turn away, not because I am nauseated but because I am outraged at how dehumanizing this whole process is. It seems to me that we should have started this autopsy with some sort of acknowledgment of our patient, to thank her for donating her body. I imagine that she did this out of some sense of altruism, to help medical students learn or perhaps to help some unfortunate woman years from now who might be stricken with cervical cancer. Don't we owe our patient something? Is it too much to ask that we pause for a minute and acknowledge her gift to us and to humankind?

I start to wonder if I am skirting the real issue. Maybe it isn't her autopsy I regret—it's her death. And not just *her* death, but death in general. Maybe that's what's bothering me. Her cold, gray body is whispering to me, *Come, medical student, look on your future. See where all your striving, all your fire, all your pretensions lead.*

Valinskas' voice drones on, but I find myself ignoring his dispassionate description of each organ: its weight, its firmness, its appearance. I keep thinking about death. This woman was alive yesterday. She is dead today. What is different about her today compared to yesterday?

Doctors used to believe that a functioning heart is what determines whether or not you are alive. If your heart's beating, you're alive. If your heart stops, you're dead. But medical and legal scholars have now decided that it is a functioning *brain,* not a functioning heart, that determines whether or not we are alive. But is it only the brain that makes us human? If I suffer a serious brain injury, am I suddenly less human? What if medical science someday develops the ability to chop off the head but then pump blood to the brain with a machine—is that bodiless head still a person?

Maybe I'm confusing "life" with "human." Lots of things—golden retrievers, redwood trees, and staphylococci—are alive, but they're not human. What, then, makes us human? A beating heart? A cogitating brain? Or is there something more, something, for want of a better word, we call a soul? "We are the summation of our synapses," the neuroscientist tells us. But is it merely egoism that prompts me to reject this notion and to insist that we are more than a series of chemical reactions?

And why, I wonder, do we never talk about this stuff in med school? People are going to look to us someday for help in deciding important issues like abortion, infanticide, the death penalty, assisted suicide, and euthanasia. Why do we spend weeks on lysosomes, membrane channels, and protein synthesis and not one day on the definition of life?

Valinskas, in the center of the room, is displaying, piece by piece, the delicate organ systems that contribute to human homeostasis—and yet it all seems so far removed from our humanity. He is showing us what makes up a bag of organs. How different that is from defining what makes us *us.* You can describe my liver and my adrenal gland and my Islets of Langerhans all you want, but you haven't come close to describing *me.*

"Dissect her essence," I want to tell Valinskas. "Perform an autopsy of *her.* Show us why she, why we are more than a bag of organs." But perhaps a pathologist is the wrong person upon whom to impose such a burden. Perhaps it is the poet who is better equipped to dissect and isolate the elusive essence that defines us.

Valinskas has completed his autopsy. Body parts lie scattered on the surrounding tables. Technicians are busy making sections of the liver and pancreas and other organs for histologic examination. As Valinskas strips off his gloves, a lab tech tears open a packet of suture and begins to close the incision, preparing the body for the wake and funeral.

"Well done, Doctors," Valinskas tells us. "You have now peered into the deepest recesses of the human body and discovered the secrets of life."

As we file out of the room, I feel that we haven't even come close.

CHAPTER FOURTEEN

As my first year drags on, I keep wishing we had at least one easy course. I keep wishing we had the medical school equivalent of Rocks for Jocks or Quarks for Dorks—maybe something like Stiffs for Biffs or Microscopes for Total Dopes, a course where all you have to do is show up and you get an A. Unfortunately, there is no such course. But I am determined to get through this year. If there is one thing I can do, it's work. No matter how hard it is, no matter how much time it takes, I will master these courses.

I spend my days and nights hunched over a microscope, trying to learn how one weird little cell differs from another. I have to keep reminding myself that with each day I am a step closer to finishing first year and getting out into the real world of wards and patients and operating rooms.

My life narrows down to two things: studying and Patti. The problem is that Patti is 350 miles away. So every other weekend I pile my books into the Beater and point it north to Rochester. By now the Beater has assumed legendary status at Loyola med school. Brian Clark says the Beater burns so much oil that it has been made a national monument in Kuwait. Dog says I have been nominated for Man of the Year by OPEC. A couple months ago the antenna fell off, so I jammed an upside-down hanger into its rusted stump. Fortunately, I can still get the Sox games. Every couple months I crawl under the car with a pair of pliers, several old hangers, and some Hawaiian Punch cans to patch what little remains of the exhaust system.

Before I leave for Rochester, I always stop at the Kmart across from the med school to pick up a case of the thickest oil they have. The guys in the automotive section are getting to know me. When I walk in, one elbows the other: "Dude, here comes that guy with the car that burns more oil than gas."

"For sure."

The two of them smile and nod their heads. They point to the back corner. "The WD-90 is back there, man. We got a special shipment just for you. It's most excellent."

These trips to Rochester are expensive. The Beater burns a tank and a half of gas and four quarts of oil each way. The only way I can cut down on expenses is to get someone to come with me. I put up signs looking for riders on the med school bulletin board a couple times a month. The fact that Patti has seven roommates this year and the fact that Rochester, with all its Mayo Clinic nurses and IBM secretaries, has a 3:1 girl:boy ratio help my recruiting efforts immensely. Dog, Jack, and Brian have all made the trip with me at various times.

But occasionally none of my med school friends can come, and I don't always have enough money to pay for the gas and oil myself. To my eternal shame, if I am desperate enough, if I am ruthless enough, there is one way I can always get someone to come with me. This involves going to Sportsman's around closing time when a lot of my old friends are coming out. At two o'clock in the morning, after a night of drinking beer, driving to Rochester, Minnesota with one of your old friends doesn't seem like such a bad idea.

"Minnesota? At two A.M.? In a death-trap old beater? Sounds like a good idea! When do we leave?"

I feel like one of those old British First Mates who used to drug unsuspecting young Irish plowboys and shanghai them into Her Majesty's Navy. Poor Paddy wakes up the next morning in the middle of the ocean with a splitting headache and the order to, "Shape up there, lad. All hands on deck."

My behavior is shameless. It is exploitive. It is taking advantage of my friends' temporary inability to make rational decisions. It is also highly effective.

The Beater is always on empty. Once my victim has given his informed consent to the trip, our first stop is always the gas station. I have to be sure my passenger doesn't "fall asleep" before we get there.

"You get this one," I say as we pull into the Shell station. "I'll get the rest."

Once the gas is paid for, my fellow traveler plops into the front seat and immediately falls asleep (that is the polite term for keeling over with your tongue lolling out of the side of your mouth and saliva dripping down your chin). Only once does one of my traveling companions awaken before we actually get to Rochester. That is John Arnott. The rising sun stabs him in the eye just as we are crossing the Mississippi River at La Crosse. Arnie sits up, wipes a hand across his face, and asks where we are and what we're doing here. I explain that we are on the way to Rochester. He winces. "Rochester? Why would anyone want to go to Rochester?" He rubs his eyes, looks first left, then right, desperately trying to convince himself that this is a bad dream. Finally, he makes me drop him off in Winona at 6:00 A.M. so he can start hitchhiking his way back home.

"How in the hell did I ever let you talk me into this?" he wails as he stumbles out of the car, holding his head in his hands.

"Don't you remember? You practically *begged* me to take you," I reply, acting as affronted as I possibly can. "I told you I didn't think it was such a good idea. 'What will your mother say?' I asked."

Arnie shields his eyes from the sun. He crosses to the other side of the road and sticks out his thumb. "Tell Patti to give me a call after she dumps you!" he shouts to me.

.   .   .

Patti and her seven roommates live in a big old frame house on First Street, just north of St. Mary's Hospital. They are all good-looking young women in their last year of nursing school. The eight of them are, if anything, even poorer than I am. They each work as a nurse's aide in their free time, and they each kick in seven dollars a week for food—a dollar a day. Each girl is expected to get her own lunch. That means that fifty-six dollars has to cover fifty-six breakfasts and fifty-six dinners. Something tells me they don't eat a lot of *clafoutis aux pommes*.

It is a terrible culture shock for me to arrive at Patti's place on a Friday night. Music is blaring from the stereo. Girls are getting dressed, taking showers, putting on makeup, and heading out for the night. Two of them are going out with guys from the West Side where I grew up. Although occasionally one of the girls will stay home to study, usually by eight o'clock Patti and I have the house to ourselves. She prepares whatever dinner I managed to appropriate from my mother's pantry and we sit for hours at the dinner table studying or listening to the Clancy Brothers and talking about work.

I usually head back to Chicago on Sunday around noon. It seems there is always a test or assignment due the next day. Patti walks me slowly to the car, holding my hand. She gives me a couple peppermints for the ride home, tells me to drive carefully, to stay out of Duane's Sand Bar in the Dells, and to remember to put in the oil. I tell her how much I am going to miss her, but I say that I have to stop coming up here so often. I just can't afford it, and I have to study. I tell her there is no way I will be able to come again for a couple months.

But always, either that Friday or the next, with or without a passenger, I am in the Beater heading north again.

Two weeks later, on a beautiful fall afternoon, Patti and I are at Mayowood, Dr. Charles Mayo's old estate on the outskirts of Rochester. We are walking along the banks of the Zumbro River, watching the ripple of ducks shimmering on the surface of the water, when Patti casually mentions something about how many kids we will have. We have never talked about marriage, but I go right on with the conversation as if it were the most natural thing in the world. We don't even have to discuss it. We both know we are going to get married.

The question is how to break it to her parents—both of whom are still skeptical of this construction worker/cabdriver who is courting their daughter. Patti decides we should announce our engagement over Thanksgiving. "I'll be home for a week and we can tell my parents then," she says.

When I get back to Chicago that Sunday night, I take stock of my financial situation. I have three hundred dollars in the bank. If we are going to announce our engagement over Thanksgiving, that means I have two months to raise enough money to buy Patti a ring. Fortunately, I am able to get in four days with Scalese and a few more nights driving the cab. By early November I am ready.

Murph knows a guy named Johnnie who knows a guy who has a friend whose barber has a neighbor whose cousin's husband is a jeweler on the West Side. "Harry'll take care of you," Johnnie tells me.

"An engagement ring, huh?" Harry muses when I finally find his jewelry store on Cermak Road. He is slowly rubbing his chin, his eyebrows furrowed. "So let me ask you a question. Do you love this girl?"

"Of course."

"No, I mean do you *really* love her?"

"Yes," I say, "absolutely. She's great. She's awesome." I am too dumb to see where this is leading.

" 'She's great. She's awesome,' " Harry repeats. "Then there is only one ring that will do." He stares at me, nods slowly, then opens a drawer in front of him. He takes out a silver box and spins it around so that it faces me.

"Open it," he says.

I slowly lift the cover of the box. Inside there is a ring the size of Rhode Island. It looks like the Hope Diamond. My throat goes dry and for a moment I can't speak.

"How much?" I finally croak.

"How much? *How much?* I show you the ring made for the girl of your dreams and all you can say is, 'How much?' Do you love the girl or not?"

"Of course I—"

"Maybe you aren't so sure, eh?" He looks at me skeptically over the top of his glasses.

"No! I'm *very* sure. She's a wonderful person. I'm lucky to be marrying her. I just don't—"

"You don't want to give her what she deserves."

"No, that's not it. I was just thinking about something a little smaller, that's all."

"You want smaller? We can do smaller. I only showed you this one because I thought you really loved this girl of yours."

"I *do* love her, but I'm just a med student. I don't have any—"

"A med student! *A med student!* You're going to be a doctor and you don't want to buy your wife a decent ring?"

It is getting very hot in there. I slide a finger under my collar. "How much is it?" I ask, pointing at the Hope Diamond.

"Sonny boy, that ring retails for eighteen thousand dollars."

He sees the look on my face and immediately adds, "But since you're a friend of Jimmy's—"

"Johnnie's."

"Yeah, right. Johnnie. Since you're a friend of Johnnie's I'm going to let you have it for eight g's."

I shake my head. There is no way.

He rolls his eyes. "All right, seven. But you're cutting me open from here to here," he says, indicating a midline thoracotomy incision. "It's only on account of Jerry that I'm doing this for you."

"Johnnie."

"Yeah, Johnnie. Love that kid like a son."

"Listen," I say. "Maybe I'm at the wrong place. I can't afford—"

His hand snakes out and pins my arm to the counter. "Never mind what you can't afford. You let me worry about that. I'm here to make your little girl's dream come true. Now tell me how much money you want to spend."

"I was thinking eight hundred to a thousand," I say. That is every cent I have in the world.

"Eight hundred to a thousand? *Eight hundred to a thousand?* Whatta ya wanna get this girl, something out of a Cracker Jack box?"

I don't need this. I'm sorry I can't buy her the Hope Diamond, but I can't even afford the box it comes in. I tell Harry I think a mistake has been made. I turn to leave, but he won't let go of my arm.

"Listen, here, Mr. Doctor. I think I might have just the thing for you." He snatches the Hope Diamond away and whips out another box, this one quite a bit smaller. He opens it and spins it around to face me. The ring has a single small diamond. Compared to the Hope Diamond it *does* look like it came out of a Cracker Jack box.

"How much?" I ask.

"Money. Why is it always about money? We're talking about the ring your wife is going to wear to your funeral someday, and all you want to do is talk about money."

I am beginning to see what is going on here. "You mean it's *free*?" I ask in my most innocent voice. "You're just going to *give* it to me?"

He snatches the box from me. "Whaddo I look like, junior, the B'nai B'rith? In life the only thing someone just *gives* you is the clap." Having imparted this useful bit of information, he waits for my response.

I say nothing and turn to walk out the door.

"Two thousand," he says.

"Eight hundred," I reply.

"Eight hundred? *Eight hundred?* What, I don't got a wife and kids? I don't gotta eat? You want me to give you this ring for eight hundred dollars?" He shakes his head. "Look," he says finally, "because you're a friend of Joey's I'm gonna let you have this ring for a grand, but I'm losing my shirt on this deal, I can tell you that."

We argue back and forth for another fifteen minutes, finally settling on thirteen hundred dollars for both an engagement ring and a wedding ring.

"I'm getting too old for this business," Harry tells me as I am leaving.

"Here I let some wet-behind-the-ears medical student take me for all I got. Thirteen hundred dollars! These rings are worth two grand at least. I don't know how I'm going to live."

Something tells me Harry is going to live just fine.

On the night before Thanksgiving, I go to Patti's house to take her out for dinner. This is the night we are going to get engaged. We have reservations at the Mill Race Inn out in Geneva. It's a long drive, but the inn is a romantic spot on the bank of the Fox River. I took Patti there once before and she loved it. Unfortunately, tonight it is snowing like crazy. We already have three inches on the ground and another six are expected by morning.

"Mike," Patti says as we get in the car. "I don't think we can risk going out to the Mill Race Inn. If we get stuck out there in the snow my parents will go bonkers."

Patti is right. We don't want to do anything to upset her parents on this of all nights, so we decide to stay local. I stop at a phone booth and make a few calls. Since this is the night before Thanksgiving, most of the restaurants are booked up. The only place I can get a reservation is the Homestead on North Avenue. The Homestead is a nice enough place, but it is a favorite with the over-seventy set. Patti and I won't exactly fit right in there. Of course we could always go to the Gossage Grill. They're never busy until around 3:00 A.M. when my brothers and all the rest of the drunks stumble in for steak and eggs. I wisely decide that The Homestead would be a better choice for an engagement dinner.

I pull the Beater into The Homestead's parking lot next to all the big Cadillacs, Town Cars, and Buicks. We go inside and weave our way through the walkers and portable oxygen tanks to our table. At the table next to us is an eighty-year-old guy who is trying to cough up one of his lungs. I thank the waiter and tell him we will take the regular menu, not the menu of specialty puréed dishes.

Patti turned twenty-one back in August, so she is finally legal to drink. I order two glasses of champagne, and we both try to act nonchalant, as though drinking champagne and getting engaged are things we do all the time.

When we finish our meal and are walking out, I ask Patti to stop for a moment. I have been wracking my brain trying to figure out some romantic way to propose. I'm running out of time. I don't want to do it in the parking lot, so next to the line of old ladies waiting for the restroom I take the ring from my pocket, slide it onto Patti's finger, and ask her to marry me. We both have tears in our eyes when she throws her arms around me and whispers, "Yes," in my ear. The four old ladies next to us don't know what's going on, but when they see I have made Patti cry, they smile sympathetically at her and scowl at me.

Back in the car, Patti and I cuddle for a few minutes, girding ourselves for the next step: telling her parents. It is traditional for a man to talk to the girl's father and ask for his daughter's hand in marriage, but there was no way I was going to ask Patti's father for anything. I already knew what his answer would be. I figured it would be better to tell him after the fact, when the engagement was a done deal.

It is only eleven o'clock when we get back to Patti's house. Her parents are watching TV in the family room. Patti keeps her left hand over her right to hide the ring. Her parents know something is up since I never bring Patti home this early. I ask Patti's little brother, Terry, if he would step out of the room so I can talk to his parents.

"How come I always gotta—"

Patti grabs him by the elbow and marches him out of the room. I wait a few minutes, but she doesn't come back. I can't believe she is leaving me alone in the lion's den.

There is no sense beating around the bush. I clear my throat, wipe the hair back from my forehead, and scratch my right armpit. "Mr. and Mrs. Burns," I begin, "I want you to know that tonight I asked Patti to marry me."

There is a very long pause before Mrs. Burns says, "Not soon, I hope."

Okay. So much for the warm, embracing, "welcome to the family, son" response I was hoping for. Nevertheless, I plunge on.

"Well, we were thinking about next summer."

Her eyes bulge. "Next summer! Patti doesn't even graduate until next summer."

"Yes, but we—"

Mr. Burns jumps into the fray. "How do you think you are going to support her? You're a medical student. You have no money."

"I still work part-time, and Patti'll be able to get a job as a nurse."

"You're not living here; I'll tell you that," Mrs. Burns says.

Well, that's one thing we can agree on.

The argument rages for over an hour, with them spouting logic and practicality, me replying with idealism and naïveté. They don't seem to understand that Patti and I love each other and that all the other stuff (money, food, shelter) doesn't matter.

Finally Mr. Burns says to me, "Have you spoken to your parents about this?"

"No, I haven't."

"And just what do you think they are going to say about this whole crazy idea?"

Twenty minutes later, Patti and I find out. By then it is close to 1:00 A.M. My parents are in bed. I ask if they could come downstairs for a minute— Patti and I want to talk to them. They are the parents of eight boys. They are used to getting up at night for weird reasons. They are glad that this time it isn't the police wanting to talk about the mailman being bitten, underage drinking, vandalism, garage fires, or fisticuffs. They pull on their bathrobes and trudge downstairs with me to where Patti is waiting.

"Mom and Dad," I say, "Patti and I got engaged tonight. We're gonna get married."

My mom lets out a whoop and crushes Patti with a hug. My dad pumps my hand and says, "Congratulations." In two minutes they have opened a bottle of champagne. My mom and Patti are chatting away about wedding dresses and honeymoons and receptions.

I go upstairs and wake up my brothers. The bars must have run out of beer, because Den and Rog are both home. Their room smells like a brewery. They aren't thrilled about getting up, but they drag themselves out of bed. Jack and Pete are in high school. Joe and Bill are still in grammar school. The only one missing is Tim, who married Diane last summer. The remaining six brothers grouse, grumble, and tumble down the steps asking, "What's the big deal about two dopes getting married?" and, "What is Patti's problem anyway? Can't she find someone better than *that* dork?"

But they all love Patti. They each give her a big hug and kiss. Joe and Bill tell her to come to her senses before it's too late. Den and Rog tell her this is the biggest mistake she's ever made. Jack and Pete, though, say it might not be that bad an idea and if Patti does decide to go through with it, would it be okay for them to drink beer at the wedding?

Finally, about two o'clock in the morning there is almost a foot of snow outside and it is still coming down. I tell Pat maybe she should just spend the night at our house.

"Oh God, Mike, if I don't come home tonight my parents will kill me."

My dad makes my brothers get dressed and go shovel out my car so I can take Pat home.

The streets are deserted—and unplowed. We slither and slide our way down Division Street to Patti's house. I am afraid to pull up to the curb in front of her house for fear of getting stuck in the snow. I leave the car in the middle of the street with the engine running and walk her to the door.

"I love my ring," she says, twisting it so it catches the light from the street lamp.

"It's not too small?"

"No," she says, "it's perfect. I love it."

We stand at her door, snow falling silently around us, two kids with scarcely a nickel between us, holding each other and wondering how we ever got so lucky.

CHAPTER FIFTEEN

It is the class we have all been looking forward to: Human Sexuality with Dr. Helen Bickford. Dr. Bickford is an Englishwoman with a high-pitched voice and a very proper British accent that makes her sound like Julia Child on acid. She also is a nationally renowned expert on sex and is always getting herself on radio talk shows, explaining to hyper mothers things like "Why Little Johnny Likes to Look at Ladies' Underwear Catalogues."

Despite my classmates' puffed-up assertions that they already know everything there is to know about sex, I'm not so sure. Most of us are immature young men with little or no experience sexually. A month ago I was observing a surgery. The patient, a woman, had just been put to sleep, but before the operation could begin, she needed to have a catheter inserted. I watched as first the junior medical student, then the intern (both male) tried unsuccessfully to catheterize the patient. Finally, the anesthesia resident (female) came around and peered over their shoulders. "That's the clitoris, not the urethra," she said. "You're never going to get a catheter in there."

Dr. Bickford takes her job seriously. Unfortunately, 80 percent of her class are young men half crazed from having their heads stuck in a microbiology text for the last six months. They are hoping the course will be something out of the Letters to the Editor section of *Penthouse* magazine or maybe a giant poster of some top-heavy centerfold. Instead, it is a serious discussion of clinical sexuality—at least that is Dr. Bickford's plan.

The problem is that her students are less interested in education than in titillation. There are constant interruptions for questions like, "Can you go over that part about the stimulation phase in more detail?" or, "We won't really go blind or grow hair on our palms, will we?"

The class covers a lot of ground. We spend the first day going over the basics, a sort of Birds and Bees for Medical Students. It must be difficult for Dr. Bickford, who does her best to stay scientific and matter-of-fact. As in all our other classes, we are given facts and are expected to regurgitate them at test time. We learn that the average married couple has sex 2.2 times per week, which most of us find scandalously low. "Are they talking about octogenarians or eunuchs or what?" We learn that the average ejaculate of a human is 5cc. The average ejaculate of a horse, on the other hand, is 100cc. Rich DiPietro arches his eyebrows and says, "Girls, they don't call me the Italian Stallion for nothing." The women groan and try to ignore him.

Like most classes in medical school, Human Sexuality is less about how to appreciate what's right than about how to diagnose what's wrong. We learn less about sexual function than about sexual *dys*function. As we get deeper into this subject I am surprised to discover how many people are, if you'll excuse the expression, screwed up by sex.

I learn more about sexual perversions that I ever wanted to learn. Rodriguez the Mexican Pervert is an altar boy compared to some of the characters we learn about. Incest, pedophilia, bestiality, exhibitionism, fetishisms, bondage, voyeurism, necrophilia, sadomasochism—after a while it all starts to sound the same: weird guys wanting to do weird things to (or on, or under, or near, or with) other weird people (or animals, or bodies, or inanimate objects—usually vinyl). It is enough to make even the horniest of us want to follow Hamlet's advice and get himself to a nunnery—or a monkery. After this part of the class we are all thinking that the life of a penitential monk on a desert mountaintop is looking better all the time.

We learn about guys who can't get erections (impotence) and guys who can't get rid of them (priapism). I wonder if Bean Pole might have a variant of this disease. We learn about women who don't enjoy sex (frigidity) and women who can't get enough sex (nymphomania). Jack Brennan says every woman in the world with frigidity lives on the South Side of Chicago and he has dated most of them. Brian Clark then says there is no such thing as nymphomania. He says nymphomania is a figment of the imagination made up by frustrated guys who dated girls from the South Side of Chicago.

It's hard to have a discussion of sexuality without at some point talking about guilt. Dr. Bickford tells us that guilt over sexual matters is rampant in our society. Brian Clark tells us at lunch that he knows what she means. "I've always felt guilty that my wang is so much bigger than everyone else's," he says. For most of us, guilt has been the chastity belt restraining our sexual ardor. Sex and guilt have been locker partners forever.

But guilt I understand. Heck, guilt was one of the cornerstones of my moral upbringing—and it wasn't such a bad cornerstone. I could be guilted into doing (or not doing) just about anything. And it wasn't just about sex. "Clean up your room—or would you rather that your forty-year-old mother with her bad back and varicose veins that she got from giving birth to all you ungrateful kids did it for you?" Or, "Eat your food. There are starving babies in China who would give anything to be eating that lima bean casserole." Or, "Stop fighting with your brothers or you're going to drive me insane." Or, my personal favorite, "It won't be so funny when I'm dead. Don't bother bringing your laundry out to Queen of Heaven Cemetery because once I'm gone, you're on your own."

But a lot of the stuff Dr. Bickford talks about is neither funny nor titillating. Sexual dysfunction is very often an indication that something else is wrong: a problem with circulation, or drugs, or depression. And even if it is an isolated problem, I am guessing that if you had that problem you wouldn't think it was so funny.

Perhaps by design, as Dr. Bickford's lectures become more graphic and detailed they lose whatever salacious twist her students might have put on them. By the time our little class on Human Sexuality ends we have become sufficiently desensitized. Sexual dysfunction is just one more clinical problem.

.   .   .

Dr. Bickford's class, although more than just theoretical, still doesn't strike me as something I am likely to use a lot in my day-to-day practice of medicine. As much as I would like to think that someday hordes of young women will be fighting to confide their sexual secrets in me, I just don't see that happening.

One of the few ways I can get some exposure to real medicine is to attend Grand Rounds. Grand Rounds is the medical equivalent of *Stump the Stars*. Usually a visiting professor is invited to listen to an intern read a brief synopsis of some difficult case. The professor then tries to make the diagnosis and suggest appropriate treatment.

Although almost all the cases are too difficult for me, it helps to be there. I am starting to learn the language. I am starting to get a feel for how things are done, for what is appropriate behavior on the wards. I dream of the day when I will get to take care of patients. It is the carrot that has been dangling before me ever since I laid down my pick and shovel and started taking pre-med courses.

Our guest today, the star we are trying to stump, is Dr. David Harding. Dr. Harding is the chairman of the department of something at some medical school out east. He must be a pretty big deal, because Dean Rich gives him a particularly long and fawning introduction. When the introduction is over, I wonder if we are all supposed to kneel and kiss Dr. Harding's ring or perhaps slaughter a goat or offer some burnt holocaust or something. It reminds me of one of those Hollywood talk shows where the host keeps gushing over some slinky actress' latest release, observing with a straight face how "overwhelmed I am at the gravitas of your oeuvre."

Dr. Harding sits in the front row, clipping his nails and acting bored as the intern presents the case. It appears to involve some kind of brain tumor. The patient has several bizarre behavioral problems. Some of his endocrine glands are out of whack. He has lab values all over the place. As I listen to the intern present the case, I am furiously scribbling notes, trying to make sense of all this.

When the intern is done, our distinguished guest shakes his head and lets out a long, disgruntled sigh. It is now his turn to start asking questions.

"How long have you been a doctor?" he asks the intern.

The intern is startled to find the interrogation suddenly turn personal. "About six months," he stammers.

Our guest snorts and says this is the worst case presentation he has ever heard. The stunned intern turns red and mumbles that he is sorry.

"In *our* institution we would never tolerate such a sloppy presentation."

The auditorium is now deathly quiet. Dr. Harding has excoriated not just the intern but the medical school as well. I can see the back of Dean Rich's neck turn red. No one says anything for almost a minute before Dean Rich stands and says that perhaps Dr. Harding would like to ask some questions to help in reaching a diagnosis.

Dr. Harding leans back in his seat. His legs are fully extended in front of him and he is touching the tips of his fingers together.

"Did it ever occur to you to check the urinary seventeen-ketosteroid levels?" he asks the intern.

"Yes, sir."

"And what was it?" Harding growls out.

"It was seventy-five."

"Seventy-five *what?*"

The intern starts flipping through his notes. "Seventy-five . . . um . . . seventy-five milligrams in twenty-four hours," he says finally.

"And does that suggest anything to you?"

"Well, sir, it uh . . . it is elevated, and that means—"

"What a *brilliant* observation," Harding says. "A urinary seventeen-ketosteroid level *five times* what it should be suggests to you that it is elevated. Brilliant. Brilliant."

This is the sixth or seventh Grand Rounds I have attended. I am used to interns getting skewered, but it's usually done in a relatively good-natured fashion. This has gone too far. This is sadistic. I find myself rooting for the intern, hoping that Dr. Harding will miss something, that he will misdiagnose the problem and go on to make a fool of himself.

Dr. Harding does not miss something. He does not misdiagnose the problem, but in my mind, he certainly does make a fool of himself. What kind of insecure jerk has to treat an intern like that? It's sick, and I am ashamed of Dean Rich for not telling our distinguished visitor to take a hike. I wish I had the guts to stand up and tell Dr. Harding that although I know even less than the intern about pituitary tumors, I do know something about simple human decency—and he doesn't have any.

When Dr. Harding has hurled his last insult and Grand Rounds is over, I shuffle out of the auditorium and realize I lost something today. Some of the luster is gone from the practice of medicine, and I know it will never return. I realize for the first time that doctors are human. There are good ones and bad ones. There are saints and jerks. I have been living in a dreamworld, imagining all doctors as having somehow been shriven in their residencies of all their bad habits so that they enter the practice of medicine pure of heart and interested only in the good of mankind. Dr. Harding has shown me that even in the uppermost echelons of medicine's hallowed halls are people who are flawed, who are deficient, who are human.

CHAPTER SIXTEEN

I spend 99 percent of my life studying, 10 percent visiting Patti, and the other 5 percent in Sportsman's or The Pub with Dog, Jack, and Brian. (I'm a med student, not a math major, okay?) Dani, at Sportsman's, is like a mother to us.

We go in there Wednesday night at eleven o'clock, after having spent the last six hours studying for a pharmacology test. We each have several beers and a cheeseburger. We buy Dani a couple shots of peppermint schnapps. When we get up to leave at one o'clock, Dani hands us the bill. We owe two dollars each.

Dog tells her that can't be right. He tells her we've been drinking and eating in here for over two hours. Dani frowns, looks at the check, does a few calculations, and says, "Okay, make it a buck-fifty."

I am doing fine in all my courses, but it hasn't been easy. My grades are good, but only because I am so fanatical about studying. Despite my success, I feel that I am one bad test away from getting booted out of here.

If there are things I need to review in microbiology, I go to the library, take out my textbook, and study. If there are things I need to review in histology, I go to the MDL, take out my microscope, and study. If there are things I need to review in gross anatomy, I go to the anatomy lab, take out my cadaver, and study. But what if it's one o'clock in the morning? No problem. Like Al's Grill, the all-night diner on Madison Street with the slogan "We doze but never close," the anatomy lab is open twenty-four hours a day.

We have a big test in gross anatomy coming up on Tuesday. As I am preparing for the test I suddenly realize there are some things about the blood supply to the liver I don't quite understand. The liver, the gallbladder, and the pancreas are all mushed together in the right upper quadrant of the abdomen. Each has its own blood supply, and I am confused about which vessel comes off where. I need to get this straightened out before the test.

And so at one thirty on a Sunday morning I find myself alone in the anatomy lab. I've been studying since six o'clock this morning and I'm tired. But I'm ashamed of being tired. We've been told that residents sometimes don't sleep for forty-eight or seventy-two hours at a crack. I tell myself I damn well better quit bellyaching about not getting enough sleep. Things are going to get a whole lot worse before they get better.

It's dark in the anatomy lab. The only lights are the hooded lamp over my cadaver and the red Exit sign glowing faintly over the door where I came in. To my right, cadaver after cadaver stretches away into the darkness at the far end of the lab.

I put on a pair of gloves, whip off the sheet that covers Jimmy, and peel back the skin flap covering his abdomen. Last week, our group very carefully dissected the hepatic vasculature. I try to concentrate on the vessels in the right upper quadrant, but I'm having a hard time tonight. Ordinarily I like it quiet when I study, but tonight the silence and the darkness seem, not sinister, but somehow unsettling and oppressive.

There is a boatload of dead bodies in this room, and they seem to be demanding my attention. I am bent over my cadaver, but I keep lifting my head and gazing down the long row of corpses fading into the darkness. They seem to be saying that there is something more important than hepatic vascularity for me to contemplate tonight.

But, come on, I don't have to be Sigmund Freud to grasp the significance of a roomful of dead people, do I? Isn't the message fairly obvious?
We're all going to die. Life is short. Death beckons and the grave yawns to
receive me. Human aspirations are vain and pretentious. I am food for
worms. All right. Okay. I get it. Now can I please get back to work?

As always, I am wrapped up in the moment. I resent and ignore distractions. The moment is hepatic vascularity. That's what I need to know.
That's what I am going to be tested on in three days. The oppressive presence of the dead and their niggling insistence upon being heard may have
some sort of deeper significance, but discerning it is not going to help me
pass the test next Tuesday. It is not going to help me get out of first-year
med school. It is not going to help me be a better doctor.

Or is it?

Finally, in frustration I throw down my forceps. I tell the dead people,
*Fine. I give up. You win. I'll listen to what you have to say. But I've got a lot
of work to do. I can give you five minutes. That's it. So make it snappy, will
you?*

But there is only silence. I look down the row of cadavers. Three tables
down I see a shriveled, leathery right arm protruding from under its sheet.
That would be Bill Lowe and Monica Meadow's cadaver. The one with the
cigar clamped in its mouth.

I rub a hand across my forehead. I know there are issues here. I know
there are metaphors and symbols. I know it would be nice if I could take
time to think about them. There are truths to be gleaned, wisdom to be
gained—and I'd like to do those things, but for the love of God, I can't. I
can pass gross anatomy without having a firm grasp on the significance of
life and death, but I can't pass gross anatomy if I don't get a firm grasp on
the vascularity of the liver.

I would like to take a few hours, hell, a few *weeks*, to ponder the human condition. I would like to reread Wordsworth and Shakespeare in
light of the things I have seen and done this first year of medical school.
I'd love to sit with my friends and discuss what life is all about, what purpose medicine actually serves, in whose vineyard we ultimately toil.

I look down at the row of cadavers stretching away into the darkness. *I know you have important things to tell me. I know I must be careful not to lose my perspective, not to lose my sensibility. I would like to listen to you. I really would. But I can't. I can't. I can't. If I don't get back to Jimmy Hoffa's liver pretty soon, I am toast. I am history. I am back throwing rocks on Johnny Battaglia's breakout gang. And I would rather be an unenlightened medical student than an insightful rock thrower.*

This is not how I envisioned medical school. I somehow imagined that all my practical learning would come wrapped in a generous coating of philosophy and serious rational discourse. Yes, I would learn hepatic vascularity, but I would learn it in the context of that which makes it greater than itself. What I am finding is that I have to choose between the two. There isn't time for both.

There seems to be an assumption that medical students should be taught the mechanics of medicine, but the spirit of medicine they should learn on their own. And perhaps that is the Dark Tower toward which my labors should be directed.

All these thoughts run through my head, and yet I instantly realize them for what they are: not superfluous, but distractive. Yes, they are intimately associated with the profession I have chosen, and yes, a consideration of them may well prove indispensable if I am to one day become a competent, caring physician, but the fact remains that there is work to do. It is all well and good for Mary to choose the better portion, to sit at the foot of Jesus and listen to His words, but I am Martha and the house needs to be cleaned; the meal needs to be prepared.

I don't know, maybe there is a hierarchy of learning. I have been chafing this whole year about having to learn arcane facts about molecules and cells and force couples, but maybe that's where we start, and from there we graduate to the study and treatment of disease. And finally, we begin to ask ourselves what exactly is it we are treating and why?

Toward whom, toward what, is our compassion ultimately directed? When a blood vessel occludes, we don't feel sorry for the vessel. We feel sorry for the patient whose function will be compromised by the vessel's occlusion. Or, taking it a bit further, do we feel sorry for the human condition in which all organs will ultimately fail? Or, in the final analysis, are we really just feeling sorry for ourselves, seeing in the suffering of others a reflection of our own mortality and demise?

None of these questions has to be answered. None of them even has to be asked. A kid can become a med student and a med student can become a doctor without ever considering these questions. But I don't want to become that kind of doctor. I want to ask questions and seek answers, but more than anything, *I want to be a doctor*, and the obstacle in my path tonight is not understanding the paradox of healing; it is understanding the blood supply to the liver.

I turn my back to the row of cadavers stretching away into the darkness, bend my head over Jimmy's abdomen, and peer into the right upper quadrant.

I have work to do.

CHAPTER SEVENTEEN

I finish my last final on June 11. My first year of medical school has come to an end. I pass everything and even excel in a couple classes. All year I felt like the sword of Damocles was poised over my head—or was it the ax of Achilles? Or the machine gun of Al Capone? Whatever it was, it feels good to be out from under it. When one of my brothers hears me say that I have been studying my brains out, he says, "So that's where they went."

To a large extent I am finally done with academia and ready to get into the real world of medicine: delivering babies and treating heart attacks and setting fractures and removing tumors. I know I still have a lot of learning to do, and I take to heart William Osler's admonition that "we are all, and always, students," but now I will be studying things I am thirsting to learn.

Medical schools are traditionally four years, with summers off. Around the time of the Vietnam War, Loyola went to three years. This means we will be going to school year-round with no summer vacations. The longest break we will have during our three years is right now: we have three weeks' vacation before we resume again on July 6.

I called Fred at Scalese months ago to be sure I could work these three weeks. So on Monday, June 14, I am up with the robins at 4:30 A.M. and heading back to the yard.

At 5:15 I swing a leg over a stool at the counter in Mary's Grill. The yardbirds are already there.

"Well, lookie here," Brother-in-Law says. "Look what the cat dragged in."

Vito claps me on the back and says welcome back. "I thought they fired your ass last year."

I shake hands with Vito and Brother-in-Law; then I tell Mary she looks beautiful this morning.

"Ain't heard that line of shit in a while," Mary says, smiling. She runs her spatula back and forth across the grill. "You gonna order somethin' or what?"

I order a bacon and egg sandwich and a carton of milk to go. Mary has them ready in three minutes and I am at the yard by 5:30.

"Where in the hell did you get that thing?" Fred asks when he sees the Beater.

"It runs great," I say to Fred. "It just burns a little oil."

"I noticed," Fred says, glancing at the blue-gray cloud of toxic fumes now settling around the car.

Just to keep me in my place, Fred makes me stay in the yard that first day.

"Let's see how you do pulling nails and stacking lumber," he says.

Vito snickers and nudges Brother-in-Law. "Looks like we got ourselves a new yardbird," he says.

JT is still running the gun on Johnny Battaglia's crew. I see him as he is leaving the yard that first morning. "You gotta get me out of here," I tell JT. "Tell Johnny I'm back. I'm a little soft, but I'll toughen up in no time."

"Don't worry, babe," JT says. "We'll spring your funky ass."

JT is true to his word. The next morning Fred tells me to take 32 and head out to Twenty-second Street where Johnny's crew is working.

"What about The Rat?" I ask Fred. "Is it still running?"

Fred looks surprised, then shakes his head. "Jesus Christ, I forgot," he says. "No one else in this company wants anything to do with that piece of junk but you." He waves his hand at the back of the yard. "Sure, go ahead, take the damn thing if you want."

When I get to the job it is only 6:00 A.M. JT and Angelo are already there. They introduce me to a couple new men.

"Meet the doc," Angelo says. "Fuckin' guy gave up a perfectly good eight-bucks-an-hour job throwing rocks to become a millionaire doctor in Lake Forest. What the hell was he thinkin'?"

I tell the new guys I am only a second-year medical student and the only time I have been in Lake Forest was when I delivered a load of angle irons there last summer.

It's 6:30 and Johnny tells us to get off our asses and start giving to the church. "And you," he says, pointing to me, "get down there and start throwin' rocks. I don't give a shit if you are Dr. Feelgood. Today you're back in the hole, baby. Back in the hole!"

JT fires up the compressor and in two minutes I am back in my world of dust and dirt and noise, stooping, bending, and throwing rocks. All the while, Johnny is bellowing that "this is the Scalese Construction Company, goddamn it, where you gotta be an M.D. just to throw rocks. Yes sir, baby. Dr. Rock. We got him right here."

We spend the day slowly working our way west along Twenty-second Street, breaking out block after block of curb and gutter. My new partner in the hole, Marvin, is a good man—not as good as Rosie, but he keeps up. JT no sooner breaks out a chunk of concrete than one of us is right on it, rolling it toward us, grasping its jagged edges, hoisting it up, and throwing it on the back of the truck.

After a couple hours of this I am starting to feel it. I have grown a little soft this past year. JT sees me lean against the back of The Rat for a moment as I wipe my forehead. He smiles. "Come on, babe," he shouts over the roar of the jackhammer. "You ain't in school now. This ain't no time for tea and crumpets. Ain't goan *be* no tea and crumpets!"

When 5:30 finally rolls around, I am beat. My T-shirt is sopping wet and tattered; my forearms are scratched and bleeding; my hands are raw and blistered. Marvin tosses me a can of Schlitz. I pull off my gloves, lay them in my hard hat, and sink down onto the tongue of the compressor. I turn the can of beer upside down, shake the dirt off it, and pop the top. My mouth is a dry crust and when I feel the delicious coolness of the beer in my mouth and going down my throat, as tired and sore as I am, it is almost worth it just to be sitting here drinking this beer.

"Feels so good when it stops hurtin'," JT says with a laugh. He slaps me on the shoulder. "Welcome back, m'man. Welcome back."

Patti, my parents, and the guys I go to school with all feel bad for me that I am working so hard, but I tell them that it's not so bad. It's hard for them to understand, but I actually like it. I like being outside. I like the back-and-forth with Angelo and JT. I like sweating and lifting. I like stretching out in the grass at the end of a long, hard day, boots off, drinking beer. I'm pretty tired the first few days, but by the end of the week it's like I never left.

And when it comes, I like the paycheck. That first week I get sixteen and a half hours of overtime. I gross $460 and take home $310. At that rate I will bring home almost a thousand dollars for three weeks' work. I work for Scalese right up to Saturday, July 3. We only work till noon on Saturdays. As I am leaving the job I tell JT and Angelo and Johnny that they haven't seem the last of me. I still have two more years of school and I'll be back.

"Yeah," Angelo says. "Fuckin' guy'll drive by in his limo throwing hundred-dollar bills out the window."

"Leave the dude alone," Marvin says. "M'man here is goin' to cure the clap." He turns to me. "Ain't that right, Mike? You goin' to cure the clap. Ain't goan be no more clap."

JT laughs and points at Angelo. "And then maybe this big dago won't have to worry none 'bout those Cicero women he be pickin' up every Friday night."

I tell them I'll do my best.

Our second year of medical school begins on Tuesday, July 6, less than six weeks before our wedding. Patti has been hired as a staff nurse at Oak Park Hospital. She came home from school on a Monday and began work the next day. She is making eleven thousand dollars a year, a salary that is going to make us filthy rich. We find a nice one-bedroom apartment in

Forest Park, halfway between Oak Park Hospital and Loyola med school. It will be ready for us August 1, two weeks before our wedding.

With the start of our second year we med students are given white coats, not long ones like real doctors, but the shorter versions that identify us as medical personnel but not quite real doctors. All that matters to me is that we will soon be going out into the wards, seeing real patients.

We begin our second year with a course on physical diagnosis where we learn how to take the blood pressure, listen to the heart, percuss the chest, swab the cervix, and palpate the knee.

We also learn several procedures. We learn how to draw blood and start IVs by practicing on each other. I am lucky to be paired with Tim Clancy, who worked as a phlebotomist at the hospital during our first year. He can draw blood slicker than the resident who is instructing us. Tim has a rubber tourniquet around my arm, a needle in my vein, and a vial of blood out of it before most of the other students can even figure out how to put on the tourniquet.

Tim is very patient with me as he walks me through my first blood draw. "Drawing blood reminds me of what Woody Hayes used to say about the forward pass," he tells me. "Three things can happen and only one of them is good. If you get the needle in the vein, you get blood and that's good. If you're too shallow, you get pain, not blood, and that's kind of bad. But!" Here he pauses. "If you're too *deep*, you can nail something like an artery or nerve and that's *real* bad. That's lawsuit bad. That's get-kicked-out-of-medical-school bad."

Tim looks me in the eye. "I don't care if you get blood, I don't care if you're too shallow, but you for damn sure better not be too deep or, with my right hand, I will reach between your legs and perform a total orchiectomy, thus removing the possibility that you and Patti will bring more inept little blood drawers into this world."

I thank him for the vote of confidence. Tim has nice veins, so it really isn't that hard. I fill a vial full of blood in just a few seconds. Tim says congratulations and if he ever becomes a heroin addict and has both his hands cut off in a chain-saw accident, I'm the one he will ask to shoot him up.

Blood drawing and IV starting we can practice on each other, but there are some exams that are more difficult to teach. Where, for example, do you find someone willing to let forty guys do a vaginal exam? I suppose Bean Pole could find someone, but I don't think Loyola is likely to hire him as a vaginal consultant. ("Hey, Dr. Rich, what you goan do with yo' paycheck?") I guess we'll just have to learn vaginal exams as we go along.

Rectal and prostate exams, however, are another story. We have a captive male audience right next door: the Hines Veterans Administration Hospital—the VA, the VA spa—where hundreds of veterans receive free medical care.

The VA has its share of lifers, guys who have nowhere else to go and just live there, finding one medical complaint after another to justify their continued presence in the hospital. They get a bed, meals, a rec center, pretty nurses to talk to, and, unfortunately for them, hordes of young medical students who have to learn rectal exams. I can imagine the veterans' growing trepidation each year as July rolls around and a new crop of students, one hand grasping a tube of K-Y jelly, the other hand gloved, with their index fingers pointing up in the air, shows up at the doors of the veterans' hospital rooms.

One of the urology residents from Hines is our instructor. "Hello, Jerry," the resident says as he leads us into the patient's room. "I've got a few new doctors here who need to learn how to examine a prostate."

Jerry leans around the corner and sees a line of new doctors stretching down the hall and around the corner.

For propriety's sake the resident asks, "You don't mind, do you?" This, I believe, is what attorneys, *bad* attorneys, would call Obtaining Informed Consent.

Jerry realizes it is payback time. He knows here is an offer he cannot, or better not, refuse. "Do I mind? No, I don't mind. When they're done maybe they could do something like cut out my liver, or stomp on my dick."

The poor man bends over and the conga line of students, one after the other, explores the deep recesses of his body. Finally it is my turn.

"No, not like that," the urology resident says. "Deeper!" Jerry grunts as I probe deeper. "Good. Now rotate your finger so you can feel the prostate. Feel that ridge? Yeah, that's it. Next!"

When I'm done I mumble my thanks to Jerry.

"That's all right, kid," he says. "It's better than last year when I had forty guys tickling my balls learning how to check for a hernia."

Now that I am a second-year student I am assigned to a service and I have to start taking call. This is cool. This is definitely cool. Now it'll be *my* turn to sit in the cafeteria in the morning, unshaven, cup of coffee in front of me, grousing about my rough night on call and all the airplane crashes and dismemberments I fixed the night before.

But I won't make a big deal of the incredible sacrifices I will make. I'll be like John Wayne, who after getting his left arm shot off shrugs and tells the wide-eyed schoolmarm that "shucks, ma'am, it's just a flesh wound." Yes, this will be just one of the many sacrifices I will make for the betterment of mankind. It never occurs to me that mankind would be much better served if second-year medical students were kept as far away from patients as possible.

There is one other terribly chic thing about being on call: I get to carry a beeper. I know the older students and residents think of the beeper as a ball and chain, but for me it is another symbol of my growing competence, a badge that tells the world that I am the real deal and that routine methods of communication are inadequate for me. I am so important that I must be instantly available to save the lives of guys with rattlesnake bites and slashed throats.

As it turns out, the hospital isn't counting on me to save lives. My responsibilities as junior medical student on call are things like treating flatulence, starting IVs, prescribing sleeping pills, holding retractors, and inserting NG (nasogastric) tubes—all the little medical fires that flare up during the night. But to me these things seem like glorious adventures. Being called at 2:00 A.M. to start an IV makes me feel like Sir Gawain preparing to do battle with the Green Knight.

I finally get to bed that first night around midnight. One of the interns shows me where the junior medical student call room is. It is a small room with a desk, a chair, and a narrow bed with a metal headboard and crisp white sheets emblazoned with the Loyola Medical Center logo. I brush my teeth, toss my shaving kit on the desk, shut off the light, and climb into bed.

Another cool thing about being on call is that I get to wear scrubs. Scrubs function as hospital wear, surgical wear, and pajamas. With my white coat, stethoscope, scrubs, and beeper I feel like a real doctor—although God help any poor patient who has to rely on *my* expertise to pull him through.

Since it is only midnight, I'm not all that tired. I keep having all sorts of things run through my mind. Will the beeper be loud enough to wake me when I fall asleep? What if the beeper's battery dies? No one is going to page me for something important anyway, but what if some ninety-year-old guy needs an enema and they can't reach me?

It is all so new, so exciting, being out of the wards. Auscultation of the heart is especially fascinating to me: the idea that just by listening to a heart you can tell which chamber is leaking, which valve is stenosed, which arrhythmia is occurring. We are told stories of legendary cardiologists from places like the Mayo Clinic who, just by listening, are better than angiograms and EKGs at telling what is wrong with a heart. It is a fascinating game—except the stakes are so high. If I make a mistake at Scalese all that would happen is that it would take us a little longer to break out a section of curb. Make a mistake reading an EKG and someone could die. There's pressure for you.

Throughout our entire physical diagnosis course it is impressed upon us that the health and well-being of countless people will depend on the extent to which we perfect the skills we are being taught.

"You can't allow yourself to misdiagnose a heart attack. You can't allow yourself to misdiagnose a ruptured appendix. You can't allow yourself to misdiagnose meningitis. Doctors do not have the luxury of failure. Too much depends on you."

I *want* people to depend on me. I *want* to be able to auscultate and percuss and probe. I *want* people in trouble to come to me, and I *want* to fix what's wrong with them. But there is so much to learn and so little room for failure.

I also worry about how the patients will receive us. I am afraid they will resent having some ignorant medical student bothering them. Since we know so little about everything, I am afraid we will be looked upon with scorn by just about everyone—especially patients.

But when I finally get out on the wards, I am surprised how much patients like us. Perhaps they see us as a bridge between themselves and their real doctors. Perhaps, unlike their real doctors, our boat hasn't completely left the shore, and they can still communicate with us. And perhaps I am underestimating the willingness of even sick people to reach out to the underdog and help him.

The junior medical student is the first member of the medical team to talk to the patient after she is admitted to the hospital. There is a firm pecking order: The lowest of the low (medical students) sees the patient first, takes a history, does an exam, and then reports to the intern. The intern then does the same thing before reporting to the resident. The resident repeats the same process before, finally, the attending physician reviews everything and then goes in to make a diagnosis and institute treatment.

Hospitals will not admit a patient without a diagnosis. The first thing I learn to do, before examining a patient, is look at the chart to see what the admission diagnosis is. That diagnosis isn't always correct, but it is a place to start.

My first assignment as a junior medical student is Med I at Loyola. Mrs. Armour is my first patient. She is a sixty-four-year-old woman with an admission diagnosis of "migraine headache." I have never had a migraine and I haven't had much exposure to neurology, so I probably know less about migraines than Mrs. Armour does. Fortunately, like most medical students, I have a little "cheat sheet" I can turn to: *The Manual of Medical Therapeutics*, a ring-bound paperback with thumbnail sketches of common medical problems and their treatments.

I lean against the wall outside Mrs. Armour's room, reading the three-fourths-of-a-page description of migraines. I learn that migraines are usually preceded by an aura, that they are often unilateral, that they are sometimes accompanied by nausea or vomiting, and that they aren't much fun to have. Having thus become an expert on migraines, I go into my patient's room.

"Hello, Mrs. Armour, I'm Michael Collins," I say. "I'm a medical student with Dr. Leishner."

I wince a little as I introduce myself, feeling somewhat ashamed that I am nothing more than a medical student. What if this lady tells me to "get the hell out of here and send a real doctor in"?

But Mrs. Armour is nice. She says it is a pleasure to meet me, and am I related to the Connollys from Elmhurst?

"No, ma'am. My name is Collins, not Connolly."

Mrs. Armour says, "That's too bad. The Connollys are nice people."

As I go through her history, she doesn't mention anything about an aura or scintillating scotoma or nausea. Her headache is unilateral, though. I go through her exam, testing her reflexes (which are normal), her extraocular eye movements (which are normal), her mentation (which is normal). Finally I ask her if I could look in her eyes with my ophthalmoscope.

"Of course, Doctor," she says.

It amazes me that she calls me Doctor even though I told her I am only a medical student. I kind of like it, though.

Looking in eyes is a tricky business. We try to see the retinal vessels, the optic nerve, and anything else that is hanging around back there. It takes a while to get good at it, and I'm not. I do manage to focus on the optic nerve, which looks normal. I don't see anything else important, so I thank Mrs. Armour and tell her Dr. Prosser will be in soon.

First Steve Prosser, the intern, then Amanda Tass, the resident, then Dr. Leishner, the attending physician, examine the patient. Finally, we stand next to the nurses' station and have our little conference. The conference starts with Dr. Leishner asking the most junior member of the service, the medical student, what the diagnosis is. Unless the patient walks in with a hatchet in his shoulder, no one expects the medical student to make the correct diagnosis.

I'm not sure what Mrs. Armour has, but I don't think it is a migraine. I explain that she doesn't fit the usual pattern of migraine. Dr. Leishner agrees and then asks me to describe her neurologic exam. I think that since he asked me about it there must be something significant about it, but I tell him I didn't find anything remarkable. Her reflexes, mentation, strength, and sensation all seem normal.

Steve and Amanda don't have a lot more to add than I did. Nor, it turns out, does Dr. Leishner. We all agree, however, that Mrs. Armour doesn't have a migraine.

"So, what do we do next?" Dr. Leishner asks me.

"CT scan?" I venture.

"Looking for what?"

"Well, tumor or abscess or . . . something else."

It turns out to be "something else." It is a vascular malformation. Some of the blood vessels in Mrs. Armour's brain are weak. There is a chance they could burst and kill her or make her a vegetable.

We call in the neurosurgeons. They examine Mrs. Armour and then explain the situation to her. They tell her she needs surgery, a particularly delicate and dangerous surgery, to fix the damaged blood vessels. They make it all seem so routine and maybe it is to them, but to a patient, hearing that during or after the operation she may die or become a vegetable, the whole thing is terrifying.

Since I have no more experience with this sort of thing than Mrs. Armour does, I, too, am terrified. Mrs. Armour has somehow come to look upon me as her liaison with the neurosurgeons, waiting until they leave the room to ask me what *this* means and what *that* means. I want no part of this. Talk about the blind leading the blind! I do my best to explain things to her, but my knowledge seems so puny and superficial compared to the neurosurgeons'.

When Mrs. Armour asks me what *I* think she should do, I am aghast. How in the heck do I know? I'm just a junior medical student and these guys are *brain surgeons*, for God's sake. I tell Mrs. Armour that if it were me, I would do whatever the neurosurgeons told me to do. But I also tell her I don't want to be responsible for talking her into a procedure that might cripple or kill her.

Mrs. Armour nods and asks, "But if I don't have the operation, wouldn't I be even more likely to be crippled or killed?"

This isn't what I had expected when I started medical school. I somehow thought medicine was cleaner, that there would always be two choices: one right one and one wrong. The doctor's job would be to work hard, make the correct diagnosis, then treat the condition. If he makes the right diagnosis and then institutes the right treatment, everyone would live happily ever after. The idea that the decision might not be clear-cut is disturbing. I don't want to hear that life is arbitrary, that there are pros and cons, that reasonable people might well conclude different things.

For the first time I realize that medicine is, to a large extent, a crap shoot. You, the doctor, educate yourself the best you can. You try to learn the odds. You try to pick the course of action that has the best chance of success, but there is no guarantee. Sometimes you crap out—only this time instead of losing a bet, someone loses her life.

I get to watch Mrs. Armour's surgery. She is already asleep when they let me enter the operating room. Neurosurgeons are not the friendliest of people. They ignore me. The only one who speaks to me is the scrub nurse who tells me not to go near anyone or anything that is sterile. She points to a spot several feet behind the head surgeon. "Stand there and don't move," she says.

They have already shaved Mrs. Armour's head and clamped it in some sort of a vise. Now they scrub the skull, incise and peel back the skin, and cut through her skull with a weird saw that looks like it came off a construction site. Then they dissect through her brain to the area of the abnormal blood vessels. I can't see much of this since I am ten feet away from the operating table.

As the hours drag by I begin to get bored looking at the back of the surgeons' gowns. But I am afraid to leave for fear that someone will yell at me, so I just stand there until they are done.

The surgeons seem satisfied. I follow them out to the waiting room, where they talk to the family. They say everything went well and that we will all have to wait until Mrs. Armour wakes up to see how she fared.

I have already been away from my service for four hours, so I can't wait in the recovery room to see how she does. I go back to the floor and begin following through on all the scut work my intern left for me. When I go home at six, Mrs. Armour still hasn't come back to the floor.

I take Patti out for dinner that night to Horan's for a burger and a beer. I tell her about my patient. It is wonderful having a nurse as my fiancée. She knows so much more about everything than I do. She tells me what to look for the next day. She tells me what are good signs, what are bad.

"Do you think you would ever want to be a surgeon?" she asks me.

I laugh. Me? A surgeon? I still haven't gotten over the wonder of being accepted at medical school. I feel more like a rock thrower than I do a doctor. I feel like I am still on double secret probation and that at any moment Dr. Rich is liable to call me into his office and say this little experiment is over and Cinderella can go back to sweeping fireplaces again.

When I get to the hospital the next morning, the head nurse tells me that Mrs. Armour is still up in the neuro ICU. We round on her up there. She has come through the surgery reasonably well, but she has a little right-sided weakness and some slurred speech. The neurosurgeons are noncommittal about her chances. She might get better. She might not. There is nothing to do but wait and see.

I don't think they mean to come across as callous as they do. I suppose they have been through this a hundred times before. But Mrs. Armour and I have not been through it before.

And what makes it worse for me is a feeling that it is inappropriate for me to express my concern, that it is somehow unprofessional, that if I want to be a good doctor I should learn to be more like the neurosurgeons: They do what they can, they give it their best shot, and then they let it go. If they have effected a cure, great. If the patient dies, too bad.

The neurosurgeons have learned to give their expertise, their skill, their time, but they cannot, they will not, give themselves. They don't allow themselves to get too high with their successes or too low with their fail-ures. They can't let a tragedy from six days, six months, or six years ago af-fect them. It is not prudent. It is not efficient. It is not professional.

This insistence on staying detached has the paradoxical result of being good for patients in general but never good for the individual patient. It is good for the forest but bad for the tree.

The naïve medical student in me doesn't like that. I want it both ways. I want doctors to be intimately and deeply involved with each patient. I want them to feel her pain, to walk in her shoes, to laugh and cry with her. But I also want them to be able to be objective, to be analytical, to be al-ways prepared to make the difficult decisions. And that isn't all. Despite their having poured their hearts and souls into the care of their patient, I want them to be able to go home and put all that stuff in a different place and be able to have a normal home life, to retain the capacity to laugh and love with their family and not be drained emotionally.

I want it both ways. I want everything. I want too much.

Mrs. Armour does get better. They have her on steroids for a while to bring down the swelling, but she slowly and steadily improves. The speech pathol-ogists work with her, the therapists work with her, and each day the neuro-surgeons come around less and less. In a way I feel sorry for them. They accomplished a miracle. They not only rid Mrs. Armour of her headaches; they also removed the threat of the vessels bursting and killing her.

It is a remarkable achievement, but the neurosurgeons seem oblivious to it all. They have a job. The job requires skill. The job does not require emotional involvement. They do the job. They do not get involved.

Surgery was a success? That's nice. Next.

CHAPTER EIGHTEEN

Father Fahey, the chaplain at Loyola med school, is a strict old Boston Irishman. He readily agrees to marry us but has several stipulations, including an insistence that there be no strippers or stag films at the bachelor's party.

"That's not the way to begin your married life," he tells me.

He's right, and I give him my word we'll keep it clean.

Traditionally the best man organizes the bachelor's party. But I don't have one best man; I have seven: all my brothers. Having my brothers in charge of the bachelor's party worries me. Anything is possible with those goofballs at the wheel. I tell them what Father Fahey said—and I say I'm not kidding. Whether or not Father Fahey forbids it, strippers and stag films would cheapen our wedding and be disloyal to Patti, so I don't want them.

My brothers chafe about being told what to do. "Do you suppose the padre would mind a little alcohol?" Tim asks. "Or can we serve only sarsaparilla and buttermilk?"

Rog is less concerned with alcohol than he is about gambling. "What about crap games?" he asks.

I knew Rog was going to ask that question. That's because Rog has a special talent. As the result of years of training, he has become one of the few people in the world who can actually talk to dice. He has assured me of this fact on more than one occasion. In fact, the more beer he drinks, the surer he is of it.

I tell Rog that I do not think the good father would object to our rolling a few bones.

The bachelor's party is held in the room above Doc Ryan's bar on Madison Street. Only three of my brothers—Den, Tim, and Rog—are old enough to drink legally. Jack is twenty. Pete is eighteen. They aren't in the place for two minutes before they each have a bottle of Old Style in their hand. Joe and Bill come to the party for a little while, too. They are still in grammar school and have been enlisted to be the altar boys at the wedding. They think it would be cool to drink beer like their older brothers, but that's where we draw the line. I tell them if I catch them drinking I'll make them dance with every one of our aunts, all thirteen of them, at the wedding.

The bachelor's party is a lot of fun. There are several salacious speeches in which I am given advice on how to perform my husbandly duties. There are references to several "marital aids," none of which I ever heard of and most of which sound painful or perverted or as if they required users to be triple jointed. The guys from the hockey team promise to pay Patti and me a visit on our wedding night just to "wish us the best." Murph and a couple of my high school friends talk about spending a couple days with us on our honeymoon to see if we "need anything." The guys from medical school attempt to extract a promise from me not to miss our next softball game, which is scheduled for three days after the wedding.

I haven't had a lot of experience getting married. When August 14 rolls around, I am a basket case. The wedding is at St. Giles, where Patti made her First Communion and Confirmation. As we wait in the sacristy for the wedding to begin, my brothers do their best to calm my nerves. Tim says Patti sent him a message saying that she is calling the whole thing off. Rog says she has eloped with the milkman. Jack says Uncle Pat is drunk again and passed out in the second row. Pete peeps around the corner and looks out at the congregation. He says our cousin Eddie just mooned everyone.

I don't think any of this is funny. I look at my watch every thirty seconds and walk around with my hands in my pockets to keep them from shaking. Finally Father Fahey calls us out to the altar. The wedding goes off without a hitch. Patti is so beautiful I can't take my eyes off her. And, to make it complete, she says, "I do."

When the service is over, everyone heads six blocks south to Patti's parents' home, where the reception is to be held. Scores of relatives and friends pack the house and spill into the backyard, filling the August night with laughter, drink, and song.

I am very grateful to my brothers for not goofing off during the wedding. They held themselves admirably in check. When they get to the reception, though, all bets are off—and I don't blame them. It's time to let the big dogs hunt. The boys head for the bar and for the rest of the night make sure no beer dies of loneliness.

Uncle Sam holds a glass of Scotch at eye level, gazes at it fondly, and asks, as he always does, "How do they make it so good and sell it so cheap?" Then he plants himself in front of Patti, throws back his head, and sings "The Girl That I Marry." My brother Timmy sings "Weela Wallia." Over in a corner of the kitchen, Dick Murphy outrages several of my aunts with a few verses of "Rodriguez the Mexican Pervert." Aunt Frannie sets her old-fashioned on the counter, clasps her hands together, and, in her quavering little voice, sings "That Dear Little Town in the Old County Down." In the heel of the night, my brothers and I, arms around one another, beer sloshing out of our glasses, gather before my mother and roar out "Mother Machree."

As the party is breaking up, my brother Jack stands on a chair and announces that "Mike and Patti want to invite all of you back to their hotel room for a nightcap."

"Like hell we do," I growl. I tell them all to stay away or I'll call the cops.

"Yeah," Timmy says. "What's the matter with you guys? Don't you know Mike and Patti need their sleep?"

As they are filing out, my relatives shake my hand and tell me how lucky I am to be marrying Patti. One of Patti's sisters has been over-served. Patti and I are amused and touched by her earnest professions of affection for us. There are tearful hugs, sloppy kisses, and several "I love yous" before her husband finally guides her out to the car.

Patti's liberated older sister, however, isn't so happy. She says if the priest mentioned the word "children" one more time during the wedding ceremony she thought Patti was going to get pregnant right there on the altar.

She's not far off.

For our honeymoon I have reserved a cabin at a small resort in northern Michigan.

"How are you going to get there?" my dad asks a few days before the wedding.

When I tell him I'm going to drive the Beater, he insists that we take his car instead. "Leave that old wreck here and take mine," he says. "It's bet-ter to space out your wedding and your funeral a little bit."

We are the youngest people—by about twenty years—at the resort in Michigan. When I made the reservations, the lady asked me if I wanted twin beds. Not having a lot of experience in making hotel reservations and thinking that twin meant two—like two people in one bed—I said yes, a twin bed would be great.

Patti and I arrive at our honeymoon destination after a seven-hour drive to find two single beds in our room. Patti looks at me in consterna-tion. "Is there something you are trying to tell me?" she asks.

We are there for a week. Every night we push the two beds together. Every morning, before the cleaning ladies get there, we push the beds back apart. On the seventh day we start drifting back home. We spend a couple days in Grand Beach with one of Patti's roommates. She and her parents are so welcoming, so genuinely glad to see us, that it makes us wish our honeymoon would last forever.

When we get back to Chicago late on Sunday night, we have a surprise waiting for us. As a wedding present, our landlord, a retired Bohemian who lives down the block, has stained and varnished the hardwood floors in our apartment. Our place is pretty bare. What little furniture we have is either hand-me-downs from aunts or cousins, or purchases from second-hand shops. We have a radio but no TV. We have a toaster but no microwave. We have a record player but no stereo. We are beginning our married life just as Patti's parents warned us we would: with no money, no savings, no credit cards, and a checking account with nothing in it. All we have is each other.

Every night we fall asleep in each other's arms to the clatter of freight trains rumbling down the B&O line. In the morning we wake snuggled together to the dull hum of traffic on the Eisenhower Expressway. We share a bowl of Frosted Flakes, kiss each other good-bye, and wonder how we ever got so lucky.

I start my next rotation the morning after we get back from our honeymoon. I am assigned to a medical service at the Hines Veterans Administration Hospital. Hines is a whole different world compared to Loyola. Although Loyola takes care of its share of indigent patients, it is a private hospital with many middle-class and wealthy patients. It is clean and modern. Hines, on the other hand, is a government facility locked in a post–World War II time warp. As I pass through the dirty glass doors into the lobby on my first day, there are cigarette butts all over the floor and a pile of dirt swept into a corner.

This is not my first visit to Hines. As a cabdriver, I participated in many adventures here: sneaking guys out in the middle of the night, bringing guys back after hours, going on runs to the liquor store, and tying bottles to strings lowered from upper floors. It shouldn't come as a surprise to me, then, to learn where much of this behavior leads. One of my first patients at Hines is Nick Curran, a sixty-year-old World War II vet with cancer of the larynx—the result of smoking three packs a day for forty years. Nick had half his throat removed last week because of the cancer and now has a permanent tracheostomy. When we come into his room that first morning, he has a cigarette pinched between his thumb and index finger and is holding the cigarette up to his tracheostomy tube, smoking through it.

I am on call that first night. When I finish my work, I turn off the lights and climb into bed. Light from the hallway seeps under the door and spreads across the polished tile floor in my room. This is the first night since our wedding that I haven't slept with Patti. I don't like being apart from her. In our little bed at home, our arms are always draped around or over or under each other, but we like it that way. Here in this cold white hospital bed, I miss Patti's warmth and the sweetness of her breath.

There is a phone next to the bed. I pick it up and call her.

"Hey, hon," I say.

"Oh, hi." Her voice is warm and sleepy. "Is something wrong?"

"No. I miss you, and I just wanted to say good night."

"Again?" I can hear her quiet laugh. I called her at ten o'clock, too.

"I'm sorry," I say. "I was just laying here thinking about you."

"You're nice."

I don't have anything else to say. I already asked her what she had for dinner and how work was that day and how the Beater was running.

"Well, I guess I'd better let you get back to sleep," I say.

"Mmm-kay."

"Good night, hon. I love you."

"Love you, too," she says. "And thanks for calling."

"Really?"

"Yes, really. Now go to sleep."

On the nights I'm not on call, Patti and I have dinner together. For the first dinner in our new home, Patti makes meat loaf. Only when she is ready to serve dinner does she realize that we have no carving knives. We received many useful wedding gifts, including a matched pair of porcelain Frenchmen holding pink handkerchiefs and a set of glass beer mugs that say "Cubs Suck," but we did not get any carving knives.

I tell Patti not to worry. I dig into my camping gear and come out with a huge Buck Knife that will serve as our carving knife for the next several years. Guests are always a little intimidated when Patti walks out of the kitchen with this huge hunting knife that looks like it came out of some slasher movie.

"Don't worry," I tell them. "Now that Patti's back on her meds she's much more stable."

Dinnertime is our time to talk about what we saw and did that day. I am always a little jealous of Patti. She is the real thing. She is done with school and out practicing in the real world of medicine. I am just a student. Patti has experience taking care of things I haven't even heard of.

"The dressing came off," she tells me one night, "and the blood shot right up to the ceiling. I put pressure on his neck and held it until the doctor got him back up to surgery. It took us forever to clean up that mess."

While Patti is dealing with gushing arteries, I am dealing with things like toenail fungus and fecal impactions. "That's it, Collins," my intern would say, glancing over my shoulder but trying to stay upwind. "Clean him out real good."

But I love what I'm doing. Basic science is over and I am on the wards. Every day I put on my white lab coat with the stethoscope in the pocket. Every day I make rounds on real patients with real problems. Every day I do things to help people get better. And every night I go home and study about the diagnosis and treatment of disease.

I have been on the service for about two weeks when we get a frantic call from the ER. We tear down there to find some old guy sitting up in the cart, his hands grasping the rail on each side. His skin is the color of a moldy tombstone. His mouth is open, his head thrown back. The tendons in his neck are stretched to the point where they look like they're going to snap, and his eyes are wild with terror. Each breath is a gasping, straining wheeze. I take one look at the guy and tell myself I am about to witness my first death.

I have no idea what is wrong, no idea what to do. If this man has to depend on me to diagnose and treat him, he is going to die. My resident and intern, however, take one look at his chest X-ray, which looks like a

Wyoming blizzard, and know exactly what to do. They start some oxygen, whip in an IV, push some meds, and even before the blood gases are back the guy is leaning back and breathing easy.

I scarcely had time to realize what was happening before it was over. This guy was knock knock knockin' on heaven's door two minutes ago, and now he's cracking jokes and trying to look down the ER nurse's blouse.

I look around the room, amazed at how calm everyone is. Chuck, my resident, is adjusting the art line. The nurse is carefully taping down the IV. The intern is writing in the chart. He was on call last night and pauses for a minute to let out a huge silent yawn. The three of them act like what just happened is no big deal. *No big deal?* They just saved a guy's life, for Christ's sake! It was the greatest thing I've ever seen. Why isn't everyone jumping up and down, pumping their fists in the air, high-fiving one another, and shouting, "You da man"? What the hell does it take to get these people excited?

Although this episode scared the hell out of me, it thrilled me like nothing I have ever done before. That guy would have died without us. I say "us" even though I didn't do much of anything but follow orders. But still, I was a part, a little part, of the team that saved him—and it feels so good. All of a sudden every sacrifice I made to get here is worth it. This is where I want to be. This is what I want to do.

CHAPTER NINETEEN

A little knowledge *is* a dangerous thing. That's why medical students are a threat not only to their patients but also to themselves. Medical students learn a little bit about a disease and then convince themselves they have contracted it. On cardiology they think every twinge of indigestion is a heart attack. On neurology they think every headache is a brain tumor. On dermatology they think every freckle is a melanoma.

I started OB on January 4. As part of my assignment, I spend one afternoon a week in the infertility clinic. I am now convinced that either Patti or I or both of us are hopelessly and terminally infertile. Never mind that I am one of eight kids and Patti is one of seven. Never mind that we have only been married for five months and that the only reason Patti hasn't gotten pregnant so far is because we have been "sort of trying" not to. (If you don't know what it means to "sort of try" not to get pregnant, don't worry. It's a Catholic thing.)

All these facts go out the window when I read about low sperm counts, blocked fallopian tubes, polycystic ovaries, endometriosis, antibodies, anovulation, and my personal favorite, asthenospermia: sperm that can't swim. I picture six or seven of my sickly little sperm donning life jackets, dipping their toes in the water, shuddering, and then bravely plunging into treacherous seas infested with man-eating antibodies. They negotiate dangerous cysts only to find their way blocked by a dead-end fallopian tube. The end comes in some cold, dark corner of the uterus where they succumb to loneliness and unrequited love.

Until I started this rotation I never thought much about infertility. It never occurred to me that Patti and I might have trouble conceiving. It never occurred to me that *anybody* might have trouble conceiving. It seems the world is full of kids, gobs of kids. Two hundred kids live within one block of where I grew up—and twenty-eight of them are named Collins. I suspect that if the subject of fertility ever comes up in my neighborhood, it is in the context of having too many kids, not too few.

But now that I have become aware of the plight of infertile couples, I am deeply affected by the unfairness of it all. I realize that having children is a personal choice and that many couples don't want to have *any* kids, and that's fine, but to want them and not be able to have them—that's tragic.

Patti and I have talked about having a large family. We both love kids and want to have lots of them. But what if it turns out that we don't? That we can't? The thought that we might never be able to conceive depresses and terrifies me.

I try to reason with myself. First of all, it is highly unlikely that two people like us, having sprung from such large families, will have difficulty conceiving. And second, even if we do, we still have each other. We can adopt if we want, or perhaps we can learn to enjoy life without the encumbrance of children—except that we don't consider children an encumbrance.

Patti says I am nuts to worry about this stuff. She says as soon as we stop sort of trying not to get pregnant, she will quickly get sort of pregnant. I tell her I'm not following her very well. She says that is because I am a man.

I'm not so sure. It all seems a lot more complicated than I ever imagined. I ask Patti if what we did last night means we were sort of trying or sort of *not* trying. She checks the calendar and says last night was different because it means we were sort of trying when we should have been sort of *not* trying. I ask her if we could sort of try tonight. She says that wouldn't be a good idea. I ask if we could sort of *not* try. Patti sighs and tells me this isn't going to work if I don't cooperate.

I learn that getting pregnant is a complicated thing. It depends not only on such obvious things as the time of the month but also on a slew of endocrinological, immunological, and emotional factors. When I learn how many impediments there are to conception, it seems amazing that women *ever* get pregnant.

In the infertility clinic we take a scientific approach to getting pregnant. One of the first things we do is make lovemaking a clinical rather than a personal act. The couples are asked to chart their lovemaking, to record not just how often they do it but also things like time of the month and the woman's temperature. They are told there are certain times of the month, certain days of the week, when they *must* have sex. The old "not tonight, dear, I have a headache" just won't fly. It's easy to see how infertility can become such a divisive issue in a marriage—especially if it is one partner's "fault." The couple wants to have children, but they can't because of *him* or because of *her*.

In our clinic we see two main types of infertility: older couples (in their mid- to late thirties) who have finally gotten their lives and careers where they want them, have stopped using contraceptives, assuming they would immediately get pregnant, and don't; and couples where the woman has pelvic inflammatory disease (PID).

PID is a complication of venereal disease that causes scarring of the fallopian tubes, thus preventing the sperm from reaching, and fertilizing, the egg. The problem is not fertility. The man is fertile; he has sperm. The woman is fertile; she has eggs. The problem is fertilization. The sperm can't get to the eggs.

Shelley Stephens is a thirty-year-old receptionist. She and her husband, Dan, have been married for six years and have been trying to conceive for three. Shelley at first denies having had venereal disease, but when Dr. Hungerford tells her why he is asking, she bursts into tears and tells him her story.

Shelley contracted chlamydia when she was a freshman in college. She got drunk at a party and was, in essence, date-raped. She remembers nothing of the actual event. She never even saw a doctor until vague abdominal symptoms prompted her to make an appointment six months later. That's when she found out she had chlamydia. She received treatment and she thought the episode was over.

What further complicates things is that she hasn't told Dan about it. Except for that one night, she never had sex with anyone but Dan. She never saw any reason to tell him about this painful part of her past. When Dr. Hungerford tells her why she is unable to conceive, she realizes the trap she is in. She had no idea that one episode of chlamydia ten years before might prevent her from having a child. Doesn't she owe it to Dan to tell him why they haven't had a baby? But hasn't she already suffered enough for something that was never her fault in the first place?

We can offer her no guidance, only assuring her we will respect her decision. In the end she tells Dan, and Dan turns out to be understanding and supportive. He doesn't hold it against Shelley, and they decide to work together to see what might be done to help them have a child.

There aren't that many options available to infertile couples. In vitro fertilization is just starting but is available in only a handful of centers. The fact that ours is a Catholic hospital is somewhat of an impediment as well. The Church is still struggling with concerns about the extent to which man ought to interfere in the act of creation. There are good arguments on both sides.

I hear later from one of the OB residents that in the end Shelley and Dan opted for surgery to try to open the blocked fallopian tubes. The surgery was successful, but after six months Shelley still had not conceived.

Shelley and Dan seem like a wonderful couple. I think they would make excellent parents—and yet they are being denied the opportunity. It doesn't seem fair, but I'm learning that life isn't always fair. In fact, I'm not just *learning* it; I'm having it rammed down my throat every day. Everywhere I turn in medicine I see unfairness: guys dying of heart attacks, women dying of breast cancer, kids dying in car crashes.

I have this feeling that if I am ever to be a good doctor, I'm going to have to make sense of stuff like this. It would help if I could somehow see the hand of God in these tragedies. It would help if I could sit down and say, "Aha! Jimmy's death—which at first seemed to be such a terrible thing—really isn't because . . ." It would help if I could go to Mary's funeral and put my arm around her husband and comfort him with my wisdom and understanding, explaining why his wife was taken from him.

Medicine is making me confront, in a deeply personal way, the very nature of God and suffering. I've been thinking about it a lot, but I'm getting nowhere fast. He's God, right? So He's bigger, He's smarter, He's more powerful, He's more everything than I am. And I'm supposed to figure out why He does what He does? Unh-uh.

No, I'll leave theodicy to the theologians. It's too much for me. I'm having enough trouble getting through medical school without trying to figure out the will of God. I'm just Popeye with a stethoscope: I am what I am, and that's all that I am.

OB differs from every other service I've ever been on. Our patients aren't diseased, they are in perfect health. They don't come to us because something is wrong, they come because something is right. They are (mostly) happy, healthy people who are glad to be here. One of the OB residents tells me that most of the time the patients don't even need us. "A cabdriver could do a fine job delivering ninety percent of babies," she says.

I never thought of it that way. Maybe I should tell my attending obstetrician that I am a cabdriver and will he, therefore, let me deliver 90 percent of the babies?

I like delivering babies—not that I ever get to do the actual delivering. But I get to be there. I get to stand in the delivery room next to the obstetrician, watching, waiting, encouraging the mom. Sometimes the obstetrician lets me cut the cord and deliver the placenta. If there is no one from anesthesia in the delivery room I get to hold the newborn, check her Apgars, and hand her to the nurse who will clean her, swaddle her, and hand her to the mom.

I am told by one of the old-time obstetricians that women used to be "knocked out" for their delivery. When they were ready to deliver they were given a heavy anesthetic, and they wouldn't wake up until it was all over.

Although epidurals are occasionally performed, most of the deliveries that I participate in are done with a local anesthetic or some sort of paracervical block. Both techniques diminish, but never eliminate, the pain. This type of anesthesia is usually augmented with some intravenous analgesic like Demerol or morphine, although we have to be careful not to give the mother too much or it will affect the baby's respirations.

I have a hard time reconciling the role of pain in giving birth. One of our charges as physicians is to relieve suffering. Since giving birth is a painful process, isn't it our responsibility to get rid of the pain? If so, we aren't doing a very good job. It seems that almost every delivery I witness is accompanied by at least some degree of pain—occasionally a *great deal* of pain. And yet, when it is all over, the mothers seem to feel it was all worth it. It makes me wonder if pain is always such a bad thing.

I did some mountain climbing before Patti and I were married, and I've always thought there is something to be said for the struggle, the long exhausting hours laboring up the mountain. Getting to the summit is important, but it is the process, the struggle, that makes the attainment of the summit significant. Otherwise why not just take a helicopter to the summit, stand there for a minute, and fly back down? What you put into the climb makes what you get out of it so much more worthwhile, so much sweeter.

I know it is easy for me, as a male, to shrug off the pain of delivering a baby. It's easy for me to insinuate that women should somehow be strong, accept the suffering, and get the job done naturally. But doesn't the struggle make the act of delivery that much sweeter? I discuss this with Patti, who tells me she is appalled that I would say something like that.

"Women don't want to hear some *guy* tell them how ennobling and up-lifting their pain can be. They aren't interested in making statements. They just want to have a healthy baby in as easy a way as possible. Don't make them think they're wimps or bad mothers just because they don't want to roll around in excruciating pain for two or six or twenty hours."

"I don't want *anybody* to have pain. I just want them to think about their choices."

"Why don't you think about defecating a basketball?"

A basketball. All righty, then. This concludes tonight's argument. Patti wins. I'll just keep my mouth shut and let the moms check the menu and order whatever drugs they want. "Better living through chemistry," that's going to be my motto.

It's on OB that I get to do my first surgical procedure: a circumcision. Almost all circs are done by the residents. They do so many that they are happy to let me do some. I am surprised at the cavalier attitude the residents have about doing circs. Most of the residents are male and I would have expected them to be a little more sympathetic about some kid having a chunk of his penis chopped off. I have a pretty good idea of how the residents would feel about having a chunk of *their* penis chopped off.

We have two circs to do today. Steve Hartung says he will do the first one. I will do the second.

"It's really not that hard," Steve says. He unwraps a sterile green plastic device. "First you slip this little doohickey over the penis, like this. Then you stretch the foreskin, like this—"

"Whoa!" I say. "Aren't you forgetting the anesthetic?" Our little two-day-old patient is already going bonkers.

"Anesthetic? Are you kidding? We don't do an anesthetic for something like this. It only takes two seconds. It'll be over before junior here even knows what's happening."

Steve can't be serious. We are going to amputate a part of a kid's penis with no anesthetic? I watch in horror as Steve deftly stretches the foreskin, checks to be sure the tip of the penis is clear, and then lops off a good hunk of the kid's johnson. Our little patient does exactly what Steve or I would do if someone whacked off a good hunk of our johnson. His eyes bug out of his head, he screams, and he looks for a weapon with which to maim the guy who did this to him. Fortunately for Steve, his victim is eight pounds, twenty inches. If he were a full-grown man, Steve's facial features would have just been rearranged.

Steve removes the green plastic device, wraps the end of the bloody penis in Xeroform, and hands the baby to the nurse. Then he turns to victim number two, who is sleeping peacefully in the bassinet next to us, unaware that Dr. Mengele and his partner, the Marquis de Sade, are about to ask him to dance.

"Your turn," Steve says.

I'm not ready for this. I'm not even sure why we do circs in the first place. A lot of doctors think circumcisions are unnecessary. The only reason most fathers want their sons circumcised is because *they* are circumcised. So here I am with a scalpel in my hand, about to do a horribly painful, possibly unnecessary procedure on an unanesthetized fellow human being who just happens to be a defenseless little baby. I feel like I am violating ten parts of the Hippocratic oath at the same time.

I look at Steve. Steve looks at me. "Showtime," he says.

It takes me five times longer than it took Steve. I inflict more pain than I have ever inflicted on anyone ever before. I feel more like a butcher than a healer. I have lost my innocence and, to make it worse, when they take that bleeding, suffering baby from me, three people tell me congratulations.

It is Mrs. McAuliffe's seventh baby. Although she is pushing forty, her delivery is going smoothly. Contrary to what I thought, Dr. Amstedt tells me that for women who have multiple births, each delivery is not always easier than the one before it. I thought that with each baby the mother "greases the skids" a little more, so that by the time she has her sixth or eighth or tenth, the baby would slide right out, pick up his tool kit, and go to work.

Not so, the doctor tells me. "For the first four deliveries it gets easier, but after that the uterus gets a little tired and stretched out. Sometimes these grand multips can really have problems."

Mrs. McAuliffe, though, is sailing along. When she is dilated to eight, Dr. Amstedt tells the nurses to take her into the delivery room. "Won't be long now, Julie," he says.

In another ten minutes she is crowning. As he checks her one last time, Dr. Amstedt frowns. Something is wrong. As he leaves the room to scrub he whispers to the delivery nurse to call anesthesia—stat.

It takes another ten minutes for him to deliver the baby, and by that time we all know there is a problem. Mrs. McAuliffe is fine. Her contractions are steady, her vital signs stable, but the fetal monitors indicate something is seriously wrong with the baby.

When Dr. Amstedt finally delivers the child I am shocked at what I see. It is a monster—not monster in its colloquial sense but monster in its medical sense: an anencephalic monster, a deformed baby with no brain. Ethicists and philosophers debate whether it is even human.

"Boy or girl?" Mrs. McAuliffe chirps from the head of the bed. She is anxious to see this new member of her family.

"I'm afraid something is wrong, Julie," Dr. Amstedt says.

"Wrong?" Her hands grip the side of the delivery table and you can almost feel the terror in her voice. "What do you mean, wrong? What's happening? What's the matter with my baby?"

The baby is making cawing, gurgling sounds as Dr. Amstedt motions to me to section the cord. I do so; then he hands the child to the anesthesia resident who has just come in.

The resident looks at the child and seems perplexed, disgusted almost. The juxtaposition of *what is* with *what was expected* overwhelms all of us.

Dr. Amstedt is up at the head of the table trying to console Mrs. McAuliffe, who gasps and says, "Oh, my God," when she sees her child.

Although it contains no brain, the child's head is very large and somehow reminiscent of a fish. That it is alive there can be no doubt. It moves and makes strange noises deep in its throat. But that it is *human* is uncertain. None of us feels any kinship to it. If anything, what we feel, in spite of ourselves, is antipathy toward it. We expected a baby; instead we got . . . this.

And yet there is something in me that won't let me leave it at that. I'm not a philosopher or ethicist, but I am learning to be a doctor and here is a life (human or not) that seems to be suffering, that just might be able to sense the difference between goodwill and hostility. While the anesthesia resident suctions the child and records his Apgars, I hold out my little finger and let the child glom onto it with his left hand. I begin stroking his little forearm.

I'm not sure what to expect. Do these children die within a few minutes or do they live for thirty years? I ask the anesthesia resident if she knows. She says she thinks it depends on how much of a brain stem it has.

"They don't usually last very long," she says.

None of us knows what to do at this point. It seems futile to do much. It seems inhumane to do nothing. In the end it is Mrs. McAuliffe who shows us.

"Would you bring me my baby?" she asks quietly.

The delivery room nurse swaddles the child in a soft white blanket and brings him over to the mom.

Mrs. McAuliffe, tears running silently down her face, strokes the baby's cheek and murmurs over and over again, "My poor little darling."

The child isn't breathing very well. After a few minutes the nurse takes him to the newborn nursery, where Mr. McAuliffe gets to hold him for a few minutes before he dies.

CHAPTER TWENTY

Our clinical assignments are usually six weeks long—just long enough for us to learn a little and then move on. In the middle of February, when I finish OB, I am assigned to peds. I can't wait to get started. I love kids and am even considering a career in pediatrics.

We take call just like we do on all the other services. The main thing we do on peds call is start IVs, and that can be quite a challenge—little people, little veins. I have been on peds for a couple weeks, and am sitting in the neonatal ICU waiting room watching *Hawaii Five-O* when one of the nurses pages me.

"Heather needs another IV started," she says.

She seems surprised when I ask, "Who's Heather?"

"I thought everyone knew Heather," she says.

Obediently I trudge up to the fourth floor. When I get there, my pockets bulging with various sizes and shapes of needles, the nurse brings me to a nine-month-old baby who is lying very still in her crib.

The nurse explains that the child suffered horrible burns in a home fire when she was just a few weeks old. She has been in the hospital ever since. The nurse can't believe no one told me about this baby. Almost every service in the hospital has been involved in her care at one time or another.

She has been a patient in this hospital longer than some of the residents have been doctors.

The child's main problem now is that something is wrong with her bowels. She has had several surgeries but is still unable to take anything by mouth. Her IV has infiltrated ("Again!" the nurse says, throwing up her hands) and she has to have another IV started to continue her fluids, nutrition, and antibiotics.

The nurse has to go back to the desk, so I am left alone with the baby. I ease myself down into the rocking chair next to the crib and pick up her chart. I can't believe how big it is. It is thicker than the chart of most eighty-year-olds. I slowly page through it, fascinated by all the things that have happened to her: burns over 80 percent of her body, liver failure, bowel necrosis, electrolyte imbalances—the list goes on and on. She has had things go wrong with her that I've never even heard of. She has a list of surgical procedures half an inch thick.

I am starting to feel uneasy. This is *not* going to be an easy IV to start. This baby knows what's coming. She is going to go bananas as soon as I put down the side of her crib, and there will be no nurse to help me, no one to hold the child down when she begins thrashing and fighting. I have tried to start IVs under those circumstances, and I don't want to go through all that again.

But I am the oldest of eight kids. I have been around children my whole life and I fancy myself a real expert on them. I figure I can charm this little one into holding still for me while I start her IV. I lay my assortment of needles, tourniquets, and alcohol wipes on the table. Then I hum a little tune and smile at the baby as I lower the rail of her crib.

"Don't be scared, little Heather. Don't be scared," I say soothingly. "Everything's going to be fine."

But before the rail of the crib is down I realize something is different about this child. Little Heather doesn't struggle or cry. She doesn't even whimper. She just lies there looking at me. There is no fear in her eyes, but there is something worse, something beyond fear. She has the eyes of an old woman—and they are filled with despair. She doesn't fear me. She doesn't resist me. She just recognizes me for what I am: another stranger come to torment her.

I am hopelessly bigger than she is, hopelessly stronger, hopelessly more powerful, and I will have my way. She can struggle, she can fight, she can cry, but none of those things will matter. I will have my way, and I will hurt her. There is nothing she can do about it. All this I can see in those eyes.

And I see more. I see a glimmer of accusation. Or am I reading my own guilt reflected back at me? What, after all, am I doing here? Who do I think I am? I'm not here to help her, am I? When my beeper went off, I didn't say, "Oh, good, another child I can help." I said, "Oh, hell, another IV I have to start."

I am a student. Heather is a textbook. She is a problem to be solved. If I help her, it is secondary to my real purpose, which is to study pediatrics, to learn how to start IVs, to get a good grade. That, not compassion, is what brought me here with my pocketful of needles and syringes.

Heather's eyes tell me that she knows all this. And she knows something else, something no child should ever know. She knows that she doesn't matter. She knows that her life, her condition, her pain, are not important. How can they be important? If they were, why is a lowly junior medical student here to start her IV? Why isn't the intern here? Or the resident? Or the attending? Or, damn it, why isn't the Chief of Surgery here?

They aren't here because this little nine-month-old lump of burned flesh isn't worth their while to come. I look at her chart: Heather Staniszewski. I'll tell you what, if her name were Heather Fields or Heather Daley or Heather Palmer, if she were a member of one of those wealthy families that donate a ton of money to this hospital, she wouldn't by lying here all by herself with some junior medical student about to start her IV. You better believe the pros from Dover would be on duty around the clock, attending to her every need.

But Heather is not from a wealthy family. She is just another anonymous burned kid, another Crispy Critter as the surgery residents call them. Heather accepts this. Her eyes show no sign of bitterness, just resignation and profound despair.

I tell those eyes to be reasonable. The Chief of Surgery can't start every IV, can't change every dressing, can't perform every surgery. After all, this is a teaching hospital, isn't it? Resident and students have to be taught. That's what teaching hospitals do. How else can everyone learn? How else are we to one day become Chiefs of Surgery?

Doesn't she understand that? Doesn't she understand that she is benefiting from being here in this teaching hospital? Doesn't she understand that she has to take the good with the bad?

That is *not* what Heather understands. What she understands is that day after day, week after week, she has been made to suffer. As far back as she can remember there has been nothing but pain. That's all there is. That's all there ever will be.

The burns, the skin grafts, the surgeries, the therapy, the IVs, the endless blood drawings—like any kid she must have struggled and fought against all of it at first. She must have cried and kept on crying, but her crying didn't matter.

The big strangers came and they hurt her, and they kept coming, and they kept hurting her, and she cried and struggled, but they held her down and hurt her some more. And once a big stranger came and stabbed her first in the right arm and then in the left arm. She fought him and she cried, but he swore and slammed her arm back down and stabbed her again and he ripped at the flesh on her legs and she cried and cried until she couldn't cry anymore, but still the big strangers came.

And they came, and they came.

And they *kept* coming, and they *kept* hurting her until she went beyond the stage of reacting to the pain. Now she just lies there with those huge, empty eyes in a tortured, emaciated, ravaged little body. And who am I but the latest torturer?

There is no appeal in those eyes, no wish or hope that I would leave her alone. She must have tried that, too, long ago, until she realized the futility of fighting against her huge, powerful assailants with the white coats. Now her eyes are devoid of everything, save the knowledge of the inevitability of pain and suffering.

I have never seen such profound despair. Suddenly my charming little songs and nursery rhymes choke in my throat. This is one child who will not be amused with bird noises and flashing penlights. Her eyes never leave my face, and there is no sign of hatred or accusation or even fear in them. But that terrible, forlorn hopelessness fills her eyes, her face, the entire room.

What sort of world is this where nine-month-old children are so intimate with despair?

Suddenly I realize that our roles have now been reversed. Now I am the one who needs reassurance. I am the one who is afraid. I hesitate, my confidence shaken like it never could be from any abusive, demanding adult. But I have a job to do. I have to start this IV. I can't just stand here all night. I start to speak to Heather, my voice gentle and quiet, as I try to win her confidence and trust.

But then I stop. Win her confidence and trust—for what? So I can betray it by turning around and inflicting more pain? How can she understand that I am trying to *help* her? How many other strangers in white coats have tried to win her over, only to then stab, cut, poke, or squeeze her? And when their little exercise in pain is finished, they lift the rail of her crib and walk away.

Maybe it was after the fifth or fiftieth or five hundredth stranger had stabbed her that she stopped struggling and stopped hoping, that she realized that it is never going to end, that all her yesterdays and all her tomorrows will be filled with an endless procession of strangers who lower the bars of her crib, torture her for a few minutes, raise the bars back up, and leave.

And now I am a part of it all. I am one of them. Me!

But I protest. No! This isn't what I intended. I am here to help her (*Oh, really?* those eyes say. *I thought you were here to* practice *on me.*) I don't want to hurt anyone. I'm just doing my job. Maybe I'm not the best IV starter in the hospital, but I'm getting better. I'm learning. (*You're learning a lot more than you bargained for tonight, aren't you, Doctor?*)

I am confused, disjointed. This is just a baby. I have an IV to start. I am here to help, to heal. My heart is in the right place. I care about her. I want her to get better. I want her to grow up and find someone to hold her and love her and care for her. That's what I want. I want her pain to stop. And I want her to stop looking at me that way. *I'm* not the problem. The burns are the problem. I am helping her to get over those burns. Someday she will realize that.

But what little Heather realizes doesn't matter. The only thing that matters is that I am going to hurt her—now. Heather doesn't struggle. She lies so still, so quiet. I can't look at her anymore. I just can't. With tears in my eyes I lift her limp, withered, scarred little arm, and I stab it and stab it again, and stab it a third time, until finally the blood flows. She never budges and her eyes never leave my face.

I wrap a bandage around the IV site. (We wouldn't want there to be any bleeding, now, would we?) I have had my way. I did what I came here to do. Now, just like all the others, I raise the side of her crib, turn, and leave the room. That is, I *try* to leave the room. I have been trying ever since.

CHAPTER TWENTY-ONE

On Mother's Day, Patti tells me she has a surprise for me. She says she missed her last period. I'm not surprised. By mutual, if unspoken, consent, our "sort of trying" not to get pregnant has gradually evolved into less "trying" and more "sort of."

Patti gives me a urine specimen, and I ask Jack Payne, the resident I am working with, if he will order a pregnancy test on it. At two o'clock that afternoon Jack walks up to me, hands me the test result, and says, "Congratulations, Dad." I immediately call Patti at work and tell her the news. We are both so excited we can hardly contain ourselves.

"But you have to promise me you won't tell a soul, not a single soul," Patti says. "It's too early." I promise Patti that this secret is safe with me.

When I get home that night Patti is waiting at the door. She is still in her nurse's uniform. She throws herself into my arms, and I swing her around as we laugh and tell each other we can't believe it.

"You didn't tell anyone, did you?" Patti asks.

"Nope. I promised not to, remember?"

Patti says she hasn't told anyone, either—well, just her sister Joanne, and Cathy and Madonna, her college roommates. "But that's okay," Patti explains to me. "I tell them everything."

.   .   .

We are going to have a baby. We almost have to pinch ourselves to believe it. This is the best thing that ever happened to us. Even though we are both in the medical field and have seen some terrible obstetrical complications, that sort of thing never even gets on our radar screen. Like little kids, we blithely assume that the pregnancy will be a snap and the delivery will be a breeze.

"And she'll sleep through the night right away," Patti says.

"And she'll have her mother's eyes," I say.

"And she'll toilet train herself within a few months," Patti says

"And she'll never leave jockstraps hanging on the basement doorknob like her uncles do," I say.

Patti frowns and says girls don't wear jockstraps.

"Then it won't be that hard for her not to hang them on the basement doorknob."

Patti slowly shakes her head and says she doesn't know if I am quite ready to be a father.

My only personal experience with childbirth was driving my mom to the hospital to deliver my youngest brother. I was sixteen years old at the time and I'm not sure if I even knew how babies were born. My mom kept telling me to slow down, but I was terrified that she was going to have the baby in the car and that I would have to do something.

I roared up to the ER at St. Anne's Hospital, helped my mom out of the car and into the wheelchair the nurse was holding. And then, to my eternal shame, I got back in the car and drove away. Fast. My brother Bill was born on a cart in the hallway five minutes later.

Patti has a little trouble with morning sickness during the first trimester, but otherwise her pregnancy goes along smoothly. I do my best to be sensitive and attentive to her needs. I realize that a woman's psyche can be fragile during her pregnancy, so I try to be a supportive husband. I tell Patti she doesn't really look that much like a cow. Perhaps because pregnancy has made her emotionally unstable, her nose flares and she begins to make eerie growling noises like Bela Lugosi used to make right before he gorged himself on some poor slob's blood.

I've always been rather fond of my blood and think it is doing fine right there in my veins where it belongs, so I decide I'd better quickly think of something nice to say. I tell Patti that the tent she is wearing looks nice. Now she is snorting and pawing the ground like a wild bull. I can almost see steam coming out of her nostrils.

I start backing away. I ask Patti to control herself. I tell her this can't be good for our little unborn baby. I have never seen my wife like this. She looks like The Terminator. At any moment I think she is going to growl, "*Hasta la vista*, baby," and blow me away.

When Patti finally regains her composure, she tells me she wishes *men* were the ones who had to carry babies; then we'd see how funny I thought it was. I am relieved to see some semblance of sanity come back in my wife's eyes.

I smile weakly and say, "Yes, dear."

In July I begin my last year of medical school. It's hard to believe that in one year I will be a doctor. My first assignment as a senior medical student is the cardiology service at Hines. I like being back at Hines. The veterans are generally a nice bunch of guys. Students and residents are given a lot of responsibility there. And for the first time I will not be the lowest man on the totem pole. I will have a junior resident under me. I can't wait to get started.

When I show up the first morning, the attending cardiologist, Dr. Morton, and the cardiology fellow, Jack Wishnant, are already there. Jack and I worked together last year when he was the resident on Durkin's GI service. We have always gotten along well. I say hello to Jack and introduce myself to Dr. Morton. I tell him I will be his senior med student on this rotation.

It is then I notice that Melvin Trimble is not here. I've never met Trimble, but I know he has been assigned as the intern on the service. "Where's Mel Trimble?" I ask Jack.

Jack starts to answer, then stops and looks at Dr. Morton. Dr. Morton clears his throat and says, "Dr. Trimble is . . . not here."

"Oh," I say, "isn't he going to be our intern?"

"No."

I look at them, confused by what is going on.

"Dr. Trimble died yesterday," Dr. Morton says. "He . . . committed suicide."

Suicide? I am stunned. I didn't know Mel Trimble, but Brian Clark worked with him last summer and said he was a decent guy. I look at Jack and Dr. Morton, unsure what to say, unsure what to ask. "I'm really sorry," I say.

Dr. Morton nods. "I didn't know the young man very well, but it is a tragedy, a terrible tragedy."

It *is* a tragedy, and while I know that, I am ashamed to admit that the next thought that comes into my mind is, *Now what?* What does a service do when it loses its intern? Where, how, do they find another? It's not like there are lots of interns hanging around with nothing to do. You can't just walk down to The Pub on a Friday night and say, "Hey! Any of you guys want to cover a cardiology service for a couple months?"

While I am puzzling over all this, Jack looks at me and says, "I was just telling Dr. Morton that I had worked with you before, and that you knew your stuff."

I mumble my thanks but wonder where *that* came from.

"I told him that I thought *you* could handle the job of intern."

I am completely shocked. "Me?"

Interns are smart. Interns are competent. Interns have name tags that say *M.D.* after their name. I'm just a medical student. My name tag says "doofus" after my name. Although at times it gets old being just a med student, there is a comfort factor in being insignificant. You are never responsible for anything. No one expects much of you. If you produce, that's a nice little surprise for everyone, but everything you do is scrutinized. It is always someone else's responsibility. But an intern! He is expected to make real decisions.

Dr. Morton holds out his hand. "Dr. Collins, I would like you to take over as the intern on this service," he says.

Instinctively I grasp his hand. "Yes, sir."

Suicide. No one ever talks about it, but every now and then you hear about it—some poor resident or intern who just gets overwhelmed by his work or his responsibilities. He comes home and leaves the engine running in the garage or jumps off a bridge.

It seems so sad, so unfair. More often than not it is the sensitive ones, the ones who care too much, who cave in under the pressure. The jerks, the ones who are in it for the money or the prestige, they never buckle at all. They cruise along, unaffected by their occasional mistake or the occasional tragedy to which they are witnesses. None of it matters to them.

We were given a little talk on suicide during our first-year orientation. Doctors take their own lives at a much higher rate than the general population. Only dentists have a higher suicide rate than doctors. Alcoholism or drug abuse often plays a role, but researchers also note that doctors who take their own lives are often more critical of themselves and have a greater tendency to blame themselves when things go wrong.

I wonder sometimes if the very feeling of empathy that brought us into medicine in the first place might actually sow the seeds of our undoing. Doctors fight a losing battle. Every doctor loses every battle. We might temporarily reperfuse that heart. We might temporarily control that diabetes. We might temporarily make the pain of that knee go away, but in the end, all our efforts are for naught. The patient dies—every patient, every time. Everything a doctor does just temporizes, just delays the inevitable. And we are forced to live with the lie that we are actually accomplishing something.

And it is worse than self-deceit. We, who should know better, reinforce every patient's desire to hide from the reality of his own mortality. Yes, we tell him, come to us and let us replace that hip, let us ream out that prostate.

Yes, we tell her, come to us and let us remove those wrinkles, let us enlarge those breasts. Together we will pretend that we have cheated fate. Together we will pretend that our efforts do more than just distract us from the lengthening shadows we try so desperately to ignore.

It is easy for us doctors to delude ourselves into thinking that what we do is important. It is easy to acquiesce in society's collective blindness. Perhaps it is the most insightful, the most sensitive, in our profession who come to realize the essential absurdity of what we do; perhaps that is what leads them to despair.

Melvin Trimble's death affects me more than I thought it would. I never knew the guy, but it brings back too many painful memories. I lost one of my best friends to suicide three years ago—and I never saw it coming. Never in a million years could I have predicted it. Even after she died, even after it became common knowledge, I just couldn't believe it. Maggie was one of the finest people I have ever known: kind, moral, loving, compassionate, considerate. She was worth ten of the rest of us—and she took her own life. What could she have been thinking? What could *I* have been thinking? Why didn't I see it coming? Why wasn't I there for her?

I never learn what happened to Melvin Trimble. No one wants to talk about it. It is too painful to explore the web of depression and guilt and inadequacy that might have contributed to his taking his own life.

Worse still, I never explore the motives that led Maggie to take her life. I just can't bring myself to talk about it with her brothers and sisters, all of whom I know and like. It is too painful for them. It is too painful for me. And, in the end, how can we ever know? How can we ever get over the notion that it is, at least in part, *our* fault? If only we had seen this or done that, if only we had been more supportive or less critical, if only we cared more and judged less, if only we delighted less in the gifts she gave us and took the time to explore the pain that must have lurked below. How can I urge them to stop blaming themselves when I can't stop blaming myself?

Sometimes I think religion is the whitewash I use to disguise the rot below. But I do take comfort in prayer. And in my prayers at night, every night, I pray for Maggie. That sore has never healed. There remains the gnawing, festering suspicion that I failed her, that had I been a better friend, she would be alive today.

When we finish rounds that first day, I drop down into a chair at the nurses' station and take a deep breath. An intern! What the hell have I let myself in for this time? I'm flattered that Jack and Dr. Morton think I can handle the job, but I'm not convinced I can.

Nevertheless, I resolve to give it my best shot. I am lucky that Mimi Usher, a junior medical student, is assigned to the service with me. Mimi is great. She has already decided she wants to be a cardiologist. She is bright, hardworking, and anxious to learn.

Our typical day begins with morning report where the person on call relates what transpired during the night. Then Morton, Jack, Mimi, and I make rounds. When we finish rounds, Morton leaves and Jack gives me a list of things to do. It is up to me to delegate jobs to Mimi that I feel she can handle. She quickly shows me she can handle a lot.

The hard part is call. When I am at the hospital during the day, there is always someone I can go to with questions or problems. If someone has an MI, the whole service is there and med student input is neither requested nor required. I am never on the front line at those times. But at night things are different. At night I *am* the front line. If someone has an MI, if someone has chest pain, if someone's EKG starts looking a little funky, the cardiology intern is the guy who has to respond.

For that first week on cardiology I am rarely home. If I'm not working in the hospital, I'm in the library poring over *Marriott's Practical Electrocardiography* or devouring Hurst and Logue's *The Heart*. I'm terrified that I will get an urgent page some night to see a gasping veteran clutching his chest and complaining of chest pain, shortness of breath, arrhythmia, heart block, ventricular fibrillation, asystole, and Blue Baby Syndrome.

"Doctor, Doctor! What should we do? He's the sickest patient I've ever seen!" the nurse will shout.

I can't just stand there and say, "Comparisons are odious," or, "I asked you first." I have to *do* something.

Besides having the stress and burden of acting as an intern, I find my-self for the first time being in the role of teacher. Mimi rightly expects that I will teach her. That's how the system works: you learn from those above you and you teach those below you.

Mimi is already pretty good at reading basic EKGs. I go over some of the more subtle stuff with her, explain the rationale behind the drugs we use, teach her how to put in a CVP and an art line. It actually is fun to teach someone like Mimi, who is so eager to learn.

Being the blind fool that I am, I make the mistake of telling Patti one night how impressed I am with Mimi. Patti looks up from her nursing journal. "What does she look like?" she asks casually.

With incredible naïveté I reply that Mimi is a very attractive girl—which she is, although I honestly never look at her in that way.

"Oh," Patti says, the cold arctic winds gathering in her voice, "and I suppose little Miss Junior Medical Student has told you what big muscles you have, and wants you to come over to her place some night to catch up on a little studying."

I nearly burst out laughing—except Patti is serious. She is four months pregnant and is inclined to think irrational things. She knows I am about as clueless with women as a man can be, plus I am deliriously happy with the woman I married. The idea that I would even *look* at another woman is preposterous. Still, I was raised in a house of eight boys. One never re-sists the impulse to tease.

"Now that you mention it," I say, "she hasn't been wearing a bra to work this last week and she keeps telling me how lonely she gets at night. Poor thing. I suppose it would be difficult for her, being one of the few women in medical school."

"I suppose it would be difficult for you going through life missing an important part of your male anatomy," Patti says.

"Patti, please," I say with disgusting equanimity, "can't you see that Mimi and I commune only on an intellectual level? I've never even noticed that she is a thirty-eight double D."

"I hate you."

"Couldn't you just *dislike* me—at least until the baby is born?"

Patti throws her nursing journal on the couch, lumbers to her feet, and glares at me. "Someday God is going to give you gangrene of the heart, or brain pus or something awful. And you are going to come crawling to me, begging me for help. And I am going to tell you to stop bleeding on Pierre, who is finishing my pedicure. And then I will yawn and say that perhaps after my astrology appointment I could drop you off at Cook County ER."

A few minutes later the phone rings. It is my brother Jack. "Hey, fat boy," he says, "do you know the name of the third baseman on the '59 Sox when they won the pennant?"

"Oh, hi, Mimi," I say in a loud voice.

"Mimi?" Jack says. "Who is Mimi?"

"What's that, Mimi? You hear strange noises coming from your bedroom and you want me to come over and check it out?"

"It's one of your stupid brothers, isn't it?" Patti calls from the other room.

"Not tonight, Mimi," I say into the phone. "I have a headache."

Jack clears his throat. "Everything okay with you and Patti?"

"Tell your brother I married an idiot," Patti shouts.

"Patti says I married an idiot."

"Maybe I'd better call you later," Jack says.

"*You're* the idiot!" Patti says.

"Bubba Phillips," I say to Jack in a low voice.

"What?"

"The Sox third baseman in '59. It was Bubba Phillips."

"Thanks," Jack says. And then after a couple seconds, "Gee, I can't wait till I get married someday."

CHAPTER TWENTY-TWO

In mid-August, a few days before our first anniversary, Patti tells me she is having some pain in her left calf. Having recently completed my OB rotation, I immediately conclude the worst. I am afraid she has a blood clot, so I tell her we have to get this checked out right away.

Patti sees her obstetrician, who refers her to a hematologist with the unlikely name of Harry Messmore. Dr. Messmore in turn refers her to a vascular surgeon, Dr. Baker. The two specialists examine Patti but disagree on the diagnosis. Dr. Messmore thinks she has a blood clot. Dr. Baker thinks she doesn't.

The only way to tell for sure is to do a venogram. But nobody wants to do a venogram because the radiation would be bad for the baby. Finally Dr. Messmore says he is convinced Patti has a blood clot and he wants her to start injecting herself with heparin every day for the rest of the pregnancy.

Dr. Baker disagrees. He doesn't think she has a blood clot and he doesn't think she needs *any* treatment. Dr. Messmore merely nods and tells us that if Dr. Baker is right, but Patti takes the heparin anyway, there is a chance she will bleed a bit more at the time of delivery. But Dr.

Messmore says that if *he* is right and Patti *doesn't* take the heparin, there is a chance she will die.

Now there's a word young married couples don't hear very often: die. That's like when your heart stops beating and they put you in a box, wrap a rosary around your fingers, and your old aunts say, "My, she looks so peaceful." It's usually a pretty permanent condition.

"So what do you want to do?" Dr. Messmore asks us.

Patti starts giving herself heparin shots.

Patti is still in the hospital when our first anniversary rolls around. Father Fahey says Mass for us down in the chapel. Our families and several of my classmates, including Jack, Brian, Cathy, and Dog, gather around the altar with us. The "celebration" is a bit more solemn that we had anticipated just a week before. Even my brothers are affected. They don't give any "Chinese laundries" to the guy in the pew in front of them. They don't come up with any "Bubbles the Clown" jokes. At the Handshake of Peace, one or two of them even give Patti a kiss.

Patti is released from the hospital two days later. A week after that she goes back to work at Oak Park Hospital. But from now on, twice a day, every day, she has to give herself heparin shots. We try to laugh it off, making jokes about scoring some gnarly heparin and shooting up between our toes, but it's not funny. All of a sudden having a baby isn't such a walk in the park. All of a sudden we lose some of our childish naïveté, and we realize that shit *does* happen—and not just to other people.

I'm not thrilled about starting my psychiatry rotation. Cardiology didn't bother me. OB didn't bother me. The ER didn't bother me. But psych scares the hell out of me—probably because neither I nor anyone else really understands it. Other disease processes—infections, heart attacks, trauma—are things that happen to your body. The inner core, *you*, is not affected.

But with mental disease it isn't your leg or your spleen or your throat that is messed up; it's *you*. Mental disease takes something from you that no other disease does. Oh, sure, some mental diseases are more understandable, less threatening: Susie is depressed because her husband left her. Jimmy is eighty years old and keeps pissing on the geraniums. But the flat-out craziness that makes people howl and rage, that makes them think they are Napoléon, that makes them curl up in a ball in a corner and whimper—I don't know what to make of any of that. How can anyone, especially some goofy medical student, do anything to help that kind of behavior?

The Madden Mental Health Center is located right next door to Loyola. It is an intimidating place. Jack Brennan tells me you have to be pretty crazy before they put you in there. On my first visit, I have to go through a series of locked doors. I glance uneasily behind me as I pass through each door, watching them lock it behind me, wondering what's going to happen if some guy with a hatchet starts chasing me yelling, "Red rum! Red rum!"

And the guards and workers here aren't terribly reassuring, either. They seem like an equally strange brew. They all have weird facial tics and ways of jerking their eyeballs back and forth. I half-expect to see some hunchbacked Igor dragging his leg behind him, holding a blazing torch, and telling me to follow him down a dark stone passageway to the laboratory where the Master is waiting.

Psychiatry turns out to be more like a class than a medical rotation. We study the *Diagnostic and Statistical Manual of Mental Disorders* and learn how schizophrenia differs from psychosis. We learn about personality disorders and various types of depression.

I am appalled to see some of the things that go on in psychiatry. I realize that pills are an important part of medicine, but in psych they have pills up the wazoo (as well as in the mouth): pills to calm you down, pills to jack you up, pills to help you remember, pills to help you forget. No matter which pole you're at, there is a pill to take you to the opposite one. I keep wondering when Grace Slick is going to show up singing, "Feed your head."

It is all well intentioned, but the use of pills in psychiatry doesn't seem as closely scrutinized and isn't subject to the same investigational rigor that pills in other branches of medicine are. Psychiatrists seem freer to engage in a cavalier sort of experimentation to see what works and what doesn't—not that I blame them. Neurobehavioral studies are in their infancy, and there is very little science to guide them. Contradictory evidence can be found almost everywhere. For instance, I learn that hyperactive kids are often given speed because it paradoxically slows them down.

But the real kicker for me is electroshock therapy. I can't believe doctors still do it. I thought electroshock therapy was outlawed by the Geneva Convention or the Supreme Court or *Mister Rogers' Neighborhood* or somebody, but I find out it is done all the time. I have visions of young college boys who have been found guilty of chugging beers and participating in late-night panty raids being dragged kicking and screaming to a soundproof bunker deep under the Administration Building. There they are strapped to a metal table under a giant transformer that crackles and sparks with electricity while some seven-foot zombie awaits word from Herr Professor to pull the switch that will turn the boys into pacified eunuchs who enjoy chick flicks and ballet.

After observing several electroshock therapy sessions, I actually am fairly impressed. It is not an inhumane procedure used to subjugate strong-willed individuals. It is a very successful treatment for a severe type of depression.

But there is no way I can get away from being uncomfortable with all this messing with people's minds. I realize that some minds are already messed up and *something* has to be done, but all this prescribing and counseling and analyzing and shocking seems so haphazard. One doctor tries one thing; another doctor tries something entirely different. One disparages analysis. The other swears by it. It is all very confusing to a young man who desperately seeks straight answers and no equivocation. I keep wishing I were on some service like general surgery where diagnoses are easily made and treatment follows rationally. The bowel's ruptured: repair it. The appendix is infected: remove it.

In psych, everything is a mystery. Nothing—not the diagnosis, not the treatment, not anything—is straightforward. You don't know if Thomas really hates his mother or not, and even if he does, is that the reason why he wants to dress like a chicken?

Part of my psych rotation involves some exposure to addiction medicine. And guess what? People get screwed up from taking drugs. Boy, there's a shocker. I don't know, maybe it's a chicken-and-egg thing. Maybe they were screwed up *before* they took drugs. All I know is that most of them are pretty whacked-out by the time we see them. There is very little med students can *do* for addicted patients. Sometimes I think there is very little any doctor can do for addicted patients. If they don't want to stop, all the advice and counseling and cajoling in the world accomplishes little.

I am discouraged and a bit outraged at the haphazard way these people are treated. I wonder if doctors are really the people to treat them. The counselors say these people need motivation, but I wonder if that goes deep enough. Sure, they have to *want* to quit, but what flaw made them start in the first place?

And what do we do for them? To start with, we lock them up. We call it Inpatient Therapy, but basically it is "Shut up and welcome to The Big House." Once we have our captive audience, we give them assorted drugs. By definition, the drugs we give them are Good Drugs. The drugs *they* take are Bad Drugs. However, if a patient ever takes the Good Drugs without our permission, then they become Bad Drugs.

Once the patients are suitably medicated (when they take our drugs they become medicated; when they take their own drugs they become intoxicated) we put them in a room with similarly afflicted individuals, where we assume they will not share information about highs or sources or pushers. Instead we encourage them to "tell their story" in such a way as to emphasize the sordidness of their lifestyle and the depth of their commitment to "sin no longer." After a while, if they are good boys and girls, we let them continue in the program as outpatients. When they have jumped through the prescribed number of hoops, when they can speak, roll over, and give us a paw, we pat them on the head and send them on their way, cured.

Treatment consists of group sessions where the patients, the group leader, and one or two medical students sit in a circle. Everyone except the med students smokes—a lot. So there we sit, telling our stories or sharing our feelings, a thick cloud of smoke hovering above us.

It is scary to hear their stories, scary to see how quickly and how completely people can sink once the compulsion gets its hooks in them. I feel this a little more keenly than the other students since I have more alcoholics in my family than you can shake a swizzle stick at.

Jeannine likes cocaine. She likes it a lot. And according to her chart, after a while she got to liking all kinds of other stuff, too. Her chart says she is twenty-eight, but she looks fifty. When it is her turn to tell her story, I am in turn fascinated and horrified: The college kid who decided to experiment a little. The young executive who had no trouble managing her habit, certain that she could compartmentalize her life indefinitely. Then the growing dependence, the failed stints in rehab, the inexorable descent, and the final abandonment of everything but the drug.

I hardly move while she tells her story. My eyes are glued to her face. I marvel at the depth of her newfound understanding and I'm impressed with her determination to get better. Med students are not allowed to be passive observers. The patients know we are med students. They know we, presumably, aren't struggling with any addictions, but Dr. Hester tells us that it is unfair to ask the patients to open up in front of us if we don't open up in front of them. By opening up, he doesn't mean we are to make up some BS story about our rampant heroin use but to share our feelings and our impressions. When it is my turn, I tell Jeannine how impressed I am with her struggle. I tell her I'm glad she seems to be getting her life back on track.

When the session is over and the patients have gone back to their rooms, Dr. Hester asks me what I think about Jeannine.

"It's amazing what she has been through," I tell him. "I can see how deeply it has affected her. I'm glad she is determined to get better."

Dr. Hester looks at me and says nothing.

The next day I am even more impressed by the strides Jeannine is making and by her determination to, as she says, "get clean."

Dr. Hester takes me aside that afternoon and basically asks what boat I just got off of. "Jeannine is a master manipulator," he tells me. "She has been in these programs long enough to know exactly what to say and exactly what buttons to push in order to get what she wants. She comes in here every six months or so because her father has a lot of money and pays for her to come. She is no more interested in getting clean than you are in getting dirty. I'm surprised you can't see that."

I try, but I can't. When Jeannine goes into her spiel the next day, I am fascinated at the tremendous battle she is waging and the unwavering resolve she has.

"She says the same thing every time she comes in here," Dr. Hester tells me.

Dr. Hester is wrong. I know he is wrong. I am absolutely positive he is wrong—until Jeannine graduates to the outpatient program and promptly disappears.

"She'll be back—if she doesn't manage to kill herself this time," Hester tells me.

I was so wrong, so off-target. Doctors are supposed to have judgment. I worry that I'm never going to have any. I ask Dr. Hester if he has any insight into why Jeannine was able to con me so easily.

"We see what we want to see," Hester says. "We try to make the world fit our preconceived notions. You are like most medical students. You *want* people to get better. You *want* them to do the right thing—so you transfer that desire to the patient.

"If you want to be a good doctor you have to learn to keep yourself out of the equation. You have to learn to pay a little more attention to *what is*, rather than what you wish it were. You have to stop thinking that you live in the best of all worlds."

.   .   .

I understand what Dr. Hester is saying, but his advice negates the one thing that medical students bring to the table: their idealism. Medical students have a dream and a vision that brought them into medicine in the first place. A lot of older doctors seem to have lost that dream somewhere along the line—and who's to blame them? Maybe there is a limit to how many times you can be lied to, manipulated, and sued before that seed of idealism withers and dies under the harsh sun of reality.

Maybe Dr. Hester is right. Maybe I *will* lose my idealism. But I'm for damn sure not going to *throw* it away just because some old, cynical psychiatrist tells me to. I won't just *lose* my idealism. They'll have to tear it out of me, because I'm not going to let it go willingly. I'm going to cling to the beliefs that brought me into medicine in the first place: that one person can make a difference, that there is a common bond we all share, that some things must be opposed, and that the strong should help the weak.

If I ever learn that those beliefs have no place in the world of medicine, then *I* have no place in the world of medicine. I'll go back to throwing rocks.

CHAPTER TWENTY-THREE

It seems like an act of betrayal. The Beater is my first car. It's the car that swept Patti off her feet when we first started going out. (Although Patti doesn't quite remember it that way.) It's the car that got me back and forth to Rochester thirty or forty times when Patti was still in nursing school. The Beater is a member of the family. The heater works. The radio works. Despite the fact that it has 140,000 miles on it, has no muffler, and burns oil like crazy, it has never failed us (well, okay, once). And now Patti, ensnared in the throes of some weird sort of nesting syndrome, is insisting we get rid of it.

"It's not safe," she says. "It's fourteen years old and it's falling apart. We have a new baby coming and that car is a death trap."

"So what are we supposed to do, go down to the Cadillac dealership and pick out our new Eldorado?"

"No, my cousin Bobby is in the used-car business up in Arlington Heights. He could find us a car."

"Well, my cousin Mike is in the used-car business in Forest Park and he found us *this* one. And it's a pretty damn good car."

Patti starts crying. "Stop talking to me like that. I just want our baby to be safe."

Oh, no, not the crying thing. I can handle fighting, threats, insults, groin kicks—but not the crying thing. The only one who ever cried when I was growing up was my mom the day my brothers and I shot so many pucks at the garage that the east wall fell off. I can't handle crying. I am not genetically equipped to deal with it.

I proceed to examine my conscience: *Okay. Let me get this straight. There's this woman. She's your wife. You love her like crazy. She is seven months pregnant. She is giving herself heparin shots every day because she got a blood clot carrying* your *child, and now she is crying because she thinks you don't care enough about her or your unborn baby to get a new car. So, who's the jerk here?*

I hang my head. I am a beaten man, and I know it. The Beater is doomed. I'm going to have to take Old Yeller out behind the woodshed and shoot him.

"I'm sorry, hon," I say. "Sure we can get a new car. I'll call Bobby this afternoon and see what he can do."

Two days later we drive out of Bobby's dealership with a sea green Dodge. I paid five hundred dollars for it (*three times* what I paid for The Beater). Bobby assures me I am getting a good deal. He even rummages around and pulls out a spare tire that he throws in our trunk. My cousin Mike did the same thing when I bought The Beater. It must be one of the standard used-car salesman's tricks: get a supply of bald tires from some junkyard and give them to every sucker who buys one of your clunkers.

Patti is due in mid-January. She's still giving herself heparin shots twice a day, and her belly is a splattered palette of purple and blue. On November 15 she finishes her last day of work. Her obstetrician has ordered her to quit. He says she needs to take it easy for the last two months of her pregnancy. The nurses at work throw a combination baby shower and farewell party for her. When she gets home, she struggles up the steps to our apartment and drops into a chair.

"Well, Mike," she says, "looks like you're the breadwinner in this family now."

This is not reassuring for either of us. I kind of liked being a kept man. It was working out rather well for me. Patti's pay as a nurse was so much more than either of us had ever made before. We have actually managed to save a good bit. But now that Patti is off work, we are in trouble. I don't know how we are going to pay rent or buy food. I could drive the cab, but that won't be enough to pay our bills. Scalese has shut down for the winter. There's no work there.

Just before Christmas, Joe Higgins, the old family friend who long ago got me the job at Scalese, hears of our predicament. He tells me he can get me a job on the truck docks at Seventy-seventh and Harlem. I jump at the opportunity. We have the week off between Christmas and New Year's. Mr. Higgins says I can start then.

Christmas is a Sunday this year. We have dinner at my parents' house. When Patti and I get there, Shannon is crouched at the front door, teeth bared, waiting for the mailman. She can't get it through her head that he doesn't come on Sundays. My brothers are in the living room drinking Old Style and arguing whether Keith Magnuson has ever won a fight in his NHL career.

"The guy's fought everyone in the league and the only one he ever beat was one of the linesmen he coldcocked by accident up in Toronto last year."

Patti walks over to them and sits down next to Tim. "It's Christmas," she says. "Can't you guys find something to talk about besides hockey and fighting? How about peace and love?"

Jack looks at her like she is nuts. "How about golf and girls with big loochies?" he asks.

"How about mud wrestling and keggers?" Rog says.

Patti gives them her disappointed grandmother look and says they should be ashamed of themselves. Then she goes out to the kitchen to talk to my mom.

Two days later, after being enrolled in the International Brotherhood of Teamsters, Local 710, I begin my career on the docks at CW Transport. I will be working the night shift from midnight to 8:00 A.M.

The work isn't too hard, but it is absolutely freezing on the docks that first night. Unfortunately, I seriously underestimated the amount of clothes I should wear, or maybe my metabolism is down, but by 3:00 A.M. my teeth are chattering and I am practically running back and forth with my loads trying to keep warm. I decide to take a minute to go to the bathroom. The bathroom is heated. There are ten guys in there lounging around trying to warm up. One of them is sitting on the trash bin. His feet are in the sink, which is full of warm water. The other workers tell me to stay in here for a while and that it's too fucking cold to be out there working. I am too worried about being fired. I need this job, so I go back to work.

Our lunchroom is in one of the two towers in the center of the dock. The lunchroom, too, is heated. At 4:00 A.M. I trudge up the metal steps. I am the last guy there. The others had been slowly drifting over to the tower a few minutes before four. When the lunch bell rang, they were up the stairs and into the room in thirty seconds.

They make room for me at one of the tables and I sit down.

The guy next to me tells me his name is Dominic. He asks, "Where the hell you been, kid? It's five after four. You like it out there or what?"

I tell Dominic I thought we couldn't leave our trucks until the bell rang.

A stocky guy at the end of the table slams his fist on the table and says, "Foogging boolsheet." After a pause he adds, "Cogsooggers." He appears to have said this for no particular reason.

I look at Dominic.

"Ah, don't worry," Dominic tells me. "That's just Anton. He don't speak no English. But Jimmy, here, taught him every swearword in the English language." He leans forward and shouts down the table, "Ain't that right, Anton?"

"Sonnabeetching besterds," Anton says, nodding his head for emphasis.

Jimmy nods, too. "Fuckin' A, Anton," he says.

"Fooggeen A," Anton repeats. "Fooggeen A. Peessa cheat."

·　　·　　·

My job is pretty straightforward. The drivers back their trailers up to the dock. I hop down, block the wheels, check the support rod, throw open the door, and start unloading. Most of the stuff I can lift myself. When I find something too heavy to lift, I turn on my light, signaling the forklift driver to come over and unload it for me. The forklift drivers always come as soon as I turn on my light. I quickly learn that this is because I am a new guy. The old guys don't want the driver to come right away. The longer it takes the driver to come, the longer they can loaf.

After throwing rocks for two years, unloading trucks isn't that hard. I kind of like it. You start with a huge semitrailer loaded to the gills with stuff and you plug away until it is empty. Every crate you unload brings you that much closer to being done. For a guy who likes immediate, positive feedback this job is perfect.

When we get off work that first morning, Dominic invites me to join him, Jimmy, and a bunch of the guys who are headed for the tavern. I thank them but say I have to get home. I tell them good-bye and I'll see them tonight. Anton waves cheerfully and says, "Chub eed ubb you ess, deeck head."

The next night, and every night that week, I am at work a half hour early. I am the first guy out to my truck. I need this job, so I work like a mule.

The guys at work are intrigued when they find out that I am a medical student. They start calling me Doc.

"So what kind of doctor you gonna be?" Quinton asks me as we are unloading a load of barbecue grills from Oshkosh one night.

I tell him I'm not sure yet.

This answer doesn't sit well with my co-workers. They can't understand why any red-blooded guy who gets into medical school would want to be anything other than a gynecologist.

"What's wrong with you, man?" they ask me.

Just to appease them, I say that gynecology is high on my list.

"Well, whatever kind of doctor you're gonna be, I'd hate to be your first patient," Quinton says. "I been down to County. I know 'bout them new doctors. They mess people up, give 'em the wrong shit, that kind of stuff. They kill a few before they get it right."

I promise that when I'm a new doctor and I give people shit I will try to be sure it is the right shit.

Quinton says it don't matter none anyway. If new doctors don't fuck you up one way, they'll fuck you up another.

Sometimes, based on the things I see at the hospital, I wonder if he might have a point.

It's hard working nights, but within a few days I get used to it. Patti, however, doesn't like it. Since I take the car, she has to stay home by herself unless one of her sisters or friends picks her up. Sometimes when I am working, one of my brothers will invite himself to dinner. He devours everything Patti puts in front of him, then drinks all my beer and watches *Starsky & Hutch* on the old TV my dad gave us. My brothers like it that I am working nights. They tell Patti I should keep it up.

Patti's pregnancy is going along well, but I am learning to be careful about what I say. I don't want her to think I am an insensitive boor. That's what she called me last week when she overheard me on the phone telling my brother Joe that this pregnancy thing sucks because it is making my ankles swell and my hemorrhoids act up.

Since my brothers never say insensitive boor things (to her face, that is) and since they are always sucking up to her so they can get more free food, Patti starts thinking maybe my brothers are right. Maybe I should be working more nights.

When Patti tells me this, I say she is being manipulated by her selfish brothers-in-law. I also say that because of her pregnancy she is suffering from a severe case of hormonal flux. I tell her that she will feel better as soon as the hormones start fluxing her into a case of nesting syndrome. Then she will want to spend all day cleaning the apartment. I tell her that would be a very matronly thing to do.

Patti starts going into that change thing again. Her face looks like Lon Chaney's when the full moon comes out and he suddenly sprouts hair, howls at the moon, and starts taking leaks on fire hydrants. She grits her teeth and says if she ever spends all day cleaning the apartment it will not be because of hormonal flux but because she wants the place to look nice for the funeral—mine.

Patti and I spend New Year's Day at her parents' house. They have finally accepted our marriage and are now very supportive and solicitous—of Patti. They are nice to me, too, but occasionally I catch them looking at me the same way you would look at a Ukranian folk dancer in a St. Patrick's Day parade: "What's *he* doing here?"

I go back to work at the hospital on Tuesday, January 3. I am up early and ready to leave for work when Patti asks if I could stick around for a couple minutes. She keeps grabbing her belly and rolling back and forth in bed.

"Are you in labor?" I ask. But how could she be in labor? She isn't due for another two weeks. We haven't even gotten a crib yet.

"I don't know," Patti says. "I've never been in labor before. But something weird is happening."

Fifteen minutes later, on the basis of our combined vast experience in having babies, we decide that Patti is indeed in labor. It is still dark as I go down and pull our "new" car around to the front of the apartment building. Then I go in and help Patti down the stairs.

It is only 5:30 A.M. and the streets are deserted. We get all the way to the hospital without ever having to stop. But as I pull into the ER at Loyola, I find that our new car has lost its brakes. The car slams into the wall outside the ER. Patti and I aren't hurt, but we stare wide-eyed at each other. Ten seconds later a huge security guard waddles out the door, a chocolate donut in his hand.

"Demolition Derby's down the street," he says, pointing south.

He takes one look at Patti heaving herself out of the front seat, holding her very swollen belly, and says, "Whoa! You sit right back down there, missy, while I get you a wheelchair. You," he says, pointing at me, "try not to crash into anything else while I'm gone."

They wheel Patti up to Labor and Delivery. Patti starts heeffing and hooffing just like the Lamaze teacher told her. It all strikes me as rather bizarre, all this staring at the ceiling and breathing through your teeth. But then I tried to imagine what it would be like for me to have a softball come out my belly button. I guess I'd be heeffing and hooffing, too.

After several hours, Patti's teeth are starting to dry out from all the weird breathing. I'm at her side the whole time, doing my best to act as coach and cheerleader. But I am new at this, too. I keep telling her the wrong things.

"Push, hon," I say.

"No," the OB nurse says. "It's too early to push."

"Focus," I say.

"No, relax," the nurse says.

"Take some deep breaths," I say.

"Slow down that breathing," the nurse says.

At that moment I just give up and realize how superfluous my presence here is. I also realize that I have discovered the final proof for the gender of God: He lets men share in the moment of conception but not in the moment of delivery. Seems like a very sensible plan.

Patti's contractions get stronger and stronger. They start coming closer and closer. Now it is time for her to be wheeled into the delivery room. There is nothing fun about this part—for either of us. Patti wants only a local, so the process of delivery is hard, painful work. It hurts me to see her in so much pain. I feel helpless and inadequate as I stand next to her, holding her hand as she struggles on.

"You're almost there, Patti," her obstetrician says. "I can see the head. One more push and you'll have a baby."

Pat takes a deep breath and bears down for all she is worth.

"That's it. That's it. That's it," he says. Patti gives one last great push. Suddenly there is a gush of fluid and a squirmy little pink bundle is in the doctor's hand. When he cuts the cord, he hands my daughter to me. "Be careful," he says. "She's a slippery little thing." I stand there holding Eileen, feeling her squirm against my chest, watching her swing her little fist back and forth. I never want to let her go, but her mother is anxiously awaiting her turn. I hand Eileen to Patti. Eileen snuggles right up to her, immediately gloms onto her right nipple, and starts sucking away.

"She knows exactly what to do," Patti says in amazement.

Seeing Patti comfortable and settled, I get a handful of quarters and go out to call the parents, brothers, sisters, aunts, uncles, and friends who have been waiting all day for news of the delivery. It is forty-five minutes later when I get back to Patti's room. Before I even get in the door I can tell something is wrong. Three doctors and two nurses are crowded around Patti's bed. One of the doctors is pushing down on Patti's belly with his right hand while his left hand is deep inside her, massaging the uterus, trying to get it to contract. The sheets are soaked with blood, and blood is pooling on the floor next to the bed. The IVs are running wide open, and one of the nurses is hanging another bag of Pitocin. Patti is still conscious, moaning each time the resident pushes on her abdomen.

It is clear what happened. The heparin has thinned her blood to the point where her body can no longer control the bleeding. Patti's pressure is dropping. Techs are shuttling back and forth drawing blood samples. I have participated in several life-and-death situations in my brief medical career. I handled them all well, but this is different. The woman I love is bleeding to death right in front of me. I can hardly stand. I catch her eye and she groans.

"Oh, Mike," Patti says in a thin little voice, "I'm so scared."

I squeeze by the doctors and nurses crowded around her and go up to the head of the bed. I try to hold her hand, but there is an IV in it. All I can do is squeeze her fingers and keep repeating that she is okay and everything is going to be fine.

It seems to take forever, but eventually they get the bleeding stopped. Her pressure stabilizes. Her heart rate comes back down. She is transferred from Labor and Delivery up to the ICU. Her vital signs are stable, but her hemoglobin has dropped nine grams. She is as pale as her sheets.

They let me stay with her for half an hour before they suggest that I leave for a while. I go down to the newborn nursery and ask the nurses if I can hold Eileen. They all know what is happening with Patti. They pull a rocking chair up to the side of Eileen's bassinet. She is wrapped up in a blanket, sound asleep, with just her little pink face peeping out. As I take my daughter in my arms, I pray that she will have a mother and I will have a wife when this night is over.

I spend the night at Patti's bedside. She is conscious part of the time, but the stress of the delivery and the voluminous blood loss have wiped her out. She barely has the strength to lift her head off the pillow.

"I'm glad you're here," she says to me about ten times that night. I can hardly trust myself to speak. I am too afraid I am going to lose her, too afraid that I will burst into tears and upset her even more. I just squeeze her hand and try to smile.

I scarcely leave her bedside for twenty-four hours. But by ten o'clock the next night the OB resident tells me I should go home. "The crisis has passed," he says. "Her vitals are stable. She's alert. Her uterus is back to normal size and there's only a trickle of bleeding. You haven't slept all night and you are going to have a lot to do when Patti goes home. You better get your rest while you can."

I go back into the ICU and tell Pat I am going to head home for a little while. She smiles and says that is a good idea.

"Isn't she beautiful?" she whispers, looking at Eileen, who is lying next to her. "Aren't we lucky people?"

It seems so unfair to all the other members of the human race who have been having babies for ten thousand years, but it turns out that Eileen is the most beautiful baby in the history of mankind. We don't want to rub everyone's face in it, but it is so obvious. My brothers, of course, are very supportive of this notion.

"Huh? Eileen? Yeah, sure, she looks fine," Tim says at the christening.

Jack is a little more enthusiastic. "Thank God she looks more like her mother," he says, poking Eileen's stomach.

Denny tries to put the whole thing in perspective. "What's the big deal?" he asks. "All babies look like Winston Churchill anyway. All Eileen needs is a cigar in her mouth and you could get her elected prime minister of England."

Father Fahey, the priest who married me and Patti, baptizes Eileen in the chapel at the medical center. Then we adjourn to our apartment, where my seven brothers, Patti's three brothers and three sisters, both sets of parents, twenty or thirty aunts and uncles, plus assorted cousins and friends, gather to celebrate our daughter's baptism. It is wall-to-wall people.

We name our baby Eileen after Patti's mother. All of a sudden my stock in the family goes up, way up. Maybe I am not such a doofus after all. Patti's mother even gives me a kiss.

Patti's sister Joanne and her husband, Jerry, are the godparents. Jerry gets up, turns down the Clancy Brothers on the record player, and gives a nice toast, telling us what a blessing it is to have Eileen in the family and assuring us of everyone's love and commitment to our daughter.

When they are gone, Patti is lying in bed nursing Eileen while I finish cleaning up. I'm not making much progress. There are cards and envelopes all over the place, and I can't help but stop and read each one. Each envelope contains a five, a ten, or even a twenty-dollar bill. Most of the cards are religious themed and are meant to respect the solemnity of the occasion. Many, especially those from my aunts, are accompanied by long, handwritten notes.

In our family, people don't say, "I love you," very often, so I am very touched by what my aunts have written. I am very grateful for the money, too, since Patti and I are so broke, but suddenly the money doesn't seem that important. I stand quietly, rereading the card from Aunt Fran. Until now I always took my family for granted. All those aunts and uncles and cousins. They have always been there, but now . . .

"Hey," Patti calls from the bedroom, "it's awfully quiet out there. What are you up to? I thought you were cleaning up. You didn't fall asleep, did you?"

I go into the bedroom and sit on the bed next to Patti. The only light is from the small lamp on her side of the bed. Patti is propped up in bed with several pillows. Eileen is nestled on her shoulder, asleep. Patti is cradling Eileen's head with her left hand and gently burping her with her right.

I slowly run my left hand through Patti's hair. "Eileen could have done a lot worse," I say.

Patti cocks her head and looks at me. "A lot worse than what?"

I shrug my shoulders. "Her parents have no money. Their car has no brakes. She lives in a one-bedroom apartment above an expressway and next to some train tracks. Her dad doesn't have much of a job, and her uncles think she looks like Winston Churchill."

Frannie's card is still in my hand. I lay it on the bed next to Patti and say again, "Eileen could have done a lot worse."

My foreman at CW likes how hard I work. He says I can come back whenever I get the chance. A week after Eileen is born I call him and arrange to work another night. It is a Sunday and I have the next day off. It is snowing like crazy as I pull into the parking lot. I grab my lunch and trudge through the snow to the dock. It is only 11:30 P.M. Dominic and the guys are up in the lunchroom playing cards. They are glad to see me.

"Where the hell you been, Doc? You get into that gynecology program yet? Give us the lowdown on all that snatch you been checkin' out."

I break it to them that I have decided not to go into gynecology. They shake their heads and wonder about all those wasted years of education. To make them feel better, I say that I am still considering a career in breast implantation. The smiles come back to their faces and Jimmy says, "That's more like it, Doc."

I pass Anton on the way to my load. He smiles and says, "Eat cheat, ezzole."

Unfortunately, I have a load from Neenah Foundry. It's all cast-iron stuff and most of it is too heavy to lift. This means I will need a lot of help from Stan, who is driving the forklift tonight. By 4:00 A.M. when lunchtime rolls around, the inside of my trailer is so thick with diesel fumes that it's hard to breathe. I feel dizzy every time I go in there. But that's good because it makes me forget how cold I am.

When we get off work at 8:00 A.M. I accept Dominic's invitation to go out for a few beers. It is quarter to nine when I pull up in front of the Tip Top Tap in Bridgeview. I trudge through the slush and snow into the tavern. Dominic, Jimmy, and several others are already seated at the bar with schooners in front of them. Dominic is peeling a hard-boiled egg. He looks up and waves me over.

I sit down and order a beer. It's been two and half years since I had a beer in the morning. We used to do it at Scalese all the time. Now it feels vaguely perverted. What if Dean Rich drives by and sees me guzzling beer at nine o'clock in the morning? He'll think I am unfit to practice medicine.

A couple cops who have just finished their shift come in. They must be regulars, since they greet Dominic and the others by name. "Meet the doc," Dominic says to the cops. We shake hands and one of them buys me a beer. Over the course of the next hour I have three or four beers and five bags of pretzels. By now it's almost ten. I buy a round for everyone, including the two cops, and say I'd better get going.

Dominic leans over to the cops and says, "Yeah, Doc's gotta get over to the hospital and do some brain surgery." He turns back to me. "Hey, Doc. How about a shot of Jim Beam just to steady the old hand, huh?"

One of the cops tells his partner to remind him never to have surgery at *that* hospital.

Jimmy and Anton are shooting pool over in the corner. I shout goodbye to them as I am walking out.

"See ya, Doc," Jimmy says.

Anton waves his cue stick. "Eed me, jegg-uff," he says.

With all the snow, it takes me an hour to get home. Patti is still in her slippers and bathrobe. When I get in the door she holds her finger to her lips and tells me not to make any noise because Eileen is sleeping.

When I kiss Patti, she smells my breath and steps back in horror. "Have you been *drinking*? At eleven o'clock in the morning?"

I feel like I am back in third grade trying to explain to Sister Geraldus why I brought the dead rat to school. "Well, hon, I—"

"You're practically a doctor," she says. "What kind of doctor goes out drinking first thing in the morning?"

"Pat, it's not really morning to me. I've been up all night and the guys—"

"Not really morning? It is totally and completely morning, and it has been for several hours."

"Yeah but the guys I work with—"

"Oh, now you're going to blame it on the guys you work with?"

"Pat, it's not that big a deal. I just had a couple beers after work, that's all."

Patti must have a touch of this post-partum depression thing. The least little bump in the road seems to upset her. But I don't blame her for being upset this time. We both have so many alcoholic relatives that our family trees are flammable. I tell her I'm sorry and it won't happen again.

When I tell my brothers about it the next day, they don't understand. "You didn't offer sacrifice to the porcelain idol. You didn't start singing 'Louie Louie.' You didn't have a lamp shade on your head. So what's the big deal?"

I explain that it just doesn't look good when you come home at eleven o'clock in the morning with beer on your breath.

"*That's* what she's upset about? That's nothing. Did you ever tell her about the time after the softball game when you and Murph—"

"That never happened."

"How about that time in college when you and Jay took the golf cart and—"

"That never happened, either."

My brothers shake their heads. "So, what, Patti thinks you were Saint Michael the Archangel before you met her?"

The concept of growing up has thus far eluded my brothers. They greatly admire me for things I am now vaguely ashamed of. They laugh at some of the antics I now find embarrassing. When I tell them I don't think that stuff is so funny anymore, they say, "Oh, excuse us, Mr. Model Citizen." They start calling me Victor Mature. They offer to pick up some stool softener and denture cream for me.

I laugh in spite of myself. If there is one thing the Collins boys know, it is how and where to stick the needle. No one was ever in danger of taking themselves too seriously in our house.

But what do my brothers expect? I *am* getting older. I'm married and have a baby. If you're still doing the same things at twenty-eight that you did at eighteen, there is something wrong with you. And besides that, I've been in medical school for two and a half years now and I don't suppose anyone could see the things medical students see without changing.

I try to explain this to my brothers. They listen seriously for a couple minutes; then Jack asks if any of my female patients has ever asked me for a slipadicktomy.

CHAPTER TWENTY-FOUR

I'm excited to start general surgery. We have some of the best trauma surgeons in the world at Loyola. Guys like Bob Freesson and Jack Winkleman, who cut their teeth down at Cook County Hospital back in the days when it was one of the premier trauma centers in the country. Their lectures are always exciting, always stimulating, always full of blood and guts and moving fast and thinking on your feet.

You play for big stakes when you do trauma. In other specialties you have time to contemplate choices, weigh evidence, and mull possibilities. You can go home and think about things, sleep on them, then reach a diagnosis and make a treatment plan. But in trauma everything is happening at once. Blood is pumping; people are crashing; pressures are dropping. Decisions need to be made *now*, often on the basis of insufficient evidence and unreliable histories. It is always easy the next day or the next week, when all the facts are known, to look back and criticize the way the guys on the front lines of trauma handled things. But, to their credit, Freesson and Winkleman never cut themselves any slack. They always insist that they and their residents make the right choice every time. They are tough on their residents, and on more than one occasion I've seen them ream the hell out of some poor guy who missed a finding on physical exam or failed to order the right lab test.

It is a bit intimidating for a medical student to get thrown into that kind of environment. Everyone knows you are less experienced and less knowledgeable than everyone else on the team. But to participate in the kinds of battles they do—and perhaps to win—there can be no more rewarding experience in medicine.

And there's one other thing about getting up on that stage. You are going to be either a hero or a bum. The opportunity to be an anonymous nobody in the back of the auditorium watching the whole performance is lost. You are in it this time, for better or worse, and you aren't going to be able to sit back and watch the whole thing unfold from the safety of your seat.

And, of course, you always wonder about yourself. You *think* you will be calm and cool in that kind of situation, but you don't know. What will happen when some guy is crashing and people are running around and the nurse is shouting out the vitals and the paramedic is shouting out the history and the intern can't get the ET tube in and you're trying to listen to the heart, feel the belly, and get a line in all at the same time? All you've got is a couple minutes, and if you are too flustered, too panicked, to figure out what's wrong and what needs to be done, your patient is toast.

And the very things that brought you into medicine in the first place—compassion and empathy and concern—these things do nothing but get in your way at those times. You can be paralyzed by your emotions. You don't need emotions at a time like that. You need to be a computer. You need, at least for a while, to not give a damn about the crying wife or the grieving children. They don't matter—at least not right now. Maybe it's their job to cry and wring their hands and look helpless. That's not your job. None of that stuff is going to help you save your patient. And if you really care about those other people, the ones who will be affected by this looming tragedy, then *now* is the time to help them. They don't need you to put your arm around them and look sad and tell them how bad you feel after their husband dies. Now, right now, while you have the chance, *they want you to save the son of a bitch*! And if you're too worried about the crying wife or the grieving children to think about needling the pericardial sac or burr-holing the skull or pumping the O-negative, then your "compassion" is a fraud.

·   ·   ·

You can't plan on emergencies. You can plan *for* them, and we do that all the time. We've had the ABCs of resuscitation drilled into us. First you secure the Airway; then you make sure he is Breathing; then you make sure he has Circulation. So we know *what* we are supposed to do; we just don't know *when* we will be required to do it. It's not like you can ask people to schedule their heart attack or their mugging or their car crash when it is convenient for you. ("Well, Mrs. Walsh, we have a four fifteen on Thursday. Would that work for you?") And when crunch time comes, it might be when you are in the middle of a routine gallbladder, or eating lunch, or two minutes before you are supposed to go home after being awake all night sewing up drunks. You might be fresh as a daisy or worn to bits. But it doesn't matter. None of it matters. You have a job to do and you damn well better do it regardless of whether you're tired or sick or depressed about your girlfriend.

Mr. Harkins has been complaining of back pain for a week. He's been on anti-inflammatories and hot packs and muscle relaxants and painkillers. He's been told to sleep curled up on his side in the fetal position, or on his back with a pillow behind his knees, or on the floor with a wooden pillow. He's had therapy and massage and acupuncture. He even snuck over to the chiropractor who jerked and manipulated and twisted him every which way but better.

His brother told him to quit complaining, we all have aches and pains. His wife told him she had something like this once and it just has to work itself out. His boss frowned and told him he'd missed enough work already. Finally, in desperation, he went to his local ER this morning. They IVed him and medicated him and X-rayed him and injected him and set him up for a myelogram next Tuesday.

When they discharged him, he came home, walked in the door, and promptly keeled over.

When the ambulance gets him to us, we don't know any of this. What we quickly *do* know is that he is hypotensive, tachycardic, and unresponsive. As Jimmy Crowley, the Chief Surgical Resident, likes to say, he is "circling the drain." We descend on him in a swarm. It's pretty obvious now that this guy has more than mechanical low-back pain.

Ten things need to be done at once. Dr. Carstens, the head of anesthesia, is here so he gets an ET tube in. Jimmy Crowley does a cut-down. Helen Henshaw, the intern, is working on an art line in the opposite wrist. Everyone is bumping against one another and shouting for things. "Hemostat!" "I need some retraction!" "Get some damn light in here!" "What's his pressure?" "Where the hell is X-ray?" "Get some blood down here. Now!"

I want to help, but I don't want to do the wrong thing or get in the way. I catch Jimmy Crowley's eye. "Foley?" I say, nodding at the guy's penis. Jimmy grunts his approval and I quickly glove up, tear open the Foley tray, swab the penis with Betadine, and slide in a catheter.

In five minutes Mr. Harkins has an ET tube down his throat, an IV in his forearm, an art line in his wrist, a cut-down in his elbow, a Foley in his bladder, and an NG tube in his stomach. He's been typed and crossed.

The guy is fifty-six years old. He comes into the ER crashing and burning, so my first thought is MI: the guy's having a heart attack. But from what I can see, his EKG looks fine. Now what? I wonder how in the hell we are going to find out what's wrong with this guy. It's not like we have all day to find out. He's alive, but just barely, and it's obvious he doesn't have much time left. While I am wondering what else could be the problem, the head nurse comes back with a report from the wife that the guy has been complaining of back pain for a week. I start wondering what that has to do with anything, but by this time Jimmy Crowley has already noticed that the guy's abdomen is distended and that he has no femoral pulses.

"Shit," Jimmy says, "ruptured triple A. Gotta be. Call the OR and let's get this guy upstairs."

Triple A: an abdominal aortic aneurysm. God, I should have thought of that. I've never seen one, but I've read about them. The big artery coming out of the heart has been ripping itself apart for the last week and now has burst. The heart is fine. It's still trying to pump blood to the rest of the body, but the vessel that is supposed to carry that blood has torn open. A little blood may still be getting through, but this is a guy who has only minutes to live if something isn't done.

Some O-negative blood arrives and the nurses quickly hang it. Helen Henshaw squeezes one bag to force it in quicker. Jimmy Crowley grabs the bag from her, wraps a blood pressure cuff around it, and pumps it up to 300. Blood is now roaring into our patient through the big cut-down in his elbow. But we all know that as fast as it is going in the arm it is coming out the hole in the aorta.

After putting in the Foley I haven't had much to do. I want to do something, so I push through the crowd to the head of the bed, where I can see that the bag of blood is starting to slip out of the blood pressure cuff. I squeeze the bottom of the bag to keep it from sliding out of the cuff.

With the art line in we can tell that the guy is still maintaining a pressure, even though it is awfully low. His heart is beating, so he doesn't need CPR, but Dr. Freesson, who has just arrived, says, "Goddamn it, if we don't get this guy up to surgery soon and cross-clamp that aorta he won't need CPR; he'll need RIP."

The next ten minutes are filled with screaming and shouting, surgeons bellowing orders and roaring threats. *This* isn't good enough or *that* isn't fast enough, and "where the hell is that amp of bicarb?" And "how many times do I have to ask for a simple goddamn hemostat?" And "why aren't those gases back yet?" The residents are yelling at the interns; the interns are yelling at the nurses. I come in for my share of abuse, too: "What idiot taped this Foley so close to the femoral artery?"

Finally we start heading for the elevator, fifteen white-coated, blood-spattered medical personnel surrounding a chrome cart. Everyone is bumping against everyone else. Nurses and techs are trying to keep IV poles and monitors and oxygen tanks upright. Helen Henshaw is trotting alongside the cart, holding the cap of a needle between her teeth, trying to draw another set of gases from the art line. The elevator door opens and the cart is shoved in. Everyone is yelling at everyone else to slow down or back off or get out of the way or make room. Frantic arms are reaching for tottering IV poles and monitors. We don't all fit in the elevator, so I sprint up the stairs and am waiting when the elevator gets there. I trot behind them as the entourage lurches down the hall and disappears into the OR.

I don't get to scrub in on this one. There are plenty of surgeons, residents, and interns who want to scrub in on a triple A, and no one's going to let a medical student take his place. I get to watch, but it's hard to see what's going on. The first ten minutes are a flurry of gowning up and splashing Betadine and slashing open the belly. And then there is blood everywhere, gushing in waves over the side of the belly, flowing down the front of the surgeons' gowns, and dripping onto their shoes. Dr. Freesson's presence is a blessing. He's been here before, and his coolness rubs off on the residents, who soon stop shouting for everything. He issues his orders in clipped, staccato fashion, and within two minutes of opening the belly he has cross-clamped the aorta. You can almost see everyone's shoulders sag in relief. If you can get a guy with a ruptured aorta into the OR and cross-clamp him before he exsanguinates, you're halfway home.

The operation takes another several hours. The excitement gives way to routine. The guy maintains a good pressure. His heart keeps beating away, and slowly the surgeons suture their graft in place.

So we saved the guy. Well, *they* saved the guy. All I did was shove a tube up his wiener, and I'm not sure that counts as part of the saving.

When you rupture your aorta there are a lot of bad things that can happen besides death. Your brain can be deprived of oxygen and you become a vegetable. You can throw clots and one of your legs might have to be amputated. Your kidneys can quit working—for a day or forever.

Our patient has none of these things. He recovers. One hundred percent. But his wife and his brother (the ones who told him to suck it up and quit complaining) can't leave it at that. They say Mr. Harkins almost died and someone must be responsible. The fact that Mr. Harkins is fifty-six years old, is seventy-five pounds overweight, lives on New York strips and chocolate sundaes, and smokes like a fish (that is *not* a mixed metaphor.

This is Chicago, remember? Even the fish have bad habits) doesn't seem to matter. Someone is at fault. Someone must be sued.

We're all off the hook. We're the heroes. We're the guys on the white horses who rode in and saved Dodge City. It's the guys who saw him in the week before his rupture that are in trouble: the family doc, the other ER doc, the chiropractor, the therapist, the masseuse—I don't know, maybe even the cabdriver who took him there—they're all sweating bullets.

There is no doubt that if the family doc diagnosed this problem seven days earlier, Mr. Harkins might not have come so close to death. But on the other hand, the family doc and the ER doc and all the others are only human. They are doing the best they can. Statistically less than one-tenth of 1 percent of back pain turns out to be related to an aortic aneurysm. It's not always that easy to diagnose. Most family docs go through their entire lives without ever seeing *one*.

I wish I had more faith in the legal system. I wish I could believe that guilty parties would be punished and innocent parties would be absolved. But the legal system, when it comes to medicine, seems more like a cottage industry set up to enrich lawyers. If the guy's family doc was drunk or truly negligent, then, yeah, sue his ass and nail him for all he's worth. But if the guy was doing his best and just didn't get the right answer . . . well, I'm sorry, but it happens every day in every walk of life. Are you going to sue me every time I make a wrong turn in the cab? Are you going to sue the Clancy Brothers every time they hit a wrong note in their concerts?

Mr. Harkins leaves the hospital a week later. Vertical. He walks out, thanking everyone and leaving a couple boxes of chocolates for the nurses. I'm not certain he remembers who I am, but he shakes my hand and tells me thanks. I feel pretty good about that. I mean, how many times are you going to shove a six-inch tube up a guy's johnson and have him tell you "thanks" afterward?

In the coming months there are subpoenas and depositions and disclosures and hearings and motions *in limine* and *res ipsa loquitor* and *post hoc ergo propter hoc* and *arma virumque cano* and *pog ma thon* and I don't know what all. Dr. Freesson says it will probably be years before the case comes to trial.

As far as Mr. Harkins is concerned, the whole thing might never have happened: he is back to smoking a pack a day and wolfing down his New York strips. As far as the lawyers are concerned, it's a shame Mr. Harkins didn't die: the case would be worth a lot more if he did.

I try not to let the legal groveling detract from the wonder of what we accomplished: we saved a guy who should have died—and I got to be a small part of it. It's an incredible feeling, and I can't believe that I'm going to get to do stuff like this for the rest of my life.

I think back to that scalding-hot day four years ago when I was throwing rocks on Johnny Battaglia's breakout gang and we all damn near killed ourselves in the heat. That's when Jesse first put the idea in my head to do something else. I think about Jesse a lot. I see him lying there in the dirt, tongue out, panting slowly. "I'm tellin' you God's own truth," he said to me.

God's own truth . . . Maybe it was, but I sure couldn't see it until Jesse rammed it down my throat. If it weren't for Jesse, I wouldn't be in medical school now. But why did he bother with me? Why did he go out of his way to kick some, as he would say, "dumb-ass white boy" in the butt and get him going?

I'm not sure, but I think the answer is all tied up with the reason I want to be a doctor. Guys like Jesse, and guys like Joe Higgins, who got me two jobs when I really needed them, and guys like my Uncle Jack, who is lending me money to get through med school, they just do nice things. They don't have to. Nobody makes them. They do it because it's in them—and I'd like to think that someday it will be in me, too.

CHAPTER TWENTY-FIVE

For the rest of my medical school career I work several nights a month on the docks. The company is good about it, and I often get to work more than eight hours since they don't have to pay me overtime. This job is a godsend and I know it.

My shift starts at midnight. Officially I am done at eight. Sometimes I can work longer, but sometimes I have to leave earlier in order to be at the hospital for rounds at seven. It's hard getting used to working at the hospital all day, then on the docks all night, then back at the hospital the next day. I really drag by the end of that second day. But I know I'd better get used to it. Residents do stuff like this all the time—and in five months I will be a resident.

The question is, *where* will I be a resident? You can't just graduate from medical school, hang up your diploma, and start practicing. You have to spend several more years doing a residency. *Then* you can go out into practice.

I am very tempted to stay at Loyola. I like Chicago. Patti and I have lots of ties here. But we both feel it might be good to go away—at least for a while. Our families are loving and devoted and caring, and there's no sense kidding ourselves: we would have had an even tougher time these last few years if it weren't for them. We have dinner once a week at Patti's parents' house and once a week at my parents' house. Each time we do, our mothers send us home with enough leftovers for another meal. But our families can also be a little overpowering: second-guessing every move, offering advice on every decision. Patti and I think it might be best to strike out on our own.

Despite our longing for grand adventure, we have no particular interest in going to the East or West Coast, so I look at programs in Milwaukee, Indianapolis, Ann Arbor, Iowa City, and even Rochester, home of the Mayo Clinic.

It is a bit of a stretch to think that Mayo would consider me. You have to have pretty impressive credentials to get a residency there. I wasn't all that impressive in my first-year basic science classes. But since we got out in the wards, I have excelled. Overall I have a fairly strong academic record, but the Mayo Clinic is, well, the Mayo Clinic. Nevertheless, I decide to apply there. Who knows, maybe they have a soft spot for dockworkers and rock throwers.

On February 17 we are invited to my parents' house to celebrate my dad's birthday. My mom is planning on having a small dinner, but as usual, things get out of hand, and pretty soon all my aunts and uncles and cousins are invited, too. An hour before dinner, Patti finds a quiet place up in one of the bedrooms to nurse Eileen. My little cousin Molly, who is six, is fascinated by this whole baby thing. She follows Patti upstairs and watches her unbutton her blouse.

"Why are you doing that, Patti?" she asks.

"It's time for Eileen to eat, honey," Patti explains.

Molly nods and watches as Patti unflaps her nursing bra and lifts her breast for Eileen.

At this point Molly's eyes bug out of her head. She steps back, points a trembling finger at Patti's breast, and says, "Eileen's gonna eat *that*!?"

.   .   .

If I don't get some money soon, none of us is going to have anything to eat. We were barely scraping by before Eileen was born, but we quickly find that babies need stuff. They need clothes and diapers and car seats and teddy bears and mobiles. These added expenses have put us into financial free fall. Everything I earned on the docks over Christmas is gone. Everything Eileen got for her christening is gone. Everything in our savings is gone. All of a sudden the basic necessities of life, food, shelter, and clothing become a lot more pressing.

I've called CW, but things are slow on the docks. They won't have any work for me for a couple weeks. I can always drive the cab, but that doesn't pay as well. I am thrilled, therefore, when Fred calls and says they could use me at Scalese. It's only for a day, but one day's work on construction is enough to buy food for a month.

The problem is that Scalese works during the day, not the night. I am a medical student on an infectious disease service. I can't just take off whenever I feel like it. Guys who take off whenever they feel like it often find themselves in a condition commonly referred to as "flunking your ass right out of here." I can afford to have a lot of things happen to my ass, but flunking is not one of them.

I'm going to have to ask my resident for help. This is asking a lot and I know it. Med students are generally a pain in the butt for residents. We don't know much and we are always asking questions. The only reason we are tolerated is because we do all the lousy jobs that no one else wants to do: starting IVs, trimming toenail fungus, removing fecal impactions, and irrigating colostomies.

John Holden is my resident. I call him that night and explain to him that infectious disease is really important to me—but so are food and shelter, and if I don't get some money pretty soon, Patti and I are going to have to move into the Student Lounge and live off bags of normal saline and discarded Snickers bars. I tell him it would only be for one day. I promise him it will never happen again.

John is a good guy. I have worked hard for him. He knows I am not trying to BS him. When I finish telling him my predicament, he actually treats me like a human being instead of a vacuum cleaner. He says, "Okay, do what you need to do. I'll cover for you."

The sun doesn't rise at this time of year until 6:30, but Fred wants us at the yard by 6. I am on call the night before, but Cathy Conroy, who is doing endocrine, comes in and covers the last two hours for me so I can get to work on time. Unfortunately, I only manage one hour of sleep. I am sitting in the furnace room eating an apple when JT bangs open the door at 5:45.

"*Damn*, it's cold out," he says, stamping the snow off his boots. He sees me sitting in the corner, shakes his head, and says, "I see married life ain't hurt your appetite none."

By six o'clock there are eight of us sitting there. Fred comes down and tells us it's time to start working for the church. He tells us to load up 22 and 28 with hoses, picks, jackhammers, and bits. We hook compressors to the back of each truck and head east on the Eisenhower.

It is just after seven when we get to the job site. The street is empty, the buildings abandoned, so I pull 22 right up onto the sidewalk. The street we are working on is directly under the Dan Ryan Expressway. Sixty feet above us, we can hear the dull hum of traffic and the deep *kaboom* of semis bouncing over the expansion joints. Deserted factories line the street to the east. A couple of boarded-up apartment buildings and a dingy flop-house face them on the west side of the street. With the buildings on either side of us and the concrete roof of the expressway above us, it feels like we are in a cave.

Nobody tells us why this work has to be done in February when it is ten degrees outside. Johnny Battaglia tells us this is a rush job and he doesn't want any bullshit. Everything has to be finished today. It is still half-dark under the Dan Ryan, but Johnny says to get our butts in gear. The hoses are stiff and we have to fight to uncoil them. The jackhammer, the bits, and the metal rails of the truck are all so cold it hurts our hands just to touch them.

I thought I was ready for this. I have long underwear, a flannel shirt, a sweatshirt, overalls, a woolen cap, and a jacket. I have so many clothes on I feel like the Pillsbury Doughboy. But the wind, roaring off the lake, funnels through the gaps in the deserted factories, whips around the massive concrete abutments, and rips right through me.

At 7:30, when JT fires up the compressor and lets loose with the jackhammer, the sound bounces off the buildings around us and the expressway above us. It's like working inside an echo chamber. There are no coffee trucks at this time of the year, so we work straight through to lunch at 12:30. I am wearing two pairs of gloves, but the concrete hunks JT breaks out are so cold there is no way to keep my hands warm. Steel-toed boots may be great for protecting toes, but they suck the cold out of the ground. When we break for lunch, JT and I sit in the cab of 22, the heater roaring full blast, but all that does is bring the feeling back into my toes and let me know again how cold they are. I am dying for coffee, tea, cocoa, soup, anything hot, but all I have is my water bottle, in which a thin layer of ice has formed across the top.

We go back to work at one. I jump up and down, flap my arms across my chest, blow through my gloves on my fingers, anything to stay warm. Finally at three Johnny pulls up with tall white Styrofoam cups of coffee and a dozen donuts. For the first time in my life I reach for the coffee before the donuts. The eight of us huddle behind 22, trying to get out of the wind. We hunch forward, holding the coffee against our chests in two hands. Although still steaming in the frigid air, the coffee is no longer boiling hot. There are no tentative sips here; we gulp it down in greedy mouthfuls, wishing we could make it last but unwilling to let its heat dissipate anywhere but inside our stomachs.

The buildings on either side of us and the expressway above us keep the sun's warmth from us. The only sun we get all day is at four o'clock when a thin shaft of sunlight sneaks between the roof of the flophouse and the Dan Ryan above us. The sliver of light, sharp as a laser, cuts through the dust and particles in the air and disappears into the top of an open Dumpster.

The sun sets at five thirty. By six it is so dark under the Ryan that we can hardly see. Johnny says tough shit: "I told you guys we gotta wrap this up today." Angelo and I swing the two trucks around so the headlights are pointed at the section we are breaking out. JT and Jurgis continue to blast away at the curb. Finally, around six thirty we finish the last section. Then we hustle back and forth in the dark, coiling hoses, loading picks, closing up the generators.

I started 22 as soon as we broke out the last section. By the time we finish loading the truck and head for the yard, the cab is warm and toasty. But we're at Independence Boulevard before I finally stop shivering.

JT and Melvin are in the cab with me. JT sits in the middle, straddling the gearshift lever and the emergency brake. His yellow hard hat is on his lap. In it he has placed his worn cotton gloves and his hammer. His right hand is draped over the emergency brake. His left hand is resting on his helmet to keep his hammer and gloves from bouncing out. Melvin is in shotgun. His hard hat is on the floor, wedged between his boots. The ashtray has two or three butts in it, plus a couple dozen nails that rattle and jiggle as we bounce along. Occasionally a nail will bounce out and fall on the floor with the rest of the junk.

Now that work is over, I am having a hard time keeping my eyes open. I've only had one hour's sleep in the last thirty-seven. Fortunately for me, traffic is terrible. I get in the far right lane and find myself nodding off for five or ten seconds at a time in the stop-and-go traffic. Every time traffic stops, I close my eyes. Ahead of me, an endless stream of red lights winds its way westward. For twenty minutes I never take the truck out of first. I just ride the clutch and inch along with everyone else.

Around Laramie it starts to snow—big flakes drifting slowly over Columbus Park, blurring the lights from Loretto Hospital. By the time we get back to the yard, gas the truck, unhook the compressor, dump the rocks, and park the truck in the burlap shed, it is eight o'clock. With the snow, it takes me another forty-five minutes to do the five miles home. I grab the mail from our box and trudge up the stairs. Patti is waiting at the door when I get there. She has Eileen in her arms.

"Oh," she says when she sees me, "you're a mess."

"Just another hard day in the wonderful world of medicine," I tell her. I step forward to give her a kiss. She backs up slightly to be sure that no part of my body touches her except my lips. She looks at my filthy clothes and frowns.

"Maybe you should get undressed on the back porch," she says.

I raise my eyebrows. "What have you got in mind?" I ask. "Aren't you afraid the neighbors would see us?"

"Believe me," Patti says, "what I have in mind no neighbor would be interested in watching."

Twenty minutes later I am freshly showered and sitting at the kitchen table, a huge mug of tea in front of me.

"You could have shaved," Patti says, setting a bowl of tuna casserole between us.

I hardly hear her. A fierce battle between hunger and exhaustion is waging inside me. As usual, hunger wins out. After working all day in the deep freeze, I am starving, absolutely starving—and tuna casserole is one of my favorite dinners. I try not to stare, but my eyes widen, my jaw drops, and saliva starts leaking from the corner of my mouth.

"Look at you," Patti says. "You look like Shannon getting ready to devour a mailman sandwich."

I shovel down an obscene amount of tuna casserole while desperately trying to listen to what Patti is saying about her mother's bunions. I manage to stay awake long enough to help with the dishes. Patti leaves me for a minute to get Eileen, who is fussing in the other room. When Patti returns, I am slumped over in my chair, head on my chest and arms dangling at my side. She touches me on the shoulder, and my entire body jerks, my head snaps up, and I shout, "Huh?"

Patti says I should go to bed.

"I can't," I say, struggling to my feet. "I have to read that chapter in Schwartz on hematogenous osteomyelitis."

"I hope it's a six-word chapter," Patti says.

An hour later I am asleep on the couch, Schwartz's book on my chest. "Come on, sweetheart," Patti says, taking my hand and pulling me to my feet. "It's time for me to put my two babies to bed."

I don't argue this time. By the time Patti comes out of the bathroom, my clothes are in a pile at the side of the bed and I am under the covers, lying on my side, sound asleep but with my right arm stretched forward onto Patti's pillow waiting for her to scoot in underneath it.

CHAPTER TWENTY-SIX

Patti and I spend a lot of time and burn a lot of nervous energy talking about where I might wind up doing my residency. This discussion is actually a waste of time, because applying for residency isn't the same as applying to college, where you might get accepted at five schools and then you pick which one you want. For residency, all applications go into a big pile, some computer analyzes everything, and each med student winds up being accepted at only one place. You go there, or you go nowhere. So at this point everything is out of my hands. We just have to wait for Match Day to find out where we will be going. I am still hoping the Mayo Clinic will consider me, but my advisor tells me, nicely, not to hold my breath.

In March I get my first taste of orthopedic surgery. I am assigned to pediatric orthopedics with Dr. Warren Black, the chairman of the department of orthopedics at Loyola. Dr. Black does most of his surgery at Hinsdale Hospital, a community hospital about five miles west of Loyola. I vaguely know Hinsdale. It is a wealthy western suburb founded a hundred years ago by assorted bank presidents, real estate moguls, financiers, yachtsmen, polo players, and foxhunters. The only Irishmen who ever set foot in the town were the ones who built the railroad. Over the years, however, the town has become more egalitarian. There have even been reports of people walking around downtown Hinsdale without riding crops and jodhpurs.

On my first day, I drive down the tree-lined streets and park my car in the garage across the street from the hospital. I go to the doctors' lounge, where I meet Dr. Black and the ortho resident, Jim Bishop, with whom I will be working for the next six weeks. After making rounds, we head to the locker room, don our scrubs, and troop into the OR. I am by now well used to the medical student's role in the OR, which is "hold this and shut up."

After a couple weeks I find myself enjoying this rotation immensely. The orthopedic surgeons, orthopods as they are commonly known, are a fun bunch to work with. They are more personable than both general surgeons and neurosurgeons. Orthopods tend to take themselves less seriously. Maybe this is because everyone else in medicine takes them less seriously, too. Ortho is generally considered the least prestigious of the surgical specialties. Orthopedics is thought to require neither the finesse of the neurosurgeon, the nerve of the general surgeon, nor the sensitivity of the gynecological surgeon.

I find orthopods to be just plain folks, lacking the pretension of the other surgical specialists. Neurosurgeons are the architects who arrive on the construction site in their BMWs, attired in tailored suits, being careful not to get dirt on their immaculately polished Italian shoes. They speak only to one another, and only about things like the coefficient of friction of calcium carbonate. Orthopods, on the other hand, are the carpenters who stumble out of their dented pickup trucks, tool belts slung over their shoulders, slurping coffee, trading insults with the ironworkers, and talking about how the refs screwed the Blackhawks last night. I like the orthopods. I feel right at home with them.

Kathleen Lang is twelve years old. She has been admitted to Dr. Black's service for spine surgery. I like Kathleen. She is a cute kid. Kathleen likes me, too. She can tell right away that I'm not your basic full-fledged, industrial-strength surgeon. I'm just a student. This somehow helps her to identify with me.

"You're not even a doctor!" she says in amazement the day before surgery.

"That's right," I say. "I'm just a medical student."

"Then how come everyone calls you *Doctor* Collins?"

"Tradition, I guess. But you can call me Mike if you want."

She likes that. When other people are around she calls me Dr. Collins, but when it is just the two of us she calls me Mike.

Kathleen is not thrilled about having surgery. She isn't thrilled about having scoliosis, either, but it is easy to ignore scoliosis. None of the kids at school can even tell she has it unless she is in a bathing suit. Kathleen says her parents wouldn't even know she had it if her pediatrician hadn't told them.

Dr. Black originally prescribed a brace for her, but Kathleen refused to wear it. In her mind it fairly screamed to the world that she was, in her words, "some kind of hideous freak."

Since she didn't wear the brace, her deformity progressed. At that point Dr. Black recommended surgery. "Without it," he told Kathleen's parents, "there is a significant chance her deformity will increase. It could even progress to the point where she would have respiratory problems later in life."

Kathleen digs in her heels. She doesn't care about later life. She cares about now. She refuses the surgery. When her parents ask her if she wants to grow up with a crooked spine like Quasimodo, she says she doesn't care. She just wants everyone to leave her alone. Her parents argue and cajole and bribe her, all to no avail. She says no. In the end, however, her parents say yes, and unfortunately for Kathleen, her parents have the final say.

I feel sorry for Kathleen, but I think her parents are doing the right thing. The fact that their child doesn't agree, that their child will forever hold it against them if anything goes wrong, makes it that much more difficult for them.

Kathleen refuses to speak to her parents for several days prior to the operation. But finally, as they are taking her down to the OR on the morning of surgery, she breaks down and sobs into her mother's arms, begging her to cancel the operation. Her mother is in tears, too, but shakes her head and says she is so sorry, but Kathleen has to have the surgery.

In the holding area before surgery, the anesthesiologist gives Kathleen something to calm her down. She is awake but heavily sedated when we get her into the OR. She looks at me out of blurry eyes and mumbles that she wants to go home. I smile and tell her everything is going to be fine. Once she is asleep, we flip her over onto the operating table and prep her from her shoulders to her thighs.

Dr. Black comes in and makes a two-foot-long incision in her back. Over the course of the next four hours we chew off her spinous processes, chop up parts of her iliac crest, stuff bone graft alongside her vertebral column, and hook in two steel rods to straighten her crooked spine.

It is the most bloody, brutal operation I have ever seen. I feel like I should be down on the South Side working in a slaughterhouse. "Stormy, husky, brawling . . . Hog butcher for the world." Old Carl Sandburg would feel right at home in this Chicago OR.

I am with Dr. Black when he speaks to the parents after the operation.

"It went quite well," Dr. Black tells them. "We achieved a nice correction. Of course, the next few days are going to be a little difficult for Kathleen, but we'll be watching her closely."

By this time I have a firm understanding of medical-speak. When a surgeon says, "The next few days are going to be a little difficult for you," that means you are going to feel like a cement truck just backed over you—twice.

Kathleen's parents nod their heads politely and thank Dr. Black for backing the cement truck over their daughter. It is fortunate for Dr. Black that Kathleen does not have any weapons of mass destruction immediately at hand when she wakes up from her surgery; otherwise things might have been "a little difficult" for Dr. Black.

It takes Kathleen a long time to wake up. She's had an awful lot of anesthetic. As she slowly struggles back to consciousness, the pain over-whelms her. Her arms are pinned down to the cart and she has a mask over her face, but she thrashes and moans with pain.

Pain management in the recovery room is handled by the anesthesiologists, not the surgeons. It takes them a while, but the anesthesiologists finally get her pain under control by giving her more and more drugs until she is gorked out. When they wheel her out of the recovery room two hours later, she has tubes coming out her mouth, her nose, her bladder, her spine, and her hip. She has tubes going into or attached to her arm, her chest, her finger, and her leg.

"A lot of things can go wrong after spine surgery," Jim explains to me as we change out of our scrubs and back into our street clothes. "Besides the obvious stuff like paralysis or nerve damage, there is urinary retention, ileus, pneumonia, wound infection, failure of fixation, nonunion, electrolyte imbalance, hemorrhage. You name it, it can happen after spine surgery. But Black doesn't want *any* of it to happen to his patients. That's why you and I have to watch this kid like a hawk. We can't let anything get by us."

I'm not with Kathleen in the recovery room when she comes out of the anesthetic, but when I see her in her room later that day I can tell she feels I have betrayed her. There was a tacit understanding between us that I would make sure the operation went well, that I would be there for her, that I would keep the pain down. When she wakes in the recovery room in the throes of a torment she never imagined, she feels I failed her.

She needs transfusions and electrolytes and plasma and morphine and oxygen and antibiotics and muscle relaxants, but finally, after a few days, she slowly starts returning to normal.

But, for Kathleen, surgery is only Step One.

We call it The Rack. It is a stainless-steel frame upon which we place unfortunate young girls who have had spinal fusions. The rods we insert and the bone grafts we apply are not strong enough to withstand the stress of motion, so all patients who have spine fusions also get body casts. The Rack holds them in position while we apply the cast.

Four days after her spinal fusion, we wheel Kathleen down to the basement of the hospital. We lift her onto The Rack and wrap roll upon roll of plaster from her neck to her pelvis until we have encased her in plaster.

Poor Kathleen. She just started being able to eat solid food, to urinate without a catheter, to breathe without an oxygen mask, and now we have entombed her in an ugly white shell that screams to the world that this fragile girl is different, is flawed. It feeds into every adolescent insecurity to which a young girl finds herself prey.

Since bathing in the cast is out of the question, within a few days Kathleen begins to accumulate various body odors. Wiping herself is difficult, and to make matters worse, she gets her first period. The poor thing can't even see where she is bleeding from. Her mother can't get her to understand that all this is normal, that it has nothing to do with her surgery, that it happens to all women, and that she is not a freak.

The nurses are great. They sit with her. They tell her stories of their own misadventures with periods, getting her to laugh and to find security in the secrets women tell one another. When I make rounds I often interrupt their laughter. The room falls silent and the three women in the room exchange glances, saying little until I am gone.

I find the best thing I can do for Kathleen is help her understand that all this will pass, that it doesn't make her any different from the other kids, and that after the initial curiosity wears off they will treat her much the same as they did before her surgery.

But Kathleen isn't buying it. In the past week she has felt betrayed by her surgeon, by her parents, and by the medical student she thought she could trust. She has been forced to have a terribly painful operation that she feels she didn't need and now she has been wrapped in a body cast that makes her feel like "some freakish mummy."

I try to cheer Kathleen up, but she won't talk to me or any other doctor. She refuses to get out of bed except when the therapists make her.

Otherwise she just lies there with her face turned away. She doesn't watch TV. She barely eats.

This goes on for about three days. Finally Dr. Black has seen enough. He pulls up a chair next to Kathleen's bed. He asks her if she would like him to go back in and pull out the rods.

Her parents gasp, but this gets Kathleen's attention. She doesn't say anything, but she turns to face him.

Dr. Black goes on to calmly explain that if he pulls out the rods he will still have to put her back in a cast, but this time for six months instead of six weeks. He says her deformity will return and she will likely have severe pain for the rest of her life. But he says he'll be happy to do it if that's what she wants.

Kathleen glares at him and says through gritted teeth, "I hate you."

Dr. Black just shrugs as though being hated is not that big a deal. He tells her to think about it and let him know her decision in the morning. "We could get you back on the schedule on, oh . . . Thursday," he tells her. But he says if she decides not to go through with the reoperation, then she is going to have to start cooperating with her rehab.

When we come in the next morning, Kathleen is already sitting up in her chair. She says she doesn't want her rods removed.

Dr. Black smiles and says, "Good choice."

When we finish rounds I say to Dr. Black, "You wouldn't really have taken her rods out, would you?"

He smiles and says, "You'll never know."

A couple days later Kathleen is finally receiving visitors. When I make afternoon rounds she has two friends with her. But the friends are sitting on the edges of their chairs gazing alternately out the window and at each other. They avoid looking at Kathleen, who is lying on her back staring at the ceiling. No one is speaking.

"Kathleen," I say with a smile, "are these friends of yours?"

Kathleen doesn't reply.

I look at her visitors. "Girls . . . ?"

"Yes," one of them says. "We, um, go to school together."

"It's nice of you to visit Kathleen," I tell them.

The two girls look quickly at each other and then at the floor.

First one girl rises, then the other. "Well," the first one says, "we should, uh, go."

"Oh, no," I say. "You don't have to leave. I'll only be a second."

But the girls have grabbed their purses and are already at the door. "Bye, Kathleen," one of them says. "We'll see you later."

Kathleen continues to stare at the ceiling. She says nothing. The girls look at each other, then turn and leave.

When they're gone, I tell Kathleen that her friends seem nice. When she doesn't respond I loop my stethoscope around my neck and sit on the foot of her bed, wishing I knew more about what to say to young girls.

"Kathleen, I know this whole thing hasn't been much fun for you."

This at least draws a response. Her eyes, filled with disdain, flit from the ceiling to mine and then back again.

I try again. "This isn't going to go on forever," I tell her. "The pain is getting better, isn't it?"

No response.

"The cast is only for another five weeks."

I can see her teeth clench, but she keeps staring at the ceiling. I guess when you're twelve, five weeks seems like five years.

"Kathleen, I know this probably seems like the worst thing that ever happened to you, but the worst is over. You have a cast for a while, a brace for a while, and then you're done. Forever. And you'll have a straight spine."

I tell her she has to try to get over this. I tell her there is a light at the end of this tunnel. I tell her she should be grateful for the support of her parents and friends. I tell her not to make a bad situation worse by having a bad attitude. But none of it gets through. I am the enemy and I have been tuned out.

.   .   .

Kathleen goes home two days later. I never see her again. My last memory of her is helping her into the wheelchair as she is being discharged. She never once looks at me or speaks to me. I never find out how Kathleen did, whether she overcame the ignominy of wearing the body cast for six weeks and eventually became a happy, well-adjusted young woman, or whether she wallowed in anger and self-pity until she became calloused and bitter, driving away even those few friends who tried to remain loyal to her.

We often do outcome studies in orthopedics. This is a way to track the success of our procedures and to help us improve the care we deliver. I don't know if Kathleen's case ever found its way into any outcome study, but if it did, the damage we did to her psyche and the toll the procedure took on her mental health won't even figure in the equation. As long as the spine stays straight she will be counted as a success in the medical literature.

CHAPTER TWENTY-SEVEN

I t's hard to believe, but in a few more months I will be a doctor. I will write "M.D." after my name. At times it seems I know so little, and yet I realize I am already better trained than most doctors in previous generations. I would be scared to death to do it—but in a pinch, I could remove someone's appendix. In a pinch, I could do a tracheotomy. And I could deliver a baby and run a code and manage diabetic ketoacidosis.

But there are so many gaps in my education. I know how to do an emergency burr hole for someone with a head injury, but I don't have a clue how to remove a toenail. I can put in art lines and chest tubes, but I have never taken out a tonsil. I can do a spinal tap on a newborn but wouldn't have a prayer of doing a colonoscopy on an adult.

Match Day is held every March. This is the day when senior medical students all over the country find out where they will do their residencies. At Loyola we all gather in The Pub, some of us affecting a blasé attitude, some of us nervous and tense. Patti is with me, although I have a hard time getting to talk to her. She is part mother, part big sister, and part girlfriend to half the guys in my class. They all love her. She knows where everyone wants to go. She knows the pros and cons. She knows the ins and outs. Heck, she has listened to the stories and the concerns and the dreams of almost all my friends. I have been trying to pretend that this is just another day, that it is no big deal, but I don't fool Patti. She knows where I have my heart set on going.

When it is announced that we will be going to Mayo, Patti throws her arms around me, congratulates me, and tells me she's thrilled to be going back to Rochester. I am grinning from ear to ear. I accept Mayo's offer immediately in case a mistake has been made and they want to change their minds.

A few days later I call my old high school friend John Devlahan, who finished Creighton med school four years ago and is now doing a cardiology fellowship at Mayo.

"Hey, Dev, guess what? I just got accepted up at Mayo. Any chance Patti, Eileen, and I could move in with you and Jane? It'd only be for five years."

Dev politely suggests I consider other options. "How about a cardboard box under a bridge?" he asks.

His wife, Jane, is more sympathetic. "Let me check the *Fellows Newsletter*," she says. "They always have a list of homes for sale."

A week later Jane is on the phone. "I've got the perfect house for you," she says. "It's right down the street from us." She gives us the number of Bob and Sherry Keane. Bob is finishing an oncology fellowship at Mayo and is joining a group in Maryland. I phone Bob that night, and he describes the house for us. Patti likes the sound of it, so we decide to drive up the next weekend to look at it.

The Keanes' house is a one-story rambler with a fenced-in backyard. It has a swing set and a rhubarb patch. It's perfect. Unfortunately, Bob is not an eccentric millionaire who wants to *give* his house away. He wants to *sell* it. In fact, he wants $57,000 for it.

We have $107.44 in the bank. That leaves $56,892.56 to go. I eventually negotiate Bob down to $53,000, and I get Northwestern Bank of Rochester to agree to a loan with 10 percent instead of 20 percent down, but where are Patti and I going to get $5,300? I'm working nights on the truck dock just to buy food and pay the rent each month.

I try to come up with an idea of where to get some money. There's always my mom. Maybe if she gave up drinking *and* dessert *and* TV for ten
years, God would . . . Nah, I couldn't do that to her.

I'm just about ready to call Bob Keane and tell him there's no way
when my father, who is not a wealthy man, shows up at our apartment the
next Saturday morning.

"Here," he says, handing me a folded slip of paper, "take this."

It's a check for $5,000. I look at the check and then back at my dad.

"Uh," is all I can think of saying. Collins men are not given to effusive displays of affection to anyone, especially not to one another. "Dad,
I—"

"Just shut up and take the check."

Burns women *are* given to effusive displays of affection. That's why I
married one. Patti wipes away her tears and gives my dad a big hug and
kiss. "Oh, thank you, thank you, thank you," she says.

"This is a loan," I tell my dad. "I'm going to pay back every cent of it."

"When you can," my dad says with a shrug. "The only thing I ask is
that you do the same for one of your brothers when the time comes."

Ten minutes later I'm on the phone, first to the bank, then to Bob
Keane. Patti and I sign the contract a week later. And, just like that, we
are home owners.

On April 12 I begin a clerkship in pediatric surgery at Children's Memorial Hospital. I have been assigned to the service of Dr. James Pomeroy, one
of the nation's most renowned pediatric surgeons. I like peds and I like
general surgery. This rotation seems perfect for me.

Children's Memorial is way on the other side of town, so I have to get
up at five every morning. This is when Eileen gets up, too. Patti and I hear
her in the crib next to us as she begins her morning ritual of squirming and
squeaking. I reach over and pick her up, nuzzling my chin into her neck
and kissing her. But at this hour of the morning Eileen is not interested in
her father. What she wants, nature has not equipped me to deliver. Eileen's
mouth is open and her neck straining like a little bird as I hand her to Patti,

who is by now sitting up in bed, having stuffed a couple pillows behind her. Patti and I talk quietly as I dress and she nurses our baby.

The drive from our apartment in Forest Park to Children's Memorial at Fullerton and Halsted takes about forty minutes at that time of day. There aren't many cars heading north on Lake Shore Drive at six o'clock in the morning. I drift north straddling two worlds: To my right, the vast open surface of Lake Michigan stretches east where the sun is just slipping over the horizon. To my left, rows of silent steel buildings, their tops glowing in the first rays of the rising sun, tower over me.

Children's Memorial has no parking for med students, but I get to the hospital around the time when the neighborhood residents are leaving for work, so I always find a place to park.

Children's Memorial is not a Loyola-affiliated hospital. The residents and fellows are all from Northwestern. This means I have two strikes against me right off the bat: I am not from Northwestern, and I am not a doctor. Within an hour I know exactly where I fit in: at the bottom. This isn't all bad, though. It's nice not having to worry about the pecking order. It's all laid out for me: I am the peckee. They are the peckers.

Working with Dr. Pomeroy turns out to be a worthwhile, but very different, experience. Like a lot of big-shot academics, Dr. Pomeroy has a ravenous ego that requires constant feeding. When he makes hospital rounds, he is like a rock star traveling with his peeps. He maintains a full complement of fellows, residents, students, nurses, therapists, and social workers who trail respectfully behind him. I half-expect to see a makeup artist, a PR guy, and a stenographer with a tight skirt and six-inch stiletto heels there, too. All he needs is a few scribes and Pharisees to complete the picture.

Dr. Pomeroy has several fawning residents and fellows whose primary purpose appears to be to pay him homage. They spend most of their time either courting Pomeroy's favor or cowering from his wrath. There is something about all this sycophancy that rubs me the wrong way. I resolve not to be part of it, but at the same time I am intrigued by the whole thing. These guys are about the same age I am. Where, I wonder, is their self-respect? They seem like little children competing to be teacher's pet. All this bootlicking and brownnosing—is this what residents here have to do to get ahead? I'd rather throw rocks.

Dr. Pomeroy's only contact with me that first day is to ask me some technical question about where to make the incision when doing open heart surgery on a neonate. It's a question he knows I could never answer. He just wants to make sure I know that around here he is king and I am peasant. Point made.

My day consists of following Dr. Pomeroy around: always on rounds, sometimes in the OR. I do not go to clinic with him. I remain in the hospital with the residents. There are so many interns and residents on Pomeroy's service that I am given no clinical responsibility. I don't take call. I don't admit patients. I don't start IVs. This is the first time since I started on the wards last year that I am simply an observer, not a provider, of medical care. I don't do a damn thing. All I have to do is learn—and there is a lot to learn.

Dr. Pomeroy and I develop an unusual relationship. He very quickly sees that I am not going to scrape and bow to him like his residents do. Our exchanges in the OR take on a pattern. Dr. Pomeroy attempts to em-barrass Collins by showing everyone how dumb he is. The problem is that Collins won't play along. I make it clear that when a surgeon who has been in practice for thirty years tries to make himself look good by making a medical student look bad it is the questioner, not the questioned, who should be embarrassed.

We are doing a thoracotomy on a sixteen-month-old when Dr. Pomeroy, without looking up, says, "Describe for us, Collins, the microvascularity of the embryonic thymus."

To which I immediately reply, "I am not familiar with the microvascu-larity of the embryonic thymus, sir, but I'm sure you are."

"Of course I am," Pomeroy says. "Don't they teach medical students anything at Loyola?"

"Yes, sir. They do."

He slams the hemostat back on the Mayo stand and says, "Collins, you might just be the dumbest medical student I have ever had."

"I would ask you, sir, to consider the possibility that your annoyance is leading you to speak in hyperbole."

At first Pomeroy is irritated that I remain composed despite everything he throws at me—not that I *ever* know the answer to anything he asks me, but I always act as though it really isn't that big a deal that the medical student isn't as knowledgeable as the surgeon.

On the other hand, I'm not here to cause trouble. I know my place. I keep my mouth shut. I am never rude or disruptive. Since I clearly acknowledge my inferiority to him, since I remain respectful (if not awed), Pomeroy tolerates my presence and goes back to abusing the residents, who depend on him for a good evaluation. He enjoys watching them squirm and sweat and grovel before him.

Once, after a particularly vicious skewering of one of the residents, Pomeroy concludes his sadistic diatribe by saying, "I think even *Collins* could have answered that question."

"Sir," I answer quietly, "for the first time in your life, I believe you may be mistaken."

Pomeroy's reputation is such that he is deluged with cases, not just the exotic, once-in-a-lifetime cases but the routine stuff as well. Unfortunately, Pomeroy is never content with the knowledge that by sending a patient to him the referring doctor is acknowledging Pomeroy's superior ability.

Pomeroy's behavior when a new patient comes in is always the same. He starts by making fun of the doctor who referred the case to him, blatantly misstating the facts in order to make the referring doctor look like an idiot and Dr. Pomeroy look like Obi-Wan Kenobi or Hipppocrates or something.

I learn a lot while I am on Pomeroy's service—not that I ever get to touch a scalpel or do anything in the OR. My job is to hold retractors and act as the straight man: "No, sir, I don't know the diameter of the inferior descending branch of the lymphohepaticosplenojejunal artery."

Despite his ego, despite his sick personality, Pomeroy is an excellent diagnostician. He has the ability to cut through all the smoke and figure out precisely what the problem is. And once he gets the patient to the OR Pomeroy is a surgical genius. I know it before the week is out. I might not pick him for Mr. Congeniality, but the man can cut. It is fun to watch him, flawed as he is, when he is in his element. When he gets that scalpel in his hand he becomes a Michelangelo. He has an uncanny knack for knowing where the bleeders are, and just how far to cut, and in which plane to dissect. I have been in enough ORs to know true genius when I see it.

"Sir, whatever else might be said about you," I tell him in the locker room one afternoon after a particularly impressive case, "you are an amazing surgeon."

My comment is more than a little ironic, but Pomeroy doesn't take it that way. He looks at me in genuine surprise, as though someone has just told him that ice is cold or grass is green. He knows I'm not brownnosing him, since my previous attitude has made it painfully obvious that we are never going to be BFFs.

"Collins," he says, "you have an instinctive grasp of the obvious."

I hold my tongue and let him have the last word. I don't think he is capable of understanding that my remark was not meant entirely as a compliment.

I have been on Pomeroy's service for two weeks when I notice there is a patient on our list whom we never see on rounds and never discuss at morning conference: Edward Grolling. To make it even more perplexing, he is in the ICU.

One afternoon I ask Joe Duvoisen, the resident, "Who is this Edward Grolling?"

Joe shrugs. "Haven't you ever noticed him? He's that kid in the corner of the ICU. We pass him every day."

I remember him now. He is a baby, a very sick-looking baby. "Is he one of our patients?" I ask.

"Technically."

"Technically? What does that mean? The kid is a patient in the ICU, he's our patient, and we never round on him or do anything for him?"

"Mike, the kid's a veg."

Joe's words are too strong for me. A veg is a vegetable, someone with no functioning human brain. Perhaps in years to come I will become calloused enough to refer to a sick baby as a veg, but I hope not.

"Joe, how can you say that? He's a little baby."

Joe shrugs again. "You can call him what you want. The kid choked on a peanut and was anoxic for several minutes before his parents noticed. They got him to the ER just in time to get the worst possible result: a living body and a dead brain. If you want to call him a little baby, go ahead, but for all intents and purposes, the kid is dead. And he's not coming back. Not today. Not tomorrow. Not ever."

I ask Joe how long the child has been in the ICU.

"Beats me. He's been here ever since I started the service, and that was a month ago."

Joe sees the look on my face and says, "Mike, wake up, will you? Yes, a terrible thing happened, *but it happened.* And it's permanent. And no one can fix it. I've been watching you and I'm telling you that you gotta stop thinking like a kid. You're always acting like we are fairy godmothers granting wishes, and that if we wave our magic wands everything is going to be fine and everyone is going to be well.

"I hate to tell you this, but that's not the world I've seen. I've seen amputations and stabbings and rapes and cancer and death—but I haven't seen any magic wands. You gotta come out of that dreamworld you are living in. You can't keep on pretending that Lassie and Timmy will always make it home, and that Mom is always going to bake an apple pie, and that everything is always going to be fine. Hell, even this kid's *parents* don't visit him anymore. *He's a veg!* Get over it."

I have to see this little baby. After rounds the next morning I go back upstairs. The baby is lying on his back on a warming table in the far corner of the ICU. As usual, he is all by himself. He looks so tiny, so sick. His paper-thin skin is scarred and discolored from all his IVs and needlesticks. His bony ribs flare with each hiss of the respirator. His eyes are closed, but he seems to be gagging slightly on the tube in his mouth. A plastic bag is dripping yellow fluid into the IV in his right foot.

I run a finger slowly over his emaciated little forearm, wondering if he can tell someone is near but then realizing how terrible it is if he can. He is alone and ignored 99 percent of the time. The only time he gets attention is when someone has to do something painful to him: start an IV, draw blood, or suck out his lungs.

I have seen some terrible things since I started medical school, but this is the worst. Nobody knows what to do with poor little Edward. He's a sick baby abandoned by both his parents and his doctors.

When I go back downstairs, I tell Joe that I don't think it is right to keep neglecting this little baby. Joe tells me to stop being so holier-than-thou: "If you want to go around and start making a fuss with nurses and parents and social workers by telling them they are coldhearted bastards for neglecting a sick little baby, go ahead. But you better ask yourself who you are treating—the kid, or yourself?"

I can't help letting some things affect me. I can't help taking some things home with me. When I go home that night I hold Eileen in a way I never held her before. I swear I will never forsake her if something terrible happens. I pour my heart out to Patti, telling her all my frustration and horror and guilt. I go to bed praying for this poor little kid rotting away in the ICU.

I realize that Joe Duvoisen is right about me. I want happy endings. I went into medicine because I had a dream. I want to make things better. I believe that one person can make a difference. The problem is learning how to accommodate my idealism with reality. One person can't make a difference *every* time. One person can't make *everything* better. But just because I can't save everyone doesn't mean I can't save anyone.

But I'm starting to see that the very act of trying exacts a terrible psychic cost. It's hard to pour yourself into a struggle, *lose* that struggle, and still come out emotionally unbloodied. Maybe that's one of the things we have to learn in medical school: how to become pragmatic without becoming cynical.

But I can't get Edward Grolling out of my mind. If I take Joe's advice and ignore this child, it means I have accepted something I don't want to accept. It seems an abandonment of my principles. If you love enough, if you care enough, if you try enough, shouldn't you be able to overcome the obstacles life puts in your way? If I ignore this child, am I not acknowledging that there are some fights better left unfought, some dreams better left undreamed?

Yes, I finally admit to myself, *I am.*

And it is at that point I acquiesce. I accept the judgment of people who know more than I. I accept that Edward Grolling died a few months ago. I accept that there is a body on the fourth floor of Children's Memorial Hospital with a bunch of tubes sticking in it and that body once housed the child who was Edward Grolling. I accept that young Edward is gone. And finally, for the first time, I accept that Lassie and Timmy aren't coming home and Mom isn't going to bake any more apple pies.

CHAPTER TWENTY-EIGHT

I'm getting tired of people telling me they can't understand it, Rex has always been such a good dog. He never bit anyone before. They just can't believe this happened.

I like dogs. But I like kids more, and I am really getting sick of seeing five- and six-year-old kids come into the ER with their lip torn off or their cheek shredded by some dog whose owner is always more upset that Rex might be in trouble than that their dog has just scarred a child for life. I have been working in the Resurrection Hospital ER a couple nights a week for the last few months and have seen a ton of dog bites.

More often than not it is a German shepherd. I have nothing against German shepherds. Heck, Rin-Tin-Tin was one. But I am beginning to think German shepherds have some primordial gene that makes them aggressive. Don't tell me that Rex never growled, never snapped, never barked at anyone before. Maybe he never growled, snapped, or barked at his owners, so they find it easy to ignore his behavior. After all, they aren't the ones at risk for having a chunk taken out of them. The signs were there. The owners just chose to ignore them. But wouldn't you think if there was just the slightest chance your dog might bite, you would keep it away from children?

This time I am really furious. Our patient is the sweetest little thing: Becky, a six-year-old who was visiting Aunt and Uncle Somebody. Becky wasn't in the door fifteen seconds when their dog lunged at her and ripped half her left cheek off. Aunt Somebody has come to the ER with Becky and I want to strangle her. She never once expresses any concern for Becky. All that comes out of her mouth are things like, "There is something wrong here. Poor little Rex never does things like this. Rebecca must have provoked him."

The aunt is provoking *me*. Becky is lying on the cart with her cheek hanging off her face like a hunk of baloney, and Aunt Somebody only seems interested in finding a way to blame the child for what *her* dog has done.

There is no such thing as a good laceration, but some cuts are better than others. Knife cuts or razor cuts, for example, usually have nice sharp edges that are easily approximated. Dog bites, on the other hand, are bad cuts. Besides the increased risk of infection, the bite doesn't just cut the skin; it *tears* it. The edges are jagged. Small pieces of skin may be missing. Even the world's greatest plastic surgeon won't be able to prevent a scar.

One of the Loyola residents, Frank Madden, moonlights in the Resurrection Hospital ER. I worked with Frank earlier in the year on Tentler's neurology service, and he was good about letting me do things. He told me about his moonlighting and said if I come to the ER on the nights he is working he will let me get some hands-on experience. I won't be paid, but I'll learn a lot.

The first laceration I ever sew up is in the Resurrection Hospital ER. It is on a construction worker with a deep cut on the back of his calf. Frank shows me how to clean and irrigate the wound and how to infiltrate the local anesthetic. He puts in a couple deep sutures and then leaves me to close the skin. It is a fairly simple laceration, about four inches long, with nice sharp edges.

Fortunately, the patient is lying on his stomach and thus unable to see how nervous his "surgeon" is. One of the nurses stays with me while I put in the first stitch or two; then she leaves. Everything feels strange and awkward. I have on sterile gloves and there is a sterile field around the incision, but I have to make sure I don't let the needle or any of my instruments touch anything unsterile.

On top of that, I'm not used to the needle holder. I don't have the knack Frank does of slipping the needle in one side of the laceration and twisting it out the other. He flicks his wrist, ties the suture with a couple twists of his hand, and is done.

I, on the other hand, have to think about where to put the needle in, how to let go of it and regrasp it in the middle of the wound and then try to bring it out the other side. The needle keeps slipping out of the needle holder; the forceps doesn't seem to want to grab the needle when it comes through the skin. And every time I finish tying my clumsy knot, I have to lay down the forceps and pick up the scissors to cut the suture.

Frank comes to check on me half an hour later. I am just about done.

"What have you been doing back here?" he asks with a laugh. "If you take much longer, that wound is going to heal itself."

He bends closer, looks at the repair, and then pats me on the shoulder. "Nice job," he says. Then he goes up to the head of the table. "Looks good, Benny," he tells the patient. "We'll have you out of here in a few minutes."

I put in the last stitch, then carefully dress the wound. I am immensely proud of myself. I can't stop smiling. I feel like I just performed the world's first heart transplant. Frank says I look like I just hit the Trifecta at Arlington. But I can't help it. I have actually stitched someone up. It's a big step, and it almost makes me feel like a real doctor.

I am always aggressive about trying to do things in the ER—and Frank is good about accommodating me. I look in babies' ears until I can tell what an infected ear looks like. I get to tape a few ankles, cast a few wrists, remove a few splinters. Once he even lets me snare a fish bone out of a throat. When he sees that I am reasonably competent, Frank lets me do some bigger stuff. I do a couple nonemergency cut-downs. He shows me how to put in a chest tube.

I've been working at Res for about a month when an ambulance brings in a sixty-year-old guy with a heart attack. He is basically D.O.A., but we do all the usual things to resuscitate him. They don't work. Finally, Frank calls the code.

I am helping the nurses clean up when Frank asks me if I've ever put in a subclavian line.

"No," I reply.

He tells the nurse to get a subclavian kit.

"But he's *dead*," the nurse says, pointing at the patient.

"I know he's dead," Frank says. "Now go get the goddamn kit!" I am surprised by the anger in his voice.

The nurse is back in two minutes with the subclavian kit. Frank tears it open. "You got a problem with this?" he snarls at the nurse.

The nurse says nothing. She, no less than I, is startled by Frank's ferocity. He is usually such a laid-back guy.

"This guy's dead," Frank says, pointing at the corpse. "But the next one won't be. And maybe the next one will be your father or my father. And maybe he will die if Collins doesn't know how to put in a subclavian."

Frank grabs a syringe with a large needle attached to it. "Here," he says, slapping the syringe into my hand, "take this." Then he practically jerks me into position at the patient's right side. "Do you know the landmarks for the subclavian vein?"

I tell him I do.

"Then get going. Angle the needle about thirty degrees and push through until you feel it pop into the vein."

Intimidated not just by the novelty of the procedure but also by Frank's manner, I hesitate. "Go on!" he snaps. "What are you waiting for?"

What I am waiting for is that I haven't gotten used to the fact that the object in front of me is no longer a patient but a body. His right eye is still half-open, staring blankly at the ceiling. I am almost afraid that I am going to hurt him. But of course I can't hurt him, because he's dead.

But just because he's dead doesn't mean he has no rights—does it? I feel like I am violating him, that I am *using* him, and that I have no right to use him. Shouldn't we ask the family for permission? But Frank is standing there glaring at me, and Frank is the boss.

I take a deep breath and feel for the spot below the clavicle. I slowly push the needle through the skin.

"Keep going. Keep going," Frank says impatiently.

I feel the needle enter the vein and immediately get blood return.

"Hold it!" he says. "You're in. Now you've gotta hold that needle perfectly still and unscrew the syringe."

As I do this, dark, almost black blood begins oozing from the needle and dripping down the patient's chest into his armpit.

"Never mind the blood," Frank says. "You've gotta thread the catheter through the needle."

Ten seconds later I am done.

"That's it," Frank says. "Now you've put in a subclavian. Don't forget how to do it. It may save a patient's life someday." He glares at me and the nurse and stomps away.

I look apologetically at the nurse, feeling that I have been the cause of all this ruckus. "Sorry," I say. "I didn't mean to cause any trouble."

"It's okay," she says. "You just have to get used to him. He's a very good doctor, but he always gets this way when someone dies. He takes it personally."

I know Frank isn't going to let me sew up Becky's face. It's way too difficult for a medical student and I know it, but Frank talks me through it as he goes along. He tells me what kind of skin cleanser to use. He tells me what kind of suture to use. He shows me the "corner stitch" that helps approximate jagged edges. He discusses how long to leave the stitches in and the perils of removing them too early or too late.

And, every couple minutes, he interrupts his instructions to say a few words to Becky, assuring her that everything is going well, telling her it won't be too much longer, telling her she is a brave girl to be holding so still. Becky's face is covered by our blue, sterile towels. Her monosyllabic, frightened little responses come muffled from deep under the sheets.

After Frank speaks to Becky for the third or fourth time, I start to realize what is going on. I have been so focused on the cheek that I forgot there is a little girl attached to it. Our *problem* may be the cheek, but our *patient* is Becky Matheson. Repairing the laceration is just one of the ways Frank is treating his patient. I am impressed, not just by Frank's competence but also by his compassion. I want to be like that when I am a doctor.

When the repair is done, it looks okay—just okay. I don't say anything to Frank, but I am disappointed. I was hoping that, for Becky's sake, we could make everything perfect. But then it occurs to me that I am thinking like a patient, not a doctor. Most patients believe they have a *right* to a perfect result. If the result is not perfect, it must be the doctor's fault. Maybe that's why there are so many malpractice suits.

When I think back to what Becky's face looked like when she came in, I realize that Frank has done a wonderful job. There is only so much that can be done with a cheek that looked like hamburger meat when he started. Becky's cheek is already starting to swell and Frank tells her parents how critical it is to keep the swelling down—otherwise the scar will spread. He gives them some ointment and some antibiotics.

The aunt is still flitting around, muttering nonsense about poor little Rex all alone back home. She says that she hopes Becky has learned her lesson about teasing dogs. That's when Frank snaps. He spins around and sticks his finger in the woman's face.

"Lady," he says, "it used to be that when a dog bit a little child, it would be put down. I wish to God we still did that. But don't you think for a minute I am going to let this go. I'm going to report this matter to the police, and if I find out that your goddamn dog ever bites another child I'll come over and kill the fucking thing myself."

Frank shouldn't have talked that way. Doctors aren't supposed to lose their cool. The lady is on the phone to the hospital administrators the next day, complaining that they have a rude, out-of-control doctor working in their ER. Frank is called on the carpet. He gets in a boatload of trouble. Maybe, just maybe, an attending physician could get away with talking to someone like that, but not a moonlighting resident. Frank is told that if it ever happens again, he will be fired.

I tell Frank if it ever happens again to call me. "Hell," I say, "I'll go over to the lady's house and shoot the dog with you."

CHAPTER TWENTY-NINE

B y the time I meet her, she is sixty years old but looks eighty. She is a skeleton over which a thin layer of yellow skin is tightly stretched. She can't weigh much more than seventy-five pounds. Her name is Mary, but except for the ID sticker at the bottom of each page, her name is never mentioned in her chart. Her name doesn't matter. The first sentence in her History and Physical says it all. She is an "elderly, cachectic, demented, in-continent" woman. For medical purposes she has been described and de-fined.

Three years ago she was a healthy 140-pound interior designer, with a husband and two daughters, ages twenty-eight and thirty. She goes into her doctor's office for her annual checkup. Her doctor runs some tests. Then he tells her something is wrong and she has to have a biopsy. It is a week before the surgeon can get Mary on the schedule for the biopsy. It is another four days before the pathologists render their diagnosis.

Sixteen days after she first walked into his office, her doctor calls her to tell her she has cancer, a particularly bad cancer. Mary is stunned. Sure, she was aware of that little lump in her breast, but it wasn't painful. It didn't seem to be growing.

When the doctor tells her she has cancer, she asks what can be done.

She wants a cure. Her doctor tells her she has Stage IV adenocarcinoma of the breast and there is no cure. There is treatment, and treatment will help, but there is no cure. It takes a while, but Mary finally accepts this. So she modifies her request. If she can't be cured, she wants something as close to a cure as possible. She wants longevity and she wants quality—as much as possible of both.

Mary then sets her foot on a road that leads to places she could never have imagined. I have no doubt that it all began with good intentions, that it all made perfect sense. First, let's get rid of as much cancer as we can. Fine. That seems reasonable. So she has a radical mastectomy and axillary node dissection. This leaves her with psychic and physical scars, as well as a permanently swollen and mildly painful left arm, but a whole lot of the cancer is now gone—and that's good.

The surgeons tell her that, as expected, they couldn't get rid of *all* the cancer. The oncologists say they aren't likely to get rid of all the cancer, either, but they are certain that with radiation and chemotherapy they can get rid of some more of it. Fine. That seems reasonable. So she has radiation and chemotherapy. Her hair falls out. She vomits for six months. She gets a terrible infection in her lung because her white count drops so low that she can't fight off predatory bacteria. But after another month in the isolation unit of the ICU, she is cured of the infection.

Mary is now almost a year out from her diagnosis. There is no question that she has some good days. There is also no question that without the surgery and chemotherapy she would be dead by now. So, she's alive and she has some good days—but she has paid a price for it.

Things go pretty well for a few more months. Then she notices some pain in her hip. She ignores it for a couple weeks, then finally tells her oncologist about it. He gets a scan and tells her the cancer has spread to her femur and her shoulder blade. The oncologist says they can treat the shoulder blade with radiation, but that she needs to see an orthopedic surgeon about her femur.

The orthopedic surgeon says her femur has been seriously weakened by the cancer. He says he'd better stick a rod down her femur or it will break. Fine. That seems reasonable. She has the radiation on her shoulder blade, gets the rod put down her femur, and goes home two weeks later.

Things go pretty well for another couple months, when she notices her belly is swollen. She ignores it for a couple weeks, then finally tells her oncologist about it. He gets a scan and tells her the cancer has spread to her liver. He says she needs to go back to see the general surgeon who did her mastectomy. The general surgeon says there is nothing he can do. There is too much cancer in the liver for him to operate. She goes back to the oncologist, who says more radiation should be able to kill some of the cancer cells. Fine. That seems reasonable. She has more radiation and the swelling in her belly goes down a little.

Things go well for another couple months, when her husband notices that she is saying peculiar things and is forgetting the names of common household items. He ignores it for a couple weeks, then finally tells her oncologist about it. The oncologist gets a scan and tells them the cancer has spread to her brain. He says there is no surgery for that, but that more radiation should be able to kill some of the cancer cells. Fine. That seems reasonable. Since Mary is so confused, they keep her in the hospital for two weeks. She has ten more sessions of radiation, and her mental status improves noticeably.

When she is leaving the hospital, she coughs and gets a terrible pain in her back. She can't ignore this. They bring her down to X-ray and find she has a broken vertebra. She is readmitted to the hospital. Her oncologist gets a scan and says the cancer has spread to her back, her ribs, and her ileum.

The orthopedic surgeon is called back in. He orders a brace for her back but says she "is not a candidate" for any more surgery. He says maybe radiation will help. The radiation oncologist is called back in. He says she has already had more radiation than she should have, but he'll do what he can and maybe he will be able to kill some of the cancer cells. Fine. That seems reasonable.

While she is having radiation to her spine, she gets another infection. A month later she is able to leave the hospital, but this time in a wheelchair. Her weight is down to one hundred pounds. Her oncologist suggests a special dietary supplement. She tries it, but it makes her vomit.

She is now two and a half years out from her diagnosis. There aren't many good days left now. But her definition of good has changed. Compared to what her life was like three years ago, she has *no* good days. Compared to what lies ahead, maybe they aren't so bad. When she is lucid, she spends a lot of time thinking about what lies ahead.

Her family can't leave her alone anymore. She is too weak to get to the bathroom by herself, and she often forgets where she is and who her children and husband are. She is in constant pain and is on morphine. Someone has to be with her twenty-four hours a day. Her daughters take turns staying with her during the day. Her husband insists that he can handle the nights by himself, but his daughters notice how worn and beaten he looks.

Suddenly things don't seem so fine. They don't seem so reasonable. Somewhere, somehow, things have gone awry. Three years ago she asked for treatment. She asked for help. Now she is in a wheelchair. She can't walk; she often can't think. She is in constant pain. She is defecating in her bed, draining pus on her daughter's couch, vomiting in her friend's car. When did she ask for that?

She asked for a few more months of life. She has been given a few more months of death. She asked that we leave her some small amount of dignity. Instead we find ourselves holding a leash with which we are dragging some pain-wracked, incontinent lump of humanity into and out of hospitals for yet one more round of treatment.

But it all began with such good intentions.

I only know Mary for the last three hours of her life, when her weary family brings her into the ER because she is having difficulty breathing. Her husband and daughters are bleary-eyed and dragging. There is still tenderness in the way they look at and touch Mary, but when they sink into the chairs at the side of Mary's bed it is obvious they are running on empty.

It is hard to know precisely what to do for Mary. There is no mistaking the huge red *Do Not Resuscitate* sticker on the front of her chart. But all that tells me is that we aren't going to do any extraordinary measures. We aren't going to shock her. We aren't going to code her. We aren't going to intubate her. But what *are* we going to do for her?

"We're going to try to make her as comfortable as possible," John King, the ER resident, tells me. He starts an IV and gives her some pain meds. He wavers but then decides to have the nurses put some nasal prongs on her and give her a little oxygen.

Mary doesn't regain consciousness, but she seems to breathe a little easier. I stand at the foot of her bed, flipping through her chart. Her chart tells me she is an elderly, cachectic, demented, incontinent woman—as if those four adjectives somehow diminish the noun they modify. Well, I don't want to hear that shit. Forget that she is elderly. Forget that she is cachectic. Forget that she is demented. Forget that she is incontinent. She is a woman, a human being, and her dignity does not depend on how old she is, how robust she is, how smart she is, or how continent she is.

But it is hard to see it that way. Her family, no less than I, no less than the rest of society, tends to see illness as diminishing humanity. We behave as though our dignity is dependent on our health. But we are *all* ill. Every minute of every day, we are *all* dying. Whom are we trying to kid when we refuse to acknowledge that one of our fellow human beings is dying? From what are we trying to hide when we string pejorative adjectives onto our dying patients' names?

Mary slips away a couple hours later. It is hard to know the precise moment when she is gone. Her husband and daughters and sons-in-law are all there, and they help one another through the ordeal. Tears are shed; hands are held; hugs are shared. I stand in the corner of the room, recording the time of death, doing the paperwork, taking it all in.

I can't do anything about the first entry in the chart, but I make damn sure about the last entry. I don't say "the patient." I don't say "this elderly, cachectic, demented, incontinent woman." I say "Mary." I say: "In the emergency room of the Loyola University Medical Center, surrounded by her family, Mary expired peacefully at 4:27 P.M."

CHAPTER THIRTY

I am standing at the window of our apartment looking down on the Eisenhower Expressway. Below me, a steady stream of lights flows slowly out of the city. I am staring off to the west, where a faint smudge of orange still lingers. In twenty-four hours I will graduate from medical school. I will start writing "M.D." after my name. Tomorrow night some- one is going to take a picture of me and Cathy Conroy and Jack Brennan and Brian Clark and the rest of our classmates. They are going to hang that picture on the wall next to the pictures of all those other classes of serious-looking young doctors.

I keep wondering how it all happened. Despite two years of pre-med and three years of medical school, despite all the long nights on call and the long days studying, despite the white coat and stethoscope, I still feel alien. I still feel I don't really belong. I turn and look at Patti, who is sitting on the couch rocking Eileen to sleep. Patti smiles up at me and makes a shushing sound with her lips, warning me not to speak for a minute or two.

I smile at Patti and go back to staring out the window. How can this wonderful woman be married to me? How can this beautiful baby really be mine? Five years ago I was a socially awkward, drifting kid, working construction by day and driving a cab by night. I had no idea what I wanted to do with my life. I hadn't met Patti, and I was afraid I never would. I had yet to ask myself life's great questions. I had yet to ask myself *any* questions.

I have gone from a boozing, bruising laborer on a breakout gang to a husband, father, and doctor in five years. I know it took a lot of dedication and hard work, yet I hardly feel responsible for, or worthy of, *any* of it. I feel like I have been dropped, undeserving, into a life I always dreamed of having. I'm not at all sure I have been the architect of my fate. Sometimes I think I have merely been the beneficiary of it.

Scalese Construction, Blue Cab, O'Dea's Pub, softball, hockey—all those things that comprised such a big part of my life back then are no longer a part of it at all. I have a tendency to look back on those days and to assume my life was misdirected, to assume I was marching along on the road to perdition, until I reached a critical point, my own personal epiphany. Then, realizing the error of my ways, I righted the ship, turned my life around, and lived happily ever after.

But what if I had been headed in the right direction all the time? What if rather than diminishing my life, throwing rocks and driving cabs and loading trucks actually enhanced it? What if I am a better, not a lesser, person for having done those things?

Patti is amused when I talk like this. She says it is simple. She says I was a little boy back then, doing little-boy things. Like Saint Paul, when I became a man I put away the things of a child. But I'm not so sure. Sometimes I wonder if the things of a child might be more purposeful and more utilitarian than we think. Sometimes I think the things of a child are what put us on the road to becoming better adults.

Our time as medical students is coming to an end. Jack Brennan, Brian Clark, and Cathy Conroy are all staying here at Loyola. Jack and Brian are going into general surgery. Cathy is going into ophthalmology. Dog was accepted into medical school last year and will be graduating a couple years behind us.

Not for the first time, I realize how little each of us matters in the grand scheme of things. We behave as though our existence is so incredibly important, as though things could never be the same without us, as though our departure will occasion tremors and aftershocks that will reverberate through the ages.

I somehow feel, with typical childish egocentrism, that Loyola is important because it is the place where I go to med school. The reality is that Loyola is the place where *four hundred* people go to med school, where *one hundred* professors teach, where *two thousand* employees work, and where *eight hundred* sick people are hospitalized. Mike Collins' arrival and Mike Collins' departure aren't even blips on the Loyola radar screen. Somehow Loyola will muddle through the catastrophe of my graduation. Somehow they will buck up and go on without me.

My parents throw a party for me and Patti. Since we are leaving for Minnesota two weeks from now, the party is as much a lament for our imminent departure as it is a celebration of my graduation. Just like they did two summers ago for our wedding, all our aunts and uncles, all our cousins and friends, cram into *my* parents' house this time.

Three kegs of Old Style in galvanized steel buckets are buried under mounds of ice in the garage. Tim has set up a makeshift bar in the backyard. He is always the bartender at family parties because he is the only one who knows how to make Rob Roys, Presbyterians, and all those whiskey drinks my seventy- and eighty-year-old aunts are so fond of.

None of my brothers will admit who dyed Shannon green. Nor will they admit who keeps filling her bowl with beer. Joe Muldooney says he always loves coming to our house. "Where else can you see a cross-eyed green dog who walks into walls?" My mom says whoever did such a thing to a poor animal is sick. Denny tells her to relax: "In a few hours, Shannon won't be the only cross-eyed thing walking into walls."

Uncle Sam is already loosened up. He picks up his Scotch and gives us "Danny Boy." When the applause dies down, my brother Bill, who is eleven, plucks Uncle Sam's sleeve and asks what he is drinking.

Sam holds his glass up to the light, gazes at it fondly, and says, "Whiskey, boy. *Uisge beatha*. The water of life."

Bill puts on his most innocent face and asks Sam, "How do they make it so good and sell it so cheap?"

Sam smiles, pats Bill on the head, and tells him he has a bright future in this world.

The old upright piano I bought from PJ O'Dea years before is still in my parents' garage. My brother Jack elbows everyone aside, sets his beer on top of the piano, and bangs out his medley of beer songs. Not to be outdone, I clear my throat and hack my way through "A Nation Once Again."

"Not bad, huh?" I say when I finish.

Uncle Art scowls and says if every Irishman had a voice like that, Ireland doesn't deserve to be free.

At one o'clock in the morning, when the last keg has sputtered and hissed itself dry ("A noble death," my cousin Tom says), my brothers and I gather in front of my mother, who smiles tolerantly as we begin to sing:

> *Every sorrow or care in the dear days gone by*
> *Was made bright by the light of the smile in your eye.*
> *Like a candle that's set in a window at night,*
> *Your fond love has cheered me and guided me right.*
> *Sure, I love the dear silver that shines in your hair*
> *And the brow that's all furrowed and wrinkled with care.*
> *I kiss the dear fingers so toilworn for me.*

Then everyone in the party raises a glass and roars out that last line with us:

> *Oh, God bless you and keep you, Mother Machree.*

My dad tells us that for God's sake it's the middle of the night and will we all please stop acting like a bunch of doofuses? Jack tells him that the plural of "doofus" is "doofi." Dad tells Jack to shut up and what does he

know anyway, he is the only kid in the history of Cook County who ever
got fired from a patronage job. "Generations of thugs, grafters, drunks,
and loafers sail through, and my kid gets canned."

Jack says it was all a terrible misunderstanding.

"Yeah," Tim says, "the rabble is always conspiring to tear down the
Best and the Brightest."

Jack smiles broadly, wobbles back and forth, and says, "Yeah. What he
said."

The policeman at the door is nice. He says he is sorry, but this time he really means it. It's 2:00 A.M., and we have to break it up. One of the neighbors has been complaining for the last two hours. No, he's sorry he can't
have a drink with us, but he wishes me and Patti all the best.

Patti and I stand at the door with my parents, thanking everyone for
coming. I hand Aunt Liz her stole, the one with the fox head at one end
and the claws at the other. She thanks me, pats me on the shoulder, and
tells me I should stop staring at Patti like I am a lovesick puppy.

Aunt Fran, who thinks anything north of St. Angela's might as well be
on Mars, gives Patti a big hug and kiss, then turns on me. She can't believe
I am going to take my new bride off to Minnesota.

"Heavenly day, Magee," she says. "How dare you make that girl live in
the middle of those ice fields?" The fact that *I* am going to be living in the
middle of those ice fields *with* her doesn't seem to matter. Aunt Fran says
Patti needs sisters and aunts and cousins and parents, and I am about to
deprive her of them.

I wait for Patti to jump in and defend me, but she smiles at Frannie and
says nothing.

Two weeks later I am in Rochester, living in John and Jane Devlahan's
basement. Dev tells me if I am good, he will let me take a shower every
couple days. I start work at the Mayo Clinic on June 20, but Patti and I
don't close on our home until July 3. For those two weeks, Patti remains

back in Chicago with Eileen, packing boxes and getting ready for the move. I call her every night. Three days before the move, Patti is worried. We have a U-Haul reserved for Saturday morning, but I haven't yet arranged for anyone to help her.

"What am I going to do?" she asks. "I can't load all this stuff by myself."

"Don't worry," I say. "My brothers will be delighted to give you a hand."

I call my brother Pete that night.

"Hello, Mike? You there? I can hardly hear you!" Pete shouts into the phone. "These goofy phones. You're not going to believe this, but it actually sounded like you said you wanted me to go to your apartment, pack up all your stuff, load it on a truck, and drive it up to the Arctic Circle or wherever the hell you live now."

"How nice of you to offer," I say.

"How nice of you to kiss my Irish ass," he replies.

Fortunately, the next day my mother intervenes. She adores Patti and pities her for her choice of husband. Mom slaps Pete and Rog on the back of the head and tells them to get off their big, fat duffs and "go help that poor girl—and don't you let her lift a thing."

I think Mom wants to be sure Patti has no grounds for annulment.

Patti and I don't have a lot of furniture, just a bed, a crib, a few wooden chairs from my dad's office, and two beautiful antique couches—one from my mother's mother, one from my father's mother. Our prized possession, however, is a grand piano, a wedding present from my brother Denny. Our apartment in Forest Park was too small to hold it, so for the past two years it has been moldering in the basement of an apartment building in Oak Park.

The piano actually is a piano *bar*, with a black Formica top trimmed with a six-inch black-and-white-striped vinyl pad around the edge. Cigarette burns scar the top in several places. Denny bought it in some West Side gin mill that was going out of business. After several hours of intense negotiation, he even convinced the owner to throw in three matching bar stools. It was a wonderful present and Patti and I love it, even though we haven't seen it since the wedding. I hope I will still remember how to play some of the songs I learned from Miss Wilson. Patti, whose many gifts do not include music, can't do much more than bang away at "Chopsticks" and "Heart and Soul."

On a sweltering Saturday afternoon my brothers lovingly fill the U-Haul with our belongings. ("It will, too, fit. Just shove the damn thing in there.") There is no room in the truck for Patti and Eileen. My brothers will drive the truck. Patti and Eileen will fly.

Patti's parents drive her to the airport later that day. The three of them are standing at the curb outside American Airlines, sobbing their hearts out, when a Chicago cop, his belly bulging against his blue shirt, lumbers over to see what's the matter. When he is told that this tearful young mother and her baby are going to the Mayo Clinic, he assumes she must be going there to die. And then, when he finds out that her grandparents are from Listowel, County Kerry, he insists on lending a hand.

"I'm a Kerryman, meself," he says. "From Ballyferriter, just down the coast."

He takes Patti's arm and escorts her right to the gate, constantly patting her hand and assuring her that everything is going to be just fine. "Sure, the wife and I will be praying to Saint Anthony for you."

Forty-five minutes and two boxes of Kleenex later, Patti and Eileen are in Rochester.

Patti and I are waiting at the front door when my brothers pull up in the truck. It is almost midnight. The boys have taken a little longer than expected because they stopped at Duane's Sand Bar in the Wisconsin Dells for cube steak sandwiches, a few Leinenkugels, and several games of eight ball.

"Eat me, fat boy," Rog says when I comment on how long it has taken them.

Even though it is late, Patti and I are anxious to get moved in. Eileen is sleeping in a cardboard box on the kitchen floor. We need our furniture. Pete and Rog grumble about "driving all damn day and then unloading this crap in the middle of the night," but Patti and I are able to convince them. The fact that I have a case of Olympia in the icebox helps immensely.

By two in the morning my brothers and I have unloaded the truck and finished the case of Oly. We miraculously maneuvered the piano down the basement steps with a minimum of damage to it, the house, and ourselves. Pete, however, keeps shaking his hand and saying he will never play the violin again. He says I will be hearing from his attorneys soon. I set the last box on the living room floor, toss the last empty in the garbage, and tell the boys it's time for bed.

Patti is horrified that my brothers are going to sleep on the floor.

"Don't worry about it," I say between yawns. "They're college kids. They do it all the time."

"It's not right," she says. "Those poor boys just loaded all our things, drove four hundred miles, unloaded everything, and now you're going to make them sleep on the floor like dogs."

"It won't be the first time. And if it makes you happy I'll get 'em some Ken-L Ration in the morning."

"Michael, they're your brothers. How can you treat them that way?"

I am silent for a moment and then start to get out of bed.

"Now where are you going?" Patti asks.

"I'm going to put some newspaper down in the kitchen in case they have to pee."

"You're disgusting."

I lean over and turn out the light. "Come here," I say. "I want to tell you something."

Patti laughs and slides over.

The next morning after Mass, Patti is taking breakfast orders from my brothers. She can't do enough for them. It seems like she wants to make it all up to them in eggs. "How can I ever thank you?" she says to Pete, taking his face in her hands and kissing him.

"What am I, chopped liver?" Rog asks, elbowing Pete out of the way. Patti kisses him, too.

"Hey, don't you guys have work to do?" I grumble from behind the Sunday paper.

Patti stamps her foot. "Michael!" she says. "Don't you talk to your brothers that way."

"Why not? Did you see how dirty the rug is where they slept last night?"

"How dare you!" She throws a towel at me. "Those poor boys spent the entire day and night doing *your* work."

"I am a doctor, madame. I spent *my* entire day saving the lives of innocent women and children."

"You slept till noon and then played with the baby all day."

This is a gross exaggeration, but I decide it might be best to let Patti have the last word. I put down the newspaper. From behind Patti's back my brothers are smirking. Pete pops another slice of coffee cake in his mouth while Rog pours himself another mug of tea.

"What are you guys laughing at?" I ask.

Immediately the smiles are gone from their faces. They cast their most innocent and aggrieved looks at Patti.

Like a mother hen protecting her chicks, Patti gets up, puts a hand on each of their shoulders, and glares at me. If I want to draw a line in the sand, it is obvious which side she is going to stand on.

"Okay, okay," I say, lifting a hand in defeat. "God bless the giving hand. They're angels, both of them. God's gift to Minnesota. Where would we be without them?"

After more eggs and more tea, after Patti packs them each a huge lunch to take back with them, after she makes me give them twenty-five dollars for gas and "Cokes" (who is kidding whom?), after she smothers them with tearful hugs and kisses, my brothers are on their way back to Chicago.

"I can't believe how nice they are," Patti says. We are standing in the street waving good-bye as the U-Haul drives out of sight. Patti is lifting Eileen's hand, making it wave, too.

"Yeah," I say, "I have to admit that it was pretty nice of them."

"Then why didn't you say something to them?"

"Aw, they're my brothers. They know."

Patti scowls and makes a funny sound in her throat. She tells Eileen that Daddy is a mean old grouch.

Eileen smiles and says, "Goob-goob."

I take Patti's hand, and as we turn and start walking up the driveway, I think of what Pete said to me a few minutes ago as he was getting into the truck to leave.

"That sure is some woman you're married to."

"Patti?" I said. "She's the best."

Five years ago I was the construction worker who didn't belong in pre-med. Three years ago I was the pre-med student with no chance of getting into medical school. One year ago I was the med student who couldn't get it through his thick skull that the Mayo Clinic isn't interested in dock-workers.

Now, although I am starting a residency at the finest medical center in the world, I'm back to being the outsider again. How many other Mayo Clinic residents are members of Teamsters Local 710, have their front teeth knocked out, their nose broken, and a face full of stitches? I'm the dumb kid from the West Side of Chicago who has no business being at a place like this. I've got one long, tough road ahead of me. But that's all right. I guess by now I have a pretty good idea what needs to be done.

Asses and elbows, I think. *Asses and elbows.*

AFTERWORD

This is a memoir, and memoirs are nonfiction. So everything in this book is true, right?

Everything in this book *is* true, but not everything is factual. I know this seems contradictory, so I think I owe you, the reader, an explanation.

In every memoir there are the facts, there is the story, and there is the truth. The facts are used to tell the story. The story is used to tell the truth. For the memoirist, the story and the truth are everything.

The facts of Mike Collins's life are really of very little consequence—or interest. Who cares where some kid from the West Side of Chicago worked and went to school? What matters is the *story* of the construction worker who dreamed of becoming a doctor. What matters even more is the truth that story represents.

There never was a Scalese Construction Company. But I did throw rocks for a company in Chicago whose name was very similar to Scalese. I didn't use the family's real name because I didn't ask their permission. And, in the end, what difference does it make? Does anyone feel cheated that I called the construction company Scalese instead of Scapone?

I used my brothers' real names because I know they won't mind. But I changed the names of most of the other characters. It may be well and good for me to talk about *my* life, but I don't know if "Jack Brennan" or "Joe Roselli" would mind if I talk about his. Why invade someone's privacy when you haven't asked them, and it isn't necessary? The story is the same. The truth is the same. Only the facts are different.

Everything in this book really did happen. Everything in this book really is true. I might have changed a few names or rearranged a few details, but not in any substantial way. W. S. Merwin has spoken of the illusion that one can tell the truth about one's life. "All memoir," he says, "really is fiction." Nevertheless, if you read this book, you will have a true appreciation of how I spent the twenty-fourth to twenty-ninth years of my life.

I would also like to address a brief note to young readers. It is my hope that young people will read this book, but read carefully, you guys. Writing about something is not the same as endorsing it. I would be very disappointed if impressionable minds thought I condoned everything I wrote about.

If I seem to treat certain misbehaviors lightly or with amusement, it is because time has taught me to look with understanding at the human weaknesses that prompt us to err, and to recognize the humanity that lies beneath.

Finally, some thanks are in order. First of all, to my wife, Patti. This book would not have happened without her support, encouragement, and patience. To my children—Eileen, Mary Kate, Paudh, Maureen, Sheila, Kevin, Matt, Nora, Brian, Annie, Katie, and Colleen—who every day make me realize how much I have to be thankful for, and who never tire of reminding me that prepositions are not to end sentences with. To my brothers—Den, Tim, Rog, Jack, Pete, Joe, and Bill—none of whom ever wound up in jail despite everyone's predictions, and all of whom turned out to be pretty good guys. To my dad, Mike Collins, who passed away a few years ago, and to my mom, Nancy Collins, to whom I still owe a year's worth of alcohol. To my agents, Meg Ruley and Christina Hogrebe at the Jane

Rotrosen Agency—thanks for your support and guidance. You guys are the best.

And finally, to the Loyola University Stritch School of Medicine in Chicago, who gave a dumb construction worker the opportunity to become a doctor. I know you went out on a limb by accepting me all those years ago, and I hope I have repaid your confidence. Thank you.